The Buddha and Dr Führer

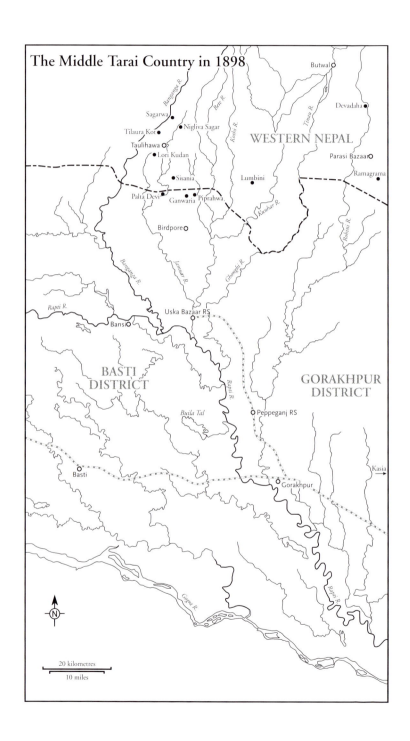

The Middle Tarai Country in 1898

Butwal
Devadaha
Sagarwa
Tilaura Kot
Nigliva Sagar
Taulihawa
WESTERN NEPAL
Lori Kudan
Parasi Bazaar
Sisania
Lumbini
Ramagrama
Palta Devi
Ganwaria
Piprahwa
Birdpore
Uska Bazaar RS
Bansi
BASTI
DISTRICT
GORAKHPUR
DISTRICT
Buila Tal
Peppeganj RS
Basti
Gorakhpur
Kasia

Banganga R.
Bee R.
Kothi R.
Tinata R.
Kanhar R.
Rohini R.
Banganga R.
Jamuar R.
Ghaghi R.
Rapti R.
Rapti R.
Gogra R.
Rapti R.

N

20 kilometres
10 miles

THE BUDDHA
AND DR FÜHRER

AN ARCHAEOLOGICAL SCANDAL

Charles Allen

Haus Publishing
London

First published in Great Britain in 2008 by
Haus Publishing Ltd
79 Cadogan Place
London sw1x 9ah
www.hauspublishing.com

A CIP catalogue record for this book is available from the British Library

ISBN 978-1-905791-93-4

Typeset in Warnock by MacGuru Ltd
Printed in Great Britain by J. H. Haynes & Co. Ltd., Sparkford
Maps by Martin Lubikowski, ML Design, London

Contents

A Winter in Nepal

The bulk of this book was written over a winter in Nepal, a country I came to know and love while as a volunteer teacher in the late 1960s. When I returned to Kathmandu in December 2007 the Nepali people were in the painful process of recovering from a civil war and transforming their country from an autocratic, caste-fixated Hindu monarchy into an egalitarian republic. It was not an easy winter for anyone, what with demonstrations, blockades on the roads and mounting shortages of electricity, diesel, kerosene, water and even food. What made my stay bearable was the good humour and resilience of the citizens of Nepal, who, to paraphrase Rudyard Kipling, watched the things they gave their life to broken, and stooped and built 'em up with worn out tools.

However, this book is not about Nepal's recent past but about more ancient and not quite so ancient times, which I had touched on in an earlier book, *The Buddha and the Sahibs*, an account of the discovery of Buddhism's Indian roots by Western Orientalists, antiquarians and archaeologists. I had ended with a chapter on the rediscovery of the last of the lost sacred sites of Buddhism: Kapilavastu, where the man whom his followers called the 'awakened one' or *Buddha*, spent the early years of his life; and Lumbini, where that same man was born. A fairly minor character in this last phase of rediscovery was a German archaeologist named Anton Alois Führer.

Two years after the book's publication in 2002 a coincidence involving a lecture at the Buddhist Society in London and Buddhist relics found in a cupboard at that same institution set me on my own path of discovery. It became apparent that Dr. Führer had precipitated a major archaeological scandal. So bizarre are some of the details that they would be laughable but for the fact that they most likely led to the death of the most eminent Sanskritist of the age as well as dealing a severe blow to Indian and Buddhist archaeology, the shock waves of which can still be felt today in the cloud of suspicion which continues to hang over the name of Piprahwa. That scandal lies at the heart of this book, recounted here for the first time with as much hard fact as I have been able to track down after more than a century of silence and neglect. At the same time this is a further celebration of Western Orientalism in India, which has had a bad press in recent years as a consequence of a regretably unscholarly book by the late Edward Said, published in 1978, which has done serious damage to cross-cultural studies.

However, this story is also about landscapes: physical and metaphysical, political and sacred. Their one constant is the setting: the borderland between the foothills of the Nepal Himalayas and the Indian Gangetic plains, which today is also the frontier between Nepal and India. Known as the *tarai*, this was not so long ago a seemingly impenetrable belt of forest fronted by a more open jungle of tall elephant grass and marshland, and riven by scores of rivers and streams running north to south. Today, after its clearance and human settlement, the tarai landscape would be relatively insignificant in the greater scheme of things – but for the fact that some 2,400 years ago, the Buddha was born and raised here as a real person of flesh and blood.

The tarai provides the geographical template for my story, a firm base upon which other more shifting landscapes have been laid, beginning with that shaped by migrants from the east who coalesced into the Sakyas and Koliyas. These two tribes settled in the tarai more than 3,000 years ago, shaping the fatherland and motherland of their most famous son, Gautama Sakyamuni, 'sage of the Sakyas'. After the Sakyamuni expired, in the act known to Buddhists as the *Maharaparinirvana*, or the 'Great Final Extinguishing', his homeland was reshaped into a sacred landscape, marked by memorials to Buddha Sakyamuni and to other earlier Buddhas. Chief among these memorialists was the emperor Asoka

Vardana or Asoka the Great, who came to these parts on what was already a well-beaten pilgrim trail to raise his own bigger and better monuments. Others followed, most notably the Kushans and Guptas, and they further ornamented this sacred landscape, drawing on the many stories or legends that grew with the Buddhist *sangha* or community as it evolved and diversified.

The next and fourth landscape was essentially a metaphysical one, where the boundaries between fact and legend blurred. This was the country of Buddha Sakyamuni as it appeared to a succession of pilgrims from China and Tibet, two of whom left detailed accounts of their travels round the Buddhist sacred places in India – accounts in which they tried to reconcile what they saw on the ground with what they had read or been told about the lives of Buddha Sakyamuni and other less tangible Buddhas.

When the last of these Chinese pilgrims entered the tarai in the year 636, that region was already reverting to its original jungle. North of the tarai, in and beyond the Himalayas, and in the countries east and south of the Indian sub-continent, Buddhism continued to flourish. But in the land in which it had first taken shape, Buddhism went into decline in the face of resurgent and sometimes militant Hinduism, a process speeded up by the advance of Islam. After the anti-Buddhist pogroms of the Muslim general Bakhtiar Khilji in 1193, in which thousands of monks were murdered and Asia's first and greatest university at Nalanda put to the torch, Buddhism all but disappeared from the Indian sub-continent, surviving only among isolated communities in the high valleys of the Himalayas: in Kathmandu Valley and in Ladakh.

Six centuries passed before a new spirit of enquiry initiated by the European Enlightenment led to the recovery of the early history and culture of the sub-continent by Orientalists – a word that has become grossly distorted in recent decades. In that process of recovery both the historical Buddha Sakyamuni and the Indian roots of the religion he founded were rediscovered. The accounts of the Chinese pilgrim-travellers were translated into French and then English and became working tools for a new species of antiquarians called archaeologists who criss-crossed the Gangetic plain in search of the lost sacred sites of Buddhism. These archaeologists created another landscape scarcely less metaphysical than that of the Chinese travellers as they searched through the tarai forests and grasslands for archaeological evidence to match what the Chinese had seen many centuries earlier. These latecomers also had to deal with the realities of a political landscape in which the tarai was in the process of being divided into nation states, leading to a line of concrete posts being hammered into the ground running east and west to form the boundary between the Kingdom of Nepal on one side and the adjacent territories of the Kingdom of Oude and the East India Company's North-Western Provinces on the other. With the annexation of Oude in 1848 and the change from Company to Crown rule in 1858, the two territories south of the Nepal frontier were united to become the North-Western Provinces and Oude (NWP&O), afterwards renamed the United Provinces. The territory east of the NWP&O was at that time part of the large province known as the Bengal Presidency but in 1904 reverted to the name by which that region had been known in earlier times: Bihar, the land of *viharas* or Buddhist monasteries.

Today, of course, there is a more modern political landscape, with the same border posts running east and west to mark the frontier between the Republic of India and the fledgling Republic of Nepal. Physically, it is being transformed mostly into open farmland, divided into countless small plots still best ploughed by a pair of oxen or buffalo, with scattered villages and hamlets, and the occasional brickworks or sugar-cane factory. Canals and reservoirs have helped to further change the scenery but the tarai's rivers and streams continue to provide a rich habitat both for migratory birds and permanent residents such as the Sarus Cranes, whose habit of pairing for life has made them symbols of good fortune and saved them from being shot to extinction. Swathes of the ancient forest have also survived on both sides of the international border and the largest of these are now national parks and wildlife sanctuaries, the last refuge of the tarai's once abundant big beasts: tigers, rhinos, elephants and wild buffalo.

What has forced these and other wild creatures to the edge is loss of habitat, now occupied by human migrants in the form of Hindu and Muslim settlers, who in three or four generations have transformed the tarai into the sub-continent's rice-bowl. These same migrants have also reshaped its culture, rejecting the word *tarai* in favour of *madesh*, meaning 'plains country', and referring to themselves as Madeshis. The Madesh has many faces. Go there in the summer and you might as well be baked in an oven, which is why the British in India developed a hat known as the 'double tarai', with two layers of felt to block the penetration of the sun. But come back in the period that the British in India knew as the 'cold weather', from October through to mid-March, and you find yourself in a delightfully temperate zone, with misty mornings, sunny afternoons and evenings when a jersey or light jumper needs to be worn. Leave the hard 'pukka' road and follow any one of the innumerable raised trackways and paths between the fields and you very soon find yourself in a rural setting seemingly at one with nature, where you will be made welcome even in the poorest human habitation.

But there are tensions on both sides of the border. In Nepal the increasingly populous Madeshis have begun to flex their political muscles and are challenging the traditional political supremacy of those they call the *Pahadis* or hill-dwellers. Yet the Madeshis are only one of many social groups or castes or tribes who believe themselves hard done by and are demanding their slice of the cake. A brutal ten-year insurgency led by self-styled Maoists and stemmed by a brutal soldiery tore the country apart and left its people impoverished, traumatised and justifiably angry at the mess they now find themselves in. On 10 April 2008, on a day when all traffic movement was banned so that everyone could come out and vote, I had the enormous pleasure of witnessing Nepal's citizens vote for a constituent assembly. The outcome was the coming to power of an all-party government with a mandate to bring about reforms which may in time allow all the people to share equally in the development process. At its first session on 28 May 2008 the Constituent Assembly voted by 564 votes to 4 to declare Nepal a federal democratic republic, giving the hated king a fortnight to clear out of his palace – a king whose late brother and forebears had been revered as living gods and avatars of Lord Vishnu. No one imagines that this is an end to the vested interests and corrupt practices that have frustrated Nepal's development, but it is surely a beginning of the end.

South of the border the situation is more complex. Here two Indian states are involved: the Bihar of British days is still Bihar but when India became independent in 1947 the United Provinces was renamed Uttar Pradesh. Bihar, to put it bluntly, is in a mess. The last national census showed that state to have India's highest birth rate, highest infant mortality figures, lowest literacy rates and lowest per capita income. In December 2007 Bihar's Chief Minister appealed to Central Government for help in combating the growing threat from home-grown Maoists, declaring that 'What used to be a minor problem in the state has now taken the shape of full-blown terrorism'. Although mild by comparison with what Nepalis suffered when their insurgency was at its height, Bihar's experience of Maoist violence has the same root causes, identified in a recent report as 'the sheer and endemic lack of human development, and crumbling administration and decaying infrastructure', all stemming from 'political lethargy'. The word that was not mentioned in this report was caste, the great unmentionable which has been the curse of the Indian sub-continent in the form of caste oppression and inter-caste rivalry.

The situation is rather better next door in the UP, India's most populous state, with a population close to 170 million. The UP also comes close to bottom in India's league table of states, but is currently undergoing a dramatic political change which may be as momentous in its own way as that taking place across the border in Nepal. In May 2007 a new government was voted into power in which a relatively new political party, the Bhahujan Samaj Party (BSP), formed the majority. What marks out the BSP as different from the others is that it was formed to give a voice to those at the bottom of the Hindu caste structure, formerly known as 'untouchables' and now more often referred to as *Dalits* or the Scheduled Castes. The BSP chose the elephant as its party symbol, a creature dear to both Buddhists and Hindus, and took its inspiration from the Dalit reformer Dr. Ambedkar, a close political ally of Mahatma Gandhi, who dedicated much of his life to trying to improve the lot of his fellow-Dalits. In 1956, frustrated by the failure of his fellow politicians to follow their words with deeds, Dr. Ambedkar staged a mass rally at which several hundred thousand low caste Hindus converted to Buddhism. Since then, for all the efforts of the Hindu extremists or ultra-nationalist parties to have religious conversion declared unlawful, more mass conversions have followed, the most recent in Mumbai in May 2007. Buddhism – or rather, neo- or Dalit Buddhism – is returning to the land of its birth.

When the UP's new government took office its cabinet consisted of five Muslims, thirteen high-caste Brahmins and Kshatriyas and no less than thirty-one Dalits. And presiding over the cabinet as Chief Minster was another Dalit: a diminutive, dumpy, but charismatic 51-year-old former teacher known either as Mayawati or as the 'Dalit Queen'. Mayawati courts controversy and as many charges of corruption surround her as any other state politician but she is now serving her fourth term as the state's Chief Minister. Despite amassing a considerable personal fortune from the donations of the faithful and despite indulging herself with jewellery, bronze statues of herself and lavish birthday parties, Mayawati has the support of the masses, not so much because of the many development projects she has so ostentatiously inaugurated but because she is one of them. The Dalit Queen may scandalise the Indian middle classes but the fact is that one-fifth of the population of the UP think of themselves as outcaste if not actually Dalit, and that figure is reflected right across the country. She and her party have learned from their mistakes, including the necessity to make alliances with former enemies and to tread lightly when it comes to religious sensibilities. The Buddhist card is in the pack but never played. It is not impossible that the next decade may see Mayawati and the BSP governing India – if she and they can look beyond petty caste loyalties. Some Hindus may see this as a threat but the wiser among them will welcome the return of the Dharma, to which Hinduism has equal claim.

But already I have taken my story too far forward. Like the best stories, this one must begin at the beginning.

Charles Allen, Somerset, England

The Return of the Wanderer

c. 405 BCE

The old man had been going home, following the highway that ran northwards across the plains towards the Himavant mountain ranges and to Kapilavastu, the fatherland on which he had turned his back almost half a century earlier. He had been born a prince of the house of Gautama and named Siddhartha, 'he whose object has been attained'; his father the tribal chieftain Suddhodana – 'pure in conduct and beloved of the Sakya like the autumn moon' – chosen by popular acclamation to rule over the Sakyas; his mother a princess of the neighbouring Koliya tribe of Koligrama and named Maya from her resemblance to the Mother Goddess.

In later years these two linked tribes would be written into the Brahminical caste system and provided with royal lineages that could be traced back to the sun. It would be written of the Sakyas that their exiled Aryan ancestors had settled *yattha Himavantapassê pôkharaniyâ tire mahâ sâkasandô*, or 'where there was a forest of *śâka* trees on the bank of a lake in the slopes of the Himâlaya.' But both the Sakyas and the Koliyas were more Mongoloid than Aryan, jungle-dwellers of the Gangetic plains driven back towards the Himalayan foothills by the advancing *Aryavanshi*. The Sakyas took their tribal name from the *saku* or *sal* forests (*Shorea robusta*) in which they lived, the seeds of which were a staple food for jungle dwellers, just as the Koliyas took their name

Queen Mayadevi's dream in which she conceives the Buddha-to-be in the form of a white elephant. A stone medallion on the carved railings of the Barhut stupa, uncovered by General Cunningham in 1874.

either from the *koila* tree (*Bauhinia purpurria*, known variously as the Mountain Ebony, Orchid or Camel's Foot) or the *kolan* tree (*Nauclea cordifolia*), the bark of which was used for treating fevers. The Sakyas of Kapilavastu occupied the western side of the Rohini river where it debouched onto the plains, with their capital at Mahanagara (more usually known as Kapilavastu), the Koliyas the eastern side with their capital at Devadaha – and for all the subsequent talk of palaces and marbled halls, and rajas and ranis, both tribes lived off the land. They used the timber of the forest to build their homes and the stockades that protected their

Scene from a relief on the eastern gateway of the Great Stupa at Sanchi, drawn by the amateur archaeologist Lieut. Frederick Maisey in about 1850 (India Office Library, British Library). The Sakyas and Koliyas would have lived in very much the same bucolic mode.

settlements, and they harnessed the rivers to water the rich alluvial soil for the paddy-fields in which they grew the rice which provided their staple diet and their wealth. They grazed their water-buffalo along the edges of the forest and in the wetlands. They also hunted in the forest and tamed its elephants, and the best of their hunters served as warriors, a role which over time became hereditary and conferred the privilege of tribal leadership.

The warrior clans of the two tribes intermarried but, in the interests of maintaining clan purity, they also practised endogamy – a custom abhorred by all good Hindus. Thus it was that Siddhartha's mother Maya and her younger sister Prajapati were both married to his father, whose mother was their aunt. Siddhartha in his turn married his cousin Yasodhara, the daughter of his mother's brother. The Sakya prince and the Koliya princess duly produced a son, Rahula, but on the evening after his birth Siddhartha, then aged twenty-nine, slipped away from his father's mote hall at Kapilavastu, abandoning wife and son to become a *paribbajaka* or wandering ascetic: a seemingly reprehensible act that afterwards became known as the Great Renunciation.

When Siddhartha had next returned to Kapilavastu he had been welcomed by his father not as his heir but as Gautama Sakyamuni, the Sage of the Sakyas, also known to his many followers as *Tathagata*, the 'One Who Has Arrived', or as Buddha, the 'Awakened One'. Both his wife and son, as well the aunt who had brought him up as his step-mother, had then followed him loyally into the ascetic life he had chosen for himself.

Now after fifty-one years of teaching the philosophy of the Middle Path the Sakyamuni knew that he would not live to see his homeland again. Two days earlier while he and his party were encamped in a mango grove a blacksmith's boy had slipped some pork into his begging bowl and, not wishing to reject the boy's offering, he had eaten.

The meat was bad and caused internal bleeding, and by the morning of the second day the Sakyamuni had become too weak to go on. His always faithful cousin Ananda had suggested they should take him back across the River Ganga to Rajgir, the centre of his teaching, but he had refused. His only son was now dead, his Sakya clansmen slaughtered, their sisters enslaved, his father's city sacked, its people scattered. Yet it was the human condition to be born into suffering, and it had been his life's purpose to understand the causes of that suffering and to find the means to end it – a philosophy encapsulated in the two phrases *Cattari Ariyasaccani*, or the 'Four Noble Truths', and *Ariyo Atthangiko Maggo*, the 'Noble Eightfold Path'. For half a century he had trod

The Sakyamuni accepts his alms bowl. A Victorian engraving of a Gandharan sculpture.

that path and here at Kushinagara he knew he had come to the end of his journey.

Beside the banks of the Hiranyavati River was a grove of sal trees. Here the old man asked to be made comfortable, saying to Ananda, 'Spread me a bed on the ground between two sal trees, with the head to the north. I am tired and will lie down on my side.' A fold of his much patched cloak was gathered up to make a pillow for his head. When his disciples began to weep he comforted them, reminding them that 'all that lives will perish' and it was not his self that mattered but his teaching. Three times he asked those gathered about him if anyone had any doubts about that teaching, and to speak up before it was too late. When no one answered the old man uttered two final sentences: 'Impermanence is in everything. Work tirelessly to achieve enlightenment.' In the last watch of the night, lying on his right side with his face turned northwards towards the hills where he had been born and raised, Gautama Sakyamuni entered that state which his followers came

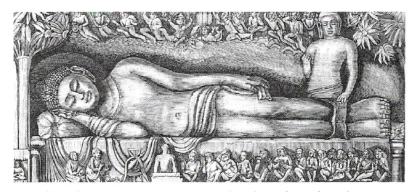

The Maharaparinirvana. An engraving based on a fresco from the Ajanta caves.

to know as the *Maharaparinirvana*, the 'Great Final Extinguishing,' sometimes translated as the 'Great Final Deliverance'.

According to the ancient Pali chronicle compiled on the island of Ceylon known as the *Dipavamsa*, the great Mauryan emperor Asoka was anointed ruler of the kingdom of Magadha 'two hundred and eighteen years after the beatitude of Buddha'. From details of diplomatic missions overseas carved on an Asokan edict rock it can be deduced that Asoka was anointed ruler within two or three years of 269 BCE [Before the Christian Era], which would mean that Gautama Sakyamuni died within a few years of 487 BCE. This is the dating of the Theravada Buddhist 'southern' tradition followed in Sri Lanka, Burma, Thailand and Cambodia. However, Sanskrit texts of the Mahayana tradition which made their way along the Silk Route to China and Japan date the gap between the Maharaparinirvana and the inauguration of Asoka to a round century, which would place the demise of Gautama Sakyamuni to around 370 BCE. Modern scholarship tends to fall between these two stools, but there is a growing consensus, based on careful analysis of the tables of succession given in the *Dipavamsa*, that the historical Buddha most probably died about 136 years before Asoka's anointing – that is to say, about the year 405 BCE.

What followed thereafter was recorded in the text known as the *Maharaparinirvana suttanta*. The earthly remains of the Sakyamuni were wrapped in cloth and covered in flowers and incense.

The cremation of the Buddha Sakyamuni, as depicted on a stone relief from the Sanchi stupa, carved in the second century BCE. The coffin bears the symbols of the wheel of the Dharma and the trident-like *triratna*, representing the 'three jewels' of the Buddha, the Dharma and the Sangha. The trees at Kushinagara were said to have flowered out of season and the gods to have showered garlands of flowers.

On the seventh day after his demise his body was placed in a coffin and cremated on a pyre of fragrant wood.

The ashes and bones were subsequently gathered up by a Brahmin named Drona. A fierce argument then broke out over who should receive these relics, which was resolved by their division by Drona into eight portions, each large enough to fill a

Drona distributes the ashes after Buddha Sakyamuni's cremation, as portrayed in an eighteenth-century Chinese history of Buddhism (From James Legge's *A Record of Chinese Kingdoms*, 1886).

small pot. The first share went to the powerful King Ajatashatru of Magadha whose kingdom lay south of the Ganga; the second to the Licchavi rulers of Vaisali, on the northern bank of the Ganga; the third to the Bulis of Allakappa, to the west; the fourth to an influential Brahmin of Vethadipa; the fifth and sixth shares to the Mallas of Kusinagara and Pava; and the seventh to the Koliyas of Koligrama, the little kingdom east of the Rohini River from which Gautama Sakyamuni's mother had come – better known in later years as Ramagrama. The last portion went to the Awakened One's own people, the Sakyas of Kapilavastu. Soon after the division of the relics an embassy arrived from the Moriyas of Pipphalivana, lying between Koligrama and Kusinagara. They too demanded a share but had to settle for the ashes of the funeral pyre.

When asked by Ananda how he should be remembered the Sakyamuni had suggested that his followers should honour four sites associated with his life and teaching: the Lumbini garden where he had been born; Bodhgaya, where he had achieved enlightenment seated under a *pipal* tree; the deer-park of Nalanda, on the outskirts of Varanasi (Benares), where he had delivered his first sermon to his first five disciples – an act known to Buddhists as the First Turning of the Wheel of the *Dharma* or Moral Order; and Kushinagara, where he had attained Maharaparinirvana. When further asked by Ananda how his ashes should be commemorated the Sakyamuni had replied that they should be buried under earth that was *thuipikata* or 'heaped up as rice is heaped in an alms bowl'. The tradition of placing the bones and ashes of a revered person under a *thupa* or mound of earth was already the established funerary practice among the peoples settled on the northern banks of the Ganges. However, the Sakyamuni further requested that this thupa should be sited beside a cross-roads so that passers-by might pause to pay their respects and by their veneration gain in understanding and merit.

Accordingly, each of the eight portions of relics recovered from the funeral pyre, as well as the Moriyas' ashes from the pyre and Drona's pot, were buried at prominent public places under what are better known today as *stupas* (from the Sanskrit form of the original Pali thupa).

As embodiments of the essence of the Buddha and his teaching, these ten stupas immediately became objects of veneration. Devotees garlanded them with flowers, lit lamps and came to pray beside them. Such important religious memorials had to be protected from the elements, so the original heaped mud mounds were strengthened with layers of crushed stone rubble. When this proved insufficiently durable the relic stupas were given an outer casing in the form of a surrounding wall and a hemispherical dome of fired bricks.

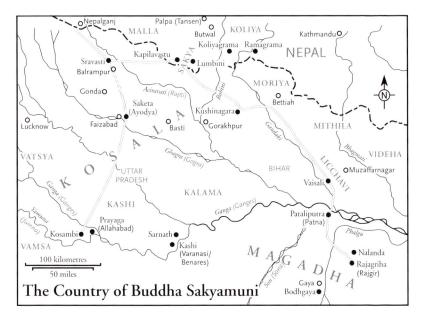

The Country of Buddha Sakyamuni

● Ancient   KALAMA – Ancient
O Modern   NEPAL – Modern

At the time of Sakyamuni Buddha the Sakya kingdom of Kapilavastu was just one of a number of minor vassal states that came within the *mahajanapada* or 'great footprint' of Kosala. With its capital at Sravasti, some three days' march west of Kapilavastu, Kosala was one of the eighteen long-established mahajanapadas of ancient India, covering much the same area as the Kingdom of Oude in the eighteenth century, the North-Western Provinces in the late nineteenth century and Uttar Pradesh in modern India. Kosala's ruler King Prasenajit became a supporter of Gautama Sakyamuni and it was through his patronage that the great monastery erected in the Jetavana garden, just north of his capital of Sravasti, became the Great Teacher's retreat during the summer rains for more than twenty years.

But even more closely associated with the Sage of the Sakyas was the rival mahajanapada of Magadha, a country roughly corresponding in its territory to the southern half of the modern state of Bihar, which owes it name from the many Buddhist *viharas* or monastic centres that for centuries dominated the landscape. Magadha's capital was Rajagriha (today Rajgir), nestling in a ring of hills two days' march south of the River Ganga and seven days' west of the ancient city of Varanasi, capital of the mahajanapada of Kasia. Here in Rajagriha the Sakyamuni and his followers enjoyed the royal patronage of King Bimbisara for more than forty years – until the king, who was five years younger than the sage, made the fatal error of abdicating in favour of his son Ajatashatru, who had him imprisoned and starved to death. This unhappy event probably took place during the last five years of the Sakyamuni's life.

Ajatashatru's cruelty led his mother, the sister of King Prasenajit of Kosala, to die of grief, which provoked Prasenajit into declaring war on Magadha. King Ajatashatru and his army were caught in an ambush and forced to surrender, but after negotiations in which the aged Gautama Sakyamuni may well have been involved as peace-maker King Prasenajit not only restored Ajatashatru's kingdom but also gave him his daughter in marriage. Soon after this act of magnanimity King Prasenajit's son Vidudhaba seized power and Prasenajit was forced to flee south to Magadha to ask for refuge from his new son-in-law – only for Ajatashatru to close the gates of his city on him, leaving Prasenajit to die of exposure outside its walls.

With the death of King Prasenajit his son Vidudhaba secured his hold on the throne of Kosala and then set out to exact revenge on the Sakyas of Kapilavastu for an ancient slight. According to the *Agganna Sutta* and the *Mahavamsa*, King Prasenajit had asked for the daughter of a Sakya to cement the alliance between their two houses but the Sakyans, who prided themselves on their racial exclusiveness, had fooled him by sending the daughter of their clan chief by a slave girl named Naga-Mtinda (perhaps from the subordinated aboriginal tribe of the snake-worshipping Nagas). Only after she had given birth to Vidudhaba did Prasenajit discover that he had been tricked by the Sakyas, leading him to deprive his son of all rights and privileges as his heir. Vidudhaba had never forgiven his father or the Sakyas, and after Prasenajit's death at Rajagriha he at once set out to avenge himself on the Sakyas. Three times he sent an army eastwards from Sravasti to destroy

King Ajatashatru leaves his palace at Rajgir to pay his respects to Gautama Sakyamuni, here represented by an empty dais and royal umbrella, since at this early period the Buddha was always represented by symbols. From the Bharhut stupa, which General Cunningham assigned to the Mauryan era 'or somewhere between 250 and 200 B. C.' but is now thought to have been built in the second century BCE under Sunga patronage.

Kapilavastu and three times, it is said, his troops were obliged to turn back after meeting Gautama Sakyamuni seated by the roadside. On the fourth occasion, however, Gautama Sakyamuni was either too far away or too close to death to hold the army back and it overwhelmed the city of Kapilavastu. The surrendered Sakyan army was destroyed in a notorious massacre that left their bodies 'scattered like straws', after which their womenfolk were carried off to Sravasti as slaves.

This slaughter ended Sakya rule over Kapilavastu, but a few Sakyas survived by fleeing into the Himalayan foothills and the jungles. Some evidently made their way to Kusinagara to claim a share of their revered kinsman's remains, which they afterwards interred in Sakya country according to his instructions. The rest never returned. Of these, some went north, including, it is said, members of the family of Gautama Sakyamuni's cousin Ananda, who crossed the mountains to reach the Nivala or Nepal Valley.

Some crossed the Rohini River into Koligrama or Ramagrama, the country of the Koliyas, while others continued further east to find sanctuary among the Moriyas of Pipphalivana. A more fanciful claim is that some of the Sakyas settled in a wild place (afterwards Champaran), which they called Moriyanage, or the 'place of peacocks', because it resounded to the cries of peacocks.

Meanwhile in Magadha King Ajatashatru resumed a programme of military expansion initiated by his late father Bimbisara. After building a great fortress of wooden walls beside the River Ganga, which he (or his successor Udayin) named Pataliputra, he crossed the great river to conquer Vaisali, the southernmost of the Licchavi states, before moving west to claim Kosala and Kashi, after which he returned to initiate a war against a confederacy of the remaining Licchavi and Malla states that continued for many years.

The Sakyamuni had warned that after his departure the country through which he had preached peace, compassion and universal brotherhood would be torn by war and suffering, and this prophecy now came about. Yet despite his cruel disposition King Ajatashatru had the highest regard for Gautama Sakyamuni and after his Maharaparinirvana, he was the first to claim a portion of the ashes, which he venerated in the stupa he raised over them at Rajagriha. Three months after the Maharaparinirvana Ajatashatru sponsored a meeting known initially as the *Pancasatika* because of the 500 enlightened monks that took part, better known today as the First Buddhist Council. Held outside a cave on the hillside just north of Rajagriha, the council formalised the moral law taught by the Buddha, the Dharma, and the rules by which his followers should live, the *Vinaya*. By virtue of his close links with the Buddha and his extraordinary memory, Gautama Sakyamuni's cousin Ananda was able to provide what was agreed to be the most perfect account of the Dharma. Those monks with the best memories then set to work to learn the whole of the Vinaya and the Dharma by heart through repeated recitation – a process that extended over six months and which became the standard means by which Sakyamuni Buddha's teaching was handed down by oral transmission generation to generation.

According to the Hindu genealogical charts King Ajatashatru, regicide and patricide, was followed by another eight descendants of his line, each son succeeding by killing his father until finally the throne of Magadha was seized by a chief minister who established the Nanda dynasty, which in turn went through nine rulers and lasted for more than a century before the arrival of a usurper named Chandragupta Mauriya. By this chronology, Gautama Sakyamuni would have had to have died well before the start of the fifth century BCE. However, the Ceylon chronicles are less fanciful: the entire Nanda dynasty turns out to have ruled for no more than twenty-two years, and the period between the death of King Ajatashatru and the arrival of Chandragupta Mauriya on the royal scene lasted little more than three-quarters of a century. In that brief span of a century the Dharma took root within the geographical bounds trodden by Gautama Sakyamuni across the Gangetic plains, but as little more than one of several competing challenges to the orthodoxy of Vedic Brahmanism that included the teaching of Gautama Sakyamuni's contemporary and sometime neighbour Mahavira, the founder of Jainism.

During that same early period the *Sangha*, or Buddhist community, initially exclusive and made up very largely of Brahmins of the priestly caste, began to evolve as the original teachings of the Sakyamuni were re-examined, re-interpreted and disputed over. Thanks to the missionary work of one of his chief disciples, Mahakatyayana of Ujjain, the Sakyamuni's teachings also began to spread into western India, and subsequently it was in the Pali dialect of western India that the sutras were preserved to become the holy texts of Buddhism.

Within the lifetimes of Mahakatyayana and his fellow disciples divisions began to appear, leading to the Second Buddhist Council held at Vaisali a century after the Maharaparinirvana. The outcome was secession by a breakaway group who rejected the strict and, as they saw it, narrow reading of Buddhism followed by their elders, the *Theras*, in favour of a more adaptable, more accessible interpretation that could also appeal to lay people – so opening the way for the development of the *Mahayana* or 'Greater Vehicle' school of Buddhism. These schismatics would eventually move away from the Magadha region to northern India, leaving behind those

Stupa worship portrayed on a panel of the Bharhut stupa.

whose more conservative beliefs became known as *Theravada*, or 'Teaching of the Elders', which can also be translated as 'Teaching of Those Left Behind'.

One early success of the reformers was the acceptance of the belief that Gautama Sakyamuni was but one of a number of emanations of Buddhahood. It was established that in the present age of humans three such manifestations of Buddhahood had preceded the Sakyamuni – Krakuchanda Buddha, Kanakamuni Buddha and Kasyapa Buddha – and one who would come after: the future Buddha Maitreya. The three predecessors of Sakyamuni Buddha, most probably renowned sages whose reputations as saints had long outlived them, were now brought into the Buddhist mainstream. Having lived and died in the same country as Gautama Sakyamuni, they too were now accorded their own memorial stupas, commemorating where they had been born, where they had died, and where their remains had been cremated and buried.

Stupa veneration now became a central element of Buddhism and as Buddhism itself evolved so too did these memorials, so that within two to three centuries of the Maharaparinirvana the original simple burial mounds of heaped-up earth had grown into magnificent monuments many times greater in height and circumference, covered in dressed and carved stone, and with additional features such as umbrellas and processional paths with railings and gates that allowed pilgrims to circumambulate the edifice.

The Buddhist stupa was a still relatively modest structure when Chandragupta Maurya, known to the Greeks as Sandracottos, seized the throne of Magadha as a teenager in or about the year 320 BCE. One account has it that Chandragupta was an illegitimate son of a Nanda prince by a concubine or slave-girl named Mura, another that he was a mercenary cavalryman from the Ashvaka tribe, known to the Greeks as the Assakenoi, who lived beyond the Indus. But there are also competing Buddhist and Jain literary traditions which claim that Chandragupta was either raised among peacocks or came from the Moriya tribe of Pipphalivana, situated in the much ravaged country between Koligrama and the Malla country of Kusinagara, within whose borders Gautama Buddha expired, so making a genealogical link between the scattered Sakyas of Kapilavastu and the new ruler of Magadha. What is indisputable is that Chandragupta was of humble stock and that he brought with him such an appetite for conquest that before he had reached his mid-twenties he had transformed the eighteen mahajanapadas of old into one mighty super-state extending from the eastern to the western seas and as far into the north-west as the country where the River Sindu or Indus debouched from the mountains onto the plains.

After two decades of conquest Chandragupta handed over power to his son Bindusara and moved to south India to become an ascetic under a Jain saint, ending his life through self-starvation in a cave. Bindusara extended his father's empire deeper into southern India, leaving untouched only the friendly Dravidian states in the far south and the unfriendly kingdom of Kalinga, in the south east. In or about the year 270 BCE Bindusara was succeeded by a son named Asoka or 'Without Sorrow', who killed his brothers and embarked on a savage campaign to subdue Kalinga. According to Buddhist history, the day after the final sack of the Kalingan capital Asoka toured the ruins and was appalled by what he saw, crying out 'What have I done?' Asoka's first wife Queen Devi was a Buddhist, and when she saw the consequences of her husband's actions she reportedly left him in disgust. Asoka returned to his capital at Pataliputra haunted by nightmares but was comforted by one of his nephews, whose father he had killed. The boy showed him the path towards Buddhism, to which he converted in the seventh year of his reign under the guidance of the fifth great elder of the Buddhist Church, 'the ancient and venerable Upagupta, recipient of all the knowledge and tradition of the faith'. The emperor then ceased to be *Chandashoka* or 'Asoka the Merciless' and became *Dharmashoka*, or 'Asoka of the Law', while on his imperial edicts he proclaimed himself to be *Devanamapriya priyadasi*, or 'Beloved of the Gods who loves all'.

Asoka now began to govern his empire on the basis of the Dharma, setting in motion what became known among Buddhists as the Second Turning of the Wheel of the Dharma. The *Divyavadana* relates how Asoka sent for Upagupta and having received him with due honour as the 'chief interpreter of the Dharma' asked him what he should do, to which Upagupta replied: 'O great king, the Lord, the Blessed Tathagata [Buddha Sakyamuni] has entrusted to me as well as to you the depository of the Law. Let us make every effort to preserve that which the Leader of the World has transmitted to us, when he was in the midst of his disciples.' Whereupon Asoka answered that it was his desire to 'visit, honour, and mark with a sign for the benefit of remote posterity all the places where the Blessed Buddha has sojourned'. The first of these sites was the birthplace of Prince Siddhartha at Lumbini, which was visited by the emperor in the twentieth year after his anointing and in great state:

> With him went four battalions of troops, and the perfumes, flowers, and garlands of due worship were not forgotten. Arriving at the garden Upagupta extended his right hand, and said to Asoka, 'Here, O great King, the Venerable One was born,' adding, 'At this site,

Veneration of the *Bodhi* tree of Buddha Sakyamuni at Bodhgaya, his particular tree being the *pippala* or *pipal* (*Ficus religiosa*). From the Bharhut stupa.

excellent to behold, should be the first monument consecrated in honour of the Buddha.' The King, after giving 100,000 golden coins to the people of the country, raised a stupa pillar and retired.

Besides making a personal pilgrimage to the thirty-two sites associated with the life and teaching of Buddha Sakyamuni and other sites associated with the earlier Buddhas, Asoka decided that the best way to spread the Dharma was to distribute the relics of the Sakyamuni throughout his empire – by opening up the eight original Maharaparinirvana stupas and reburying their sacred contents in tiny portions within thousands of new stupas built right across the land – the texts speak hyperbolically of 84,000 such stupas, representing the 84,000 sections of the Dharma and the 84,000 particles of the Buddha. According to the *Asokavadana*, there was initial resistance from the local Buddhists and when the emperor came to open up the first relic stupa, King Ajatashatru's stupa at Rajgir, he had to use force: 'Then the King, saying, "I will distribute the relics of the Exalted One", marched with an armed force in fourfold array, opened the stupa put up by Ajatashatru, and took the relics'. The text goes on to say that here and at the other original relic stupas he opened up, Asoka repaired the damaged structure: 'Having given back the relics, putting them distributively in the place whence they had been taken, he restored the stupa. He did the same to the second, and so on until he had taken the seventh bushel; and restoring the stupas, he then went on to Ramagrama'. Although unclear, the text can only mean that after removing the relic remains from each stupa Asoka returned some small part of the relics as part of his redistribution scheme.

Seven of the eight original stupas were successfully broken into, but not the eighth – the stupa of the Koliyas of Koligrama at Ramagrama. Here when Asoka arrived to open the stupa he found it guarded by the Nagas or serpent kings, who refused to allow him to remove the relics, which suggests that at Koligrama, too, the emperor's authority was challenged by the local people, probably followers of a snake-worship cult in which the sacred cobra Naag was revered as a guardian of the Buddha.

Some indication as to how the Sakyamuni Buddha relics were

re-interred by Emperor Asoka can be gained from an account in the *Mahavamsa* chronicle of Ceylon of the building of a relic-chamber within the *Mahathupa* or Great Stupa at Anuradhapura to house some bone relics of Sakyamuni Buddha obtained from the Himalayas by Emperor Asoka's missionary son Mahinda. These relics were placed at the base of the stupa within a stone box made up of six flat stones, which stood on a 'flower-offering ledge' in the centre of the stupa. As well as the relics themselves, the coffer contained various precious things including jewels, garlands and a representation of the Bodhi-tree in symbolic form.

The Opening

Piprahwa Kot, 18 January 1898

It was mid-January, most likely one of those days when the sun takes all morning to burn off the mists which cloak the Gangetic plains at that time of year. Logic suggests therefore that it was probably just after lunch when William ('Willie') Claxton Peppé marshalled his party and led them on horseback and in pony traps northwards towards the border. After five and a half miles – and just half a mile short of the Nepalese frontier – the party, consisting of perhaps half a dozen Europeans of both sexes, turned off the track and dismounted. Before them rose the largest of a number of knolls known locally as *kots*, a word derived for the Sanskrit term for a ruler's palace or fortress but which had come to be used locally to describe any unnatural mound. This particular mound Willie Peppé had named the Piprahwa Kot, after the name of the nearest village, which itself took its name from an extensive grove of *pipal* (*ficus religiosa*) trees, long regarded as sacred. The kot now swarmed with coolies – workmen drawn from Peppé's own Birdpore Estate supplemented by Tharus from across the border. Before the forty-five square mile Birdpore Estate had been laid out in the 1840s and 1850s this had all been jungle and swamp, inhabited only by wild animals – and by the Tharu forest-dwellers, whose immunity from the virulent local form of malaria now made them a valuable asset, even if they disliked manual labour.

Three generations of settlers, British and Indian, had worked on this land and many had died of fever in the process. Willie's maternal grandfather had been part of the first generation, his father William Peppé senior among the second, joining the Birdpore

William Claxton Peppé of Birdpore Estate, probably photographed in the year of his first marriage in 1884, when he was aged 32. *(Courtesy of Neil Peppé)*

Estate in 1849 as a manager and marrying Willie's mother a year later. It was William Peppé the elder who had had built Birdpore House, a palatial bungalow with a magnificent covered veranda at the front and a broad sweep of steps that led down to a garden complete with lawns, herbaceous borders and an ornamental fountain. Willie himself belonged to the third generation. He had been born in Birdpore House in 1852 but sent home at six to be educated in Scotland. At twenty-one he had returned to India, taking over the management of the estate sixteen years later when the old man had become too infirm to carry on. He was now forty-five years of age and in his prime, and there was no one within miles who would have dared dispute his authority as the raja or *zamindar* of Birdpore Estate and all its people, for he was ruler in all but name. It was, after all, the Peppés who had transformed a wilderness into a going concern and in the process given employment, security and a modicum of prosperity to a large labour force and their families. A stern man and a hard task-master Peppé-Sahib might be but he was also a just man who knew the ways of his people and who listened to their concerns.

Work had started on the Piprahwa Kot ten months earlier. Three weeks' of clearing away soil and loose piles of bricks had revealed a massive hemispherical dome some 120 feet in diameter. It appeared to be built entirely of large rectangular slabs of fired bricks, reddish in colour, the accumulated weight of which had caused the entire structure to settle and spread, so that what must originally have stood some fifty feet high or more at the centre was now half that height.

At that point Willie Peppé had suspended all work, partly because the hot season was by then too advanced to think of going on and partly because he needed expert advice.

That advice had been readily available for, by happy coincidence, two leading authorities on Indian archaeology were senior civil servants attached to the provincial division of Gorakhpur within which the Birdpore Estate lay, and a third was actively engaged in an archaeological excavation just a matter of miles away across the border in Nepal. Willie Peppé had chosen to consult the man he knew best: Vincent Arthur Smith of the Indian Civil Service (ICS), then serving as District Judge in the divisional headquarters at Gorakhpur town – sixty miles by road from Birdpore but brought closer thanks to the new branch line running north to Uska Bazaar.

Smith was the son of the well-known Irish antiquarian and numismatist Dr. Aquilla Smith and had come out to India twenty-six years earlier after graduating from Trinity College, Dublin. Having topped the final examination list for the ICS in 1871, he had been marked out as a man who would go far. He could have had the pick of the provinces but had plumped for service in the North-Western Provinces and Oude, usually referred to as the NWP&O. His first posting as Assistant Commissioner had been to the Basti District, within which lay the Birdpore Grant, and there a year later in 1873 he had met Willie Peppé, newly graduated from Edinburgh University. At that time Smith had been twenty-five years old and Peppé twenty-one.

In the years that followed the two had become good acquaintances rather than close friends. The ICS was an elite service and its members did not fraternise with those they governed. Furthermore, the mercantile and planter community to which the Peppés belonged came low in the caste system that the British in India followed, and whether gentlemen or not, those like William Peppé who were 'country born' of India-domiciled parents came lower still, however grand their estates. It would have helped if the two had shared interests outside their work, but the one was interested only in the 30,000 acres of the Birdpore Estate that he managed as his own fiefdom while the other spent his leisure-time digging into India's past in an almost literal sense.

Early on in his career Smith had made his professional mark with the publication of *The Settlement Officer's Manual for the North-Western Provinces*, and in the normal course of events would have expected to be running his own Division as a Commissioner by the time he was forty-five and a senior figure within the NWP&O Secretariat by fifty – instead of which he was now fifty-one and still stuck in the middle ranks.

The reasons for this lack of success were not easy to discern, since Smith was a most able and conscientious servant of the Raj and would afterwards be described by a friend as 'thoroughly Irish, genial, hospitable, and outspoken'. Indeed, it may have been a case of being too outspoken for his own good, to say nothing of spending too much time following his *shauq*, by which was meant a hobby that grows into an all-consuming passion. Like his father before him, Smith was fascinated by the past, and in India that fascination developed into an all-absorbing interest in every aspect of Indian history. One of the earliest of his predecessors in that same part of India had been Sir William Henry Sleeman, who had achieved fame as the official who had uncovered the murderous cult of *thugee* and had then gone on to play the leading role in its suppression. Smith now had the opportunity to go over the ground covered by Sleeman half a century earlier, an experience that led to his publishing an edited version of Sleeman's *Rambles and Recollections of an Indian Official*. But this interest in India's more recent past soon led to look deeper into India's 'lost' early history prior to the arrival of Islam. 'He early formed the resolution of writing the ancient history of Northern India,' declared an Indian contemporary. 'In the midst of heavy official duties, Dr. Smith persisted in his resolution of devoting all his spare hours to his favourite studies'.

At the time of Willie Peppé's initial clearing of the Piprahwa Kot in the spring of 1897 Vincent Smith had been too busy to spare a visit but in October of that same year, while on the way to undertake some archaeological explorations of his own, he had called in at Birdpore to examine the partly exposed knoll. He had without hesitation declared it to be a Buddhist stupa or relic mound, the bricks pointing to an unusually early date, their large size being 'specially characteristic of the Asoka period'. He had recommended further excavation and had instructed Peppé on how he should proceed, and when he had got back to his bungalow in Gorakhpur he had written him a letter explaining who Asoka was and why he was so important: 'Asoka of the Ceylonese books, who calls himself Piyadasi in his inscriptions was Emperor of India, with his capital at Patna (Pataliputra) from about BC 259–222. He visited the traditional birthplace of Gautama Buddha in the 21st year of his reign in BC 239'.

Smith's letter had contained much more besides, including references to a Chinese traveller named Huien Tsang and to various stone pillars recently uncovered close by on the Nepali side of the border. However, Willie Peppé had never had much time for history and, besides, he had far more important things to think about: his second wife, Caroline Ella, had just given birth to their third son Lionel at Birdpore.

It was not until after the Christmas festivities, with a large party of relatives staying over at Birdpore House, that Willie Peppé's

The Piprahwa stupa after excavation. *(Above)* A photograph from William Peppé's album shows the Piprahwa complex from the south after excavation, with the remains of a small monastic building exposed in the foreground. *(Courtesy of Neil Peppé) (Below)* The better photo was taken in late February 1898, and shows Willie Peppé (in white solar topee and ducks) talking to Dr. Anton Führer, while a surveyor takes measurements. *(India Office Library, British Library)*

thoughts had returned to the uncovered mound at Piprahwa. Excavation recommenced in the New Year of 1898 with the digging of a trench some ten feet wide into and across the mound from north to south. Then a square well had been sunk down into the centre of the kot to a depth of almost twenty feet, cutting through alternating layers of brick and clay mortar. At a depth of ten feet a small soapstone vase had been uncovered, badly smashed and full of clay but also containing 'some beads, crystals, gold ornaments, cut stars etc'. The vase and its contents had been put to one side and the digging had gone on – to uncover the top of 'a circular pipe, filled with clay, and encircled with brickwork'. This pipe appeared to mark the central axis of the stupa. At its head it was about two feet in diameter but as they continued to dig down so it began to shrink until finally it was no more than four inches in diameter, by which time they had descended through another eighteen feet of 'solid brickwork set in clay'. At this point the central 'pipe' widened to form a small rectangle, which the diggers took to mean they had arrived at the base of the stupa.

On the afternoon of 15 January Peppé had been called from his estate work to be shown the latest discovery: a hole in the brick-work at the bottom of the well scarcely larger than a badger's set. It was cleared to reveal a recess, inside which sat a rectangular stone chest or coffer 'of a very superior hard sandstone … cut out of one solid piece of rock … in a perfect state of preservation with its sides very smoothly cut … all but polished'. The coffer was about two and a half feet wide and about two feet high.

Peppé had then called for a lamp and by crouching down beside the hole had made out that the coffer extended more than four feet into the darkness. What he also saw was that the lid was cracked into four sections but had not collapsed. 'The chest was perfectly closed,' he recorded afterwards. 'Fortunately the deep groove in the lid fitting so perfectly on the flange of the chest prevented the lid from falling in when it was first broken and also when we were removing it.'

Peppé's training as an engineer told him that the coffer and lid together must weigh at least three-quarters of a ton. In fact, the lid alone was afterward found to weigh 408 pounds. He called a halt to the excavation, placed guards over the dig and went home to plan how the coffer might best be removed from its niche and brought to the surface without damaging whatever contents it held.

In the meantime, the coolie force was put to work clearing the surrounding area, revealing brick-built buildings on three sides of the stupa. The largest was laid out beside the stupa's north-east corner: a rectangular building 120 feet by 100, with a central courtyard surrounded by a series of small rooms or cells each ten foot square. 'I have had the walls laid bare but have not dug to any depth,' wrote Peppé of the uncovering of what seemed to be a monastery. 'At different parts of this building I have found long nails, some with broad beads, and also bits of earthen pots … The wood of the lower portion of the [door] frame was found in several of the door ways, looking black and charred and readily crumbling away.' This appeared to suggest that the monastery had been destroyed by fire.

Three days passed before all was ready for the raising of the giant stone coffer and its opening, so that it was on 18 January 1898 that Willie Peppé, manager and senior shareholder of the Birdpore Estate, brought his guests to the Piprahwa Kot to witness the event. Four adults would afterwards put their names to a deposition describing what transpired: two of Willie's cousins – Allen B. Peppé, manager of the estate of the Maharaja of Chota Nagpur, and George Tosco Peppé, who managed a tea estate in Ranchi – Mr Judson, assistant manager of the bordering Newra Estate, lying to the east of Birdpore, and a 'Madame' whose name is indecipherable but was probably Alice, wife of George Tosco Peppé. Also present was George Tosco's seventeen-year-old daughter Elfie. Missing from the scene was Willie Peppé's wife Ella; it was now three months since the birth of their son Lionel, but the boy was not doing well and she had felt unable to leave him.

A pulley and hoist had been set up and a wheeled trolley lowered into the well. The lid of the coffer was then carefully removed in its four sections and the coffer itself drawn out to rest on the trolley. The lid was then replaced and both sections winched up to the surface and set down on firm ground. The lid was then again removed.

'It so happened that we delayed opening this casket three

(Above) The stone coffer *in situ* in the Piprahwa stupa, with its lid off, prior to being lifted out of the shaft. *(Courtesy of Neil Peppé)*

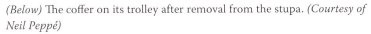

(Below) The coffer on its trolley after removal from the stupa. *(Courtesy of Neil Peppé)*

days after we had unearthed it,' wrote Peppé, 'and our curiosity was raised to the utmost. Our surprise can be imagined when on removing the lid we found an empty chest save for these few miniature vases standing up as they had been placed probably two thousand years ago'. With the younger members of the family crowding at his shoulders Willie Peppé reached into the coffer. The reason for his disappoint was that the five little receptacles in the coffer were scarcely larger than jam-jars. But then he must have caught the glint of crystal and gold, for not only was the floor of the coffer strewn with tiny, sparkling objects but the lid of one of the containers had come off and had turned the far corner of the coffer into a mass of twinkling points of light.

Reaching down into the stone chest Willie Peppé closed his fingers round the largest of the receptacles. It was smooth and almost waxy to the touch, and when he lifted it into the light of day he and the others saw that it was made of soapstone and shaped very like a *lota*, the bulbous-shaped waterpot found in households throughout the Indian sub-continent. There was a murmur of disappointment, as much from the workmen lining both sides of the cut as from the circle of Europeans crowded round the pit.

Peppé dipped into the coffer for a second time and emerged holding another soapstone container. But this was quite different in shape from the first and altogether finer: a perfect sphere divided horizontally across the middle to form a receptacle and a cover, the former set on a disc-shaped base, the latter capped by a slightly smaller disc which provided the base for a second sphere and a third even smaller disc topped by a spike. From top to bottom the object stood no more than seven inches high, a delicate piece of turned steatite stoneware almost the colour of ivory. 'Beautifully turned,' was Peppé's first observation, 'and the chisel marks seem quite as fresh as if it had been made a few days ago'.

One of the watching Europeans called for the receptacle to be opened but Willie Peppé shook his head. He was a man used to having his way and no-one challenged him. He turned his attention back to the coffer and this time brought out a third soapstone container, much smaller than the first two and shaped somewhat like a circular pill-box. It was passed without ceremony to Peppé's foreman, who wrapped it in newspaper and placed it beside the two other containers in a box lined with wood-shavings.

'This one's has some damage,' Willie Peppé declared to no one in particular and it was some moments before he straightened up, this time holding a spherical container and lid very similar in shape to the first, but smaller and slightly darker. It had evidently suffered at some time in the past, for it bore a hole the size of a new-born child's fist near the base. Again Peppé made no effort to prise top and base apart and the vessel was packed away with the rest.

'Just one more, at the far end, and it's come apart.'

Peppé now had to reach deep into the coffer. When he straightened up he held in the palm of one hand a shining object quite different from the others. It was a hemispherical lid made entirely of crystal, topped by a delicate handle in the shape of a fish. He held it up to murmurs of admiration and now for the first time his sun-tanned features softened into a smile. 'That's the cover,' he said. 'Now let us see what it covers.'

He ducked back into the coffer and there was a great deal of scrabbling and wriggling before he stood up. Now there was a broad grin on his face and he kept one hand cupped over whatever was in the other until he had straightened himself. He waited until he had the full attention of the entire assembly of Europeans, estate workers and Tharu villagers. '*Dekko*!' he exclaimed as he took away his right hand. 'Look at that!'

Cupped in the palm of Willie Peppé's left hand was the base of the crystal container, circular and some two to three inches deep. It was filled to the brim with hundreds of jewels of every shape and hue, many of them beads cut to resemble tiny flowers – and not only jewels but quantities of gold and silver flowers, each with six or eight petals. So close-heaped was this cache that it was impossible to make out any detail, but it was enough to silence those who were closest to hand and to cause those who stood at the back to shout out that Peppé Sahib had found treasure.

'Will you dig any deeper, Willie?' called out his seventeen-year-old niece Elfie. 'Oh, do go on digging.' But no one took any notice of her.

Willie Claxton Peppé was viewed by Elfie Peppé as 'rather

The five reliquary urns from the Piprahwa stone coffer, as photographed by Dr. Führer in late February 1898. *(IOL, BL)*

overbearing' and 'something of a domestic tyrant' but the fact was he liked to do things by the book. He now stayed behind to organise the operation that saw the stone coffer safely hoisted onto a bullock cart and he only left the scene after he was certain that no one would touch the coffer until it had been brought to Birdpore House, the reason being that there were still numerous beads and what looked like fragments of wood scattered about inside. That same evening, after the five urns and their contents had been locked away in a storeroom at Birdpore House, he sat down to write two letters. One was addressed to Vincent Smith at Gorakhpur. The other went to the Archaeological Surveyor to the Government of the NWP&O and Curator of Lucknow Museum, who was at this time conducting his own archaeological excavation inside Nepalese territory no more than fifteen miles away. His name was the Reverend and Doctor of Philosophy Anton Alois Führer.

Führer was a year younger than Willie Peppé, having been born in Germany in 1853. As a student he had studied theology at the University of Würzburg and after completing his doctorate had been ordained into the Roman Catholic priesthood. In about 1878 he was sent out to Bombay as Father Führer to join the teaching staff at St Xavier's College. However, while still in Germany Führer had developed an interest in Oriental studies which had led him to study Sanskrit under a group of leading Orientalists that included Dr. Julius Jolly. In Bombay he found a flourishing circle of Sanskritists that included his former mentor Dr. Jolly but was dominated by another German, the already eminent Professor Johann Georg Bühler, who had been appointed Professor of Sanskrit at the University of Bombay in 1863 at the age of twenty-six and had since then led the way in Sanskrit studies throughout the sub-continent. German scholars had already established themselves as leaders in the field of Indology and many at this time had found employment in various posts in India. Anton Führer now began to take his Sanskrit more seriously and when Professor Bühler left Bombay in 1880 to take up the chair of Sanskrit at the University of Vienna he continued his studies under Bühler's successor Professor Peter Peterson. In 1882 Anton Führer published the first of a number of seemingly learned articles in the *Journal of the Bombay Branch of the Royal Asiatic Society*. A year later he was credited as the editor of a Sanskrit *shastra* published in the *Bombay Sanskrit Series*, initiated by the man whom he always regarded as his prime mentor, Prof. Georg Bühler, with whom Führer remained in close contact throughout his career in India.

However, it seems that Führer and his employers at St Xavier's College were not in accord on matters of theology, and in about 1884 he either resigned or was dismissed and returned to Germany. Then in 1885 had come the Lucknow appointment, apparently as a result of the intervention of the then Lieutenant-Governor of the NWP&O, Sir Alfred Lyall, but almost certainly on the recommendation of Professor Bühler. So Führer had returned to India, no longer as Father Führer but as the Reverend Führer – and with a wife at his side. He was initially appointed assistant to a Major J. B. Keith, whose only qualification for the post of Archaeological Surveyor to the Government of the NWP&O was an undistinguished career as an artillery officer. However, two years later the Major retired and Führer became not only the province's new Archaeological Surveyor but also Curator of Lucknow Museum, housed in one of a complex of magnificent if decaying palace buildings in the centre of the city known collectively as the Chhutter Manzil. Although the museum was afterwards relocated in a larger building nearby known as the Lal Baradari, or 'Red Pavilion', in Führer's time it was housed in Gulistan-i-Iram, the 'Rose Garden of Heaven' (today an empty ruin), in the extensive cellars of which it was said that the dissolute King Nassir-ud-Din of Oude was poisoned by his nobles in 1837. Following the uprising of 1857 the entire complex had for months been the scene of the most desperate fighting as the British sought to hold the nearby Residency and then retake Lucknow.

Willie Peppé was just old enough to remember that hot summer of 1857, the year of the Mutiny. He had been five years old when he and his mother, elder sister and infant brother had become refugees, sailing downriver in a hired country-boat through a hostile countryside for a week before joining other fleeing Europeans at Patna and continuing on down the Ganges in a steamer to Calcutta. His father, William Peppé senior, had stayed behind to protect his estate and it had been almost a year before they saw him again. He had lost a finger in one of his numerous skirmishes with the rebels and at one point had been forced to flee his home in his pyjamas and then watch Birdpore House go up in flames. But he had survived and Birdpore House had been rebuilt.

The three children were then taken by their mother to Aberdeenshire, where the Peppés had their roots (although there were those in the family who believed that their unusual surname came from French Huguenot ancestors). Sixteen years passed before the younger Peppés saw their childhood home again. After schooling in Aberdeen Willie took a civil engineering degree at the University of Edinburgh. Then in 1873 he and his younger brother Georgie returned to Birdpore Estate to work for a father they had not seen for more than a decade.

The Birdpore Estate or Grant had been part of a curious experiment begun by the East India Company in the 1830s. Back in 1801 Nawab Saadat Ali Khan of Oude had been forced to cede a large slice of his kingdom to the East India Company to pay off his kingdom's debts. It included a block of land known as the Gorakhpur Tarai.

The word *tarai* means 'damp country' but it came to be used to describe the territory bordering the foothills of Nepal adjacent to and merging into the great Gangetic plain, a strip of land laced with scores of rivers debouching from the hills onto the plains and all running north to south. The more northerly section of the strip, which the British knew as the Upper or Nepal Tarai, was spoken of by the Nepalis as the *char khose jhaari*, meaning the forest that was four *kho*s wide, a *khos* being the furthest distance a cow's mooing might be heard, so thus about two or three miles. This eight- to twelve-mile-wide forest section was largely made up of magnificent *sal* trees, known locally as *sak*, and it marked the physical boundary where the foothills of the Himalayas ended and the central Gangetic plain began. According to one of the first Britons to travel through this forest belt, it was the haunt of 'wild beasts, especially elephants and rhinoceroses ... Tigers are not so numerous as might have been expected in a country so uncultivated. Black bears of a great size are more numerous, and are very troublesome. Wild hogs, hog-deer, hares, foxes and jackals, are to be found in abundance.'

As far as the Nawabs of Oude were concerned the Upper Tarai was of little value other than for its timber and they had been content to allow it to be taken over by the hillmen of Gorkha, who after conquering Kathmandu Valley in the late eighteenth century had begun to encroach upon the Indian plains.

South of the great forest of the Upper or Nepal Tarai was the Lower Tarai, a much broader strip of more open country: 'a wasteland covered with long grass or reeds ... intersected by numerous small rivers'. But it was a wasteland that could be grazed over by cattle in April and May 'when the periodical hot winds entirely destroyed the herbage of more southern regions'.

Human settlement in both parts of the tarai came at a price. What both the hill rajas of Nepal and the nawabs of the plains knew all too well was that the region was little short of a death-trap, due what was known locally as the *ayul* – 'a poisonous air, which many of them imagine proceeds from the breath of large serpents ... Rational men assign a more natural origin to the Ayul or bad air. They say, that the ground in the forests, in spring, is covered in fallen leaves, which are rotted by the first rains of the hot season, and, by their putrefaction, corrupt the air ... after which the unhealthy season begins, and continues until the cold weather.'

What the locals called ayul the British came to know as tarai fever, a strain of malaria so virulent that permanent human settlement in the tarai was thought well-nigh impossible. The further north you travelled the worse the tarai fever got. 'Throughout the hours of daylight the Tarai is safe enough,' wrote a contemporary of Willie Peppé's:

> It is the evening that man may not spend in this beautiful park. Sundown in the Tarai has brought to an end more attempted raids into Nepal and has buried more political hopes than has ever been known. The English learned their lesson early, for within forty years of Plassey [1757] a column withered and retreated before the miasma of this paradise. The English had been told of its dangers but they had to learn by experience what all India had known and feared for centuries.

Tarai fever was as lethal to the Gorkhas and the other hill-tribes of Nepal as it was to the British and to the Indian plain-dwellers, and they too learned to keep out, so that for centuries the tarai served as a barrier and a no-man's-land, home only to one group of people: the jungle-dwellers known as the Tharu, who by all accounts had lived there since time immemorial.

According to one of the first Europeans to view them as anthropological specimens, the Tharus 'style themselves *ban-rajas*, or "forest kings", enjoying the free and easy life of the forests'. After centuries of independence, they were now in the process of 'becoming rapidly Hinduised', particularly those who lived in the Lower Tarai. 'The women do the largest part of the sowing, weeding and harvesting,' wrote Dr. Anton Führer of them in 1897–

> whilst the men engage in hunting and fishing, which they regard as the proper occupation of their sex. Their villages are from one to two miles distant from each other, and the houses are all made of wood and grass. The outside grass walls of each house are plastered over with red mud; they never use cow-dung for this as is usual with the Indian people outside the jungle and forests. The houses are large, cool and commodious, and generally raised on poles, in order to

Two semi-Hinduised Tharu women photographed by Dr. Führer in the Nepal Tarai in 1897. The clay storage jars in the background were on display only because their mud-and-thatch dwelling had just burnt down. *(IOL, BL)*

protect the inmates from damp and malaria ... Every little village is a self-governing community. Disputes are settled by a council of elders, and this is sometimes presided over by a head-man or *chaudhari* [who] acquires the status of head-man by tacit consent and not by election. The decisions of the council or the head-man are obeyed unreservedly ... Amongst themselves the Tharus are, for the most part, a peaceful and good-natured race, following without question, as if by a law of nature, the customs and maxims of their ancestors. The honesty of the Tharus is proverbial.

By the civil code known as the *Mulki Ain* promulgated in 1854 the Rana rulers of Nepal had officially designated the Tharus as low caste Hindus, describing them as 'enslavable alcohol drinkers' and 'a degraded and ignorant people'. Like a number of other groups of low social status in India, they reacted against discrimination by claiming descent from one of the so-called royal clans of the Rajputs, the most popular explanation being that their ancestors had migrated east from their homeland in the Thar desert in the face of Islamic conquest. However, the single fact that they had developed such a high degree of immunity from the local strain of malaria pointed to a much longer residence in the tarai. There were other indicators, too – the absence of caste divisions, an abhorrence of animal sacrifice but no special respect for cows, a history of persecution by the Hindus, the building of mounds over cremated remains, a fondness for endogamy in several of their clans and a number of significant differences in the way they practised Hinduism – all of which suggested that the religion of their ancestors had been very different. There was even talk that these ancestors, among whose ruined cities they lived as hunter-gatherers, had once been great kings and had produced not one but two great conquerors of men.

What was also notable about the Tharus was the fear in which they were held by the hillmen to the north and the plain-dwellers of the south:

In the plains *Tharuhat* or 'the Tharu country' is a synonym for 'witch-land'. Every Tharu woman, after the marriageable age, is supposed by those who live outside the Tharu country to possess the power of the Evil Eye to bewitch and enchant: so that she has the power to turn a stranger into a wild animal or destroy him slowly by consumptive fever. This is one of the reasons why all natives of India outside the Tarai forests dread the Tharus and fear to live among them.

Rural scenes on a decorative frieze from the Bharhut stupa. The Tharu people store their grain and keep their fowls in clay structures similar to those shown here.

The reality, of course, was that the ayul had served the Tharus well, ensuring that for generations they remained free to roam the forests as hunter-gatherers, rice-farmers and fisherfolk. But as the nineteenth century wore on the Tharus came under ever-increasing pressure from north and south as large tracts of what they had always regarded as their ancestral lands were expropriated and turned over to cultivation. More pressure came from the growing practice of setting fire to jungle grassland in the spring so that cattle could be driven up from the parched plains to feed on the new grass. This had a damaging effect on the local wildlife on which the Tharus depended for part of their diet, to say nothing of the increased risk to their lives as large numbers of tigers, rhinos and wild buffalo were forced out from their natural habitat.

A significant part of this pressure came from the Gorakhpur Tarai, a rectangular tract of land approximately sixty miles in length and forty wide extending northwards from the town of Gorakhpur to the Nepalese border. The East India Company (EICo) made no effort to exploit this territory until after its border with Nepal had been fought over and secured in 1815. But in an effort to deprive the Nepalese of resources during that same war, the British army commander was authorised to 'remove the class of persons inhabiting the Forest of Bootwal [Butwal, 65 miles due north of Gorakhpur], denominated Taroos [Tharus], together with their families … for settling them in the district of Gorakhpoor, where it was intended to provide for them by assignments of waste lands'. As a result of this enforced resettlement the lands the Tharus had previously occupied within Nepal were abandoned: 'The forest or jungle extended itself on the high lands, and the low lands which produced the rice crops, became covered in high reeds, the habitation of Tigers, Elephants, and other wild animals. In this state it existed for fully twenty years'.

Then in 1834 the Government of the EICo's North-Western Provinces devised a plan 'for bringing the waste lands and forests in the Zillah [portion of a province, afterwards designated a 'division' by the British] of Gorakhpoor into cultivation ... by inviting European and Anglo-Indian capitalists to take leases of fifty years, bringing the land into cultivation'. Within a few years more than 650 square miles of land had been leased out, one of the earliest being the Birdpore Grant, which took its name from the originator of the scheme.

The Gorakhpur Grants scheme was a disaster. No one had considered the tarai fever, which decimated both the British grantees and their imported labour forces: 'The periodical rains brought annually malaria and fever,' wrote the son of one of this first generation of colonisers, 'and when sickness did not kill outright, it incapacitated some, and induced others to remove away to healthier regions ... No single Grantee escaped the ordeal, all equally suffered, and if a few outlived the dark period of trouble and misfortune, it was simply from having more perseverance.'

Managing the Birdpore Grant as co-proprietors were two brothers: Hugh and John Pirie Gibbon, who tried everything from indigo and sugar-cane to lac manufacture, silk weaving and horse breeding, but with very little success. So damaging was the malaria that in 1843 Hugh Gibbon and his wife Delia decided to take their three children home to Aberdeen, where they left them with his mother before returning to India. Very soon after their return, however, Hugh succumbed to malaria leaving his wife with a new-born son – who also died. Then in 1848 Hugh's brother John Pirie Gibbon died, leaving the widowed Delia to run the estate on her own. She looked around for a new manager and found him in the person of William Peppé, who had been managing a nearby estate until differences with its owners had led him to quit. Within months the two were married. Their daughter Annie was born a year later in 1850; then Willie in 1852; Sarah, who died in infancy and was buried in their garden at Birdpore, in 1854; and their last child Georgie in 1856.

Under the joint management of William Peppé and his wife's cousin William Gibbon an estate burdened with enormous debts was turned into a going concern, but not before three decades of hard work accompanied by many setbacks. Every year some 500 male labourers were brought in by train from Azimghur, Jaunpur and Chota Nagpur in Bengal. Due to malaria and disease very few returned home but enough survivors settled with their families to provide the core of the estate's labour force. It was also Peppé's good fortune that in the 1840s large numbers of Hindu and Muslim refugees from the ruinously misgoverned Kingdom of Oude migrated east into Birdpore to replace the lost labour – and that not long afterwards quinine became more widely available as a partial remedy for malaria. Peppé and Gibbon also recognised that it was in their estate's interests that these migrants should be leased plots of land to settle on and cultivate free of rent for three years. They set up dispensaries to make the quinine freely available and began to drain the swamps that, unknown to all, provided the breeding grounds for the malaria-carrying mosquitoes. 'They seemed to stand the climate better than the imported labourers,' wrote William Gibbon of these new settlers:

> The Western Grants gradually settled down and became culti-vated where the land offered the most advantages. This gradually induced others with families to join in the venture ... The soil was proved well adapted to the cultivation of rice, and profitable to the husbandman ... With tillage and cultivation the climate improved, and although the latter period of the rainy season, with its decaying vegetation still occasions malaria, bringing with it fever and ague, spleen and other disorders, the cultivator has learned the great boon of a timely dose of quinine, dispensed to him by his *malik* [chief] the Grantee. In time, dispensaries with European medicines were introduced, drainage and other sanitary arrangements attended

to, and better communications with the outside world, prospects brightened, and the life of the Grantee became a different existence altogether from what it was at the start.

Over the same period Peppé and Gibbon discovered that with proper irrigation in the form of canals and reservoirs – known locally as tanks – Birdpore's rich soil could produce some of the best, if not *the* best, rice in India, which when transported down river to Patna became better known as Patna rice.

In 1884 William Peppé's eldest son Willie returned from a home leave with his new bride, Rosalie, who never adjusted to the harsh summer environment of Birdpore and died three years later. Over this same period William Peppé senior became increasingly unwell and took to spending more of his time in a handsome cottage he had bought for the family in the hill-station of Mussoorie. The management of the main estate he left in the capable hands of his eldest son Willie, while Georgie, the younger brother, took charge of two smaller holdings nearby.

It was at this juncture – with Willie Peppé to all intents in charge of the Birdpore Estate – that the Reverend Doctor Anton Alois Führer appeared on the local archaeological scene, having been appointed in 1885 to the post of Curator of the Lucknow Museum and Archaeological Surveyor of the province that since the annexation of Oude by the EICo had been enlarged to become the North-Western Provinces and Oude (NWP&O).

In that same year of 1885 a grim struggle for succession was being fought out north of the border in the Kingdom of Nepal. Here a remarkable pattern of rule had developed under the nominal suzereinty of the royal family of the Shahs, whose ancestor Prithvi Narayan Shah of Gorkha had overthrown the Malla kings of Kathmandu Valley in 1768 and subsequently created the nation state of Nepal. The kings remained prisoners in their palaces while a succession of ministers drawn from a rival family, the Ranas, ruled in their stead as hereditary prime ministers, styling themselves maharajas and according themselves all the titles and privileges of kingship, including the possession of large numbers of wives and concubines. In 1877 the founder of this Rana dynasty of ruling prime ministers, Prime Minister Maharaja Sir Jung Bahadur Rana, died of cholera while hunting in the tarai and his brothers saw to it that the prime ministership passed not to one of his sons but to one of them, the genial but weak Maharaja Ranudeep Singh Rana, who left the running of the state to his more able younger brother Dhir Shumsher Rana, nominally his Commander-in-Chief.

Unlike his brother, Dhir Shumsher Rana was both a hard-bitten warrior and a statesman. He effectively ruled Nepal in his brother's name and through a series of purges ensured that the succession passed to his own male line. This was formidable, consisting of seventeen legitimate sons and numerous illegitimate ones. The former became notorious as the *Satrabhai* or 'seventeen brothers'. After the death of their father in 1884 the Satrabhai continued his work to strengthen their position and in 1885 five of them combined to shoot dead their uncle Maharaja Ranudeep Singh Rana and murder all other rival Rana cousins in the line of succession.

According to family legend, it was Khadga Shumsher Rana, the second oldest of the brothers and then aged twenty-four, who played the leading role in this brotherly putsch. Nevertheless, it was his older brother Bir Shumsher Rana who then became Prime Minister and *de facto* ruler of Nepal, with Khadga Shumsher at his side as his Commander-in-Chief. The other more junior members of the Satrabhai awarded themselves the rank of general and took on various roles as governors and ministers under their eldest brother.

Within two years of gaining power it had become clear to Prime Minister Bir Shumsher Rana that the growing strength of Khadga Shumsher had become a threat to his rule. He summoned his younger brother to his palace and told him bluntly that 'Two lions cannot live in one forest'. At this point the stories begin to differ: one version has it that Khadga Shumsher immediately offered to withdraw from Kathmandu Valley in the interests of brotherly unity; the other, recorded by the visiting French Sanskritist Silvain Lévi in his journal, that 'four men throw themselves on him, take him by the wrists and the Maharaja announces to his younger brother that by an overflow of affection he creates him governor of Tansen, the district west of Nepal ... And under a strong escort

Some of the seventeen Satrabhai and their less legitimate brothers. The young Commander-in-Chief Khadga Jung Bahadur Shumsher Rana is seated in the centre next to the man he hoped to depose, his elder brother Prime Minister Bir Shumsher Rana (bearded and wearing helmet). The smaller brother seated on the other side of Bir Shumsher is their younger brother Chandra Shumsher, who later thwarted Khadga Shumsher's ambitions to rule Nepal from 1901 to 1929. Detail from a photograph taken by the court photographer Chitrakar in about 1887 during a reception for the visiting Chinese Amban of Tibet. *(Photo courtesy of Kiran Man Chitrakar)*

through mountain necks and dells, they lead the Governor to Palpa in spite of himself.'

Whichever version is the more accurate, the facts are that Khadga Shumsher was deprived of his military command, removed from the roll of succession and appointed Governor of the Western Tarai. His elder brother wanted him far enough away to present no military danger yet close enough for him to keep an eye on him, so he exiled him to Palpa, several days' march to the west of

Kathmandu. As the 'Palpa Raja', after the name of the town where he had his summer capital, Khadga Shumsher's new command extended from the lower foothills of the Himalayas in central Nepal to the Indian border opposite the NWP&O and northern Bihar (at that time still part of the province of Bengal).

Although raised in relative poverty, Khadga Shumsher was among the first of the Ranas to benefit from a good English-medium education by being sent to school at what afterwards became Presidency College in Calcutta. The result was that he was well-read and had a good command of written and spoken English. According to an English visitor to Nepal, who knew his brothers better than the man himself, Khadga was 'a man of curious contrasts – a bully and a keen student of antiquarian research; useless as a leader, he was a capable enough man in carrying out readily and efficiently a scheme thought up by another ... but his impatient vanity was such that there are on record against him no less than four separate attempts to overthrow a Prime Minister of Nepal'. Fair assessment or not, the facts are that his banishment to the Western Tarai at the age of twenty-six hit General Khadga Shumsher very hard, for it was a backwater in every sense of the word. In the summer the exile and his family lived in a small palace at Palpa built at 6,000 feet in the lowest of the ranges of the Himalayan foothills; in the winter months they moved down to the town of Batauli (now Butwal) which guarded the main highway into the hills. This was an ancient highway running south from Kathmandu to Gorakhpur and beyond, and one of the few trade links connecting Nepal with the outside world.

Ever since the days of Maharaja Jung Bahadur Rana, the rulers of Nepal had recognised the power of the British Raj in India and the threat it represented to their country's independence. To maintain that independence meant remaining on the best of terms with the British Government of India while at the same time keeping the British at a distance. By the terms of their original peace treaty with Britain in 1815 they had been forced to accept a British Resident in Kathmandu Valley but they kept him on a very tight leash and only in exceptional circumstances, such as a hunting party in the Nepal Tarai, were other Britons allowed to trespass across their borders. To this same end, no effort was made to open up Kathmandu Valley or to develop trade routes by building roads or railways linked to India. As the Satrabhai Ranas strengthened their hold on the government of Nepal in the late 1880s the tarai, with its forests and swamps and mosquitoes, came increasingly to be seen as a defensive shield, used principally as a hunting ground to which the Ranas repaired in the mosquito-free cold weather months from mid-October to mid-March to hunt tiger, rhino, elephant and lesser game.

It now became General Khadga Shumsher Rana's responsibility to organise these cold-weather shikars – and to exploit the Nepal Tarai's natural resources. British India needed railway sleepers for its fast-growing rail network and the sal timber from the tarai proved ideal for the purpose. When the Tharus declined to co-operate with the destruction of their forests the General brought in immigrants from India, many of them Muslims. Considerable numbers of *pahadis* or 'hill people' from Nepal also took the gamble of moving down into the unhealthy plains. More ancient forest not required by the Ranas for big-game hunting were cleared, followed by settlement and the planting of crops. Sufficient numbers of these new settlers survived the ayul to transform large swathes of the tarai jungle into open farmland. The losers were the Tharus. They rarely fought back, but they viewed these invaders with hostility, while the settlers for their part regarded the jungle-dwellers as little better than savages. Whereas the Tharu had always built with mud, timber and thatch the newcomers began to build with brick, often using old bricks recovered from the large kots that their clearances of the jungle exposed. These excavations frequently brought to light stone images, some of which were incorporated into new Hindu temples and some destroyed as manifestations of idolatry. Stories of Muslim iconoclasm have frequently been exaggerated – not least by boastful Muslim historians – but enough instances have been recorded by neutral observers such as Francis Buchanan and Brian Hodgson to show that idol-breaking and the building of new places of worship over infidel ruins was common-place in the Gangetic plains as late as the nineteenth century. Yet nineteenth-century progress, in the form of clearing away old ruins or recycling their materials, was at least as damaging as religious intolerance in obliterating the past.

As for General Khadga Shumsher, the accounts of his enemies say that he never stopped plotting his return to Kathmandu and power. Nevertheless, after a decade in exile as the Governor of Palpa he had become not only an expert in shikar but also an authority on the Western Tarai and everything it contained.

The Reading

Birdpore House, 19 January 1898

On the morning of 19 January Willie and Ella Peppé sat down with other members of their family at Birdpore House to examine the five vessels from the Piprahwa kot and their contents.

The Peppés' were planters and not archaeologists, and as the lid of each vase or pot was removed and its contents spread out on the table the excitement was so great that afterwards no one could quite recall what had come from where. The overall impression was of myriads of tiny, glittering gems – amethysts, cornelians, topazes, garnets, beryl, malachites, lapis lazuli, crystals, corals and pearls – mostly cut to resemble six- or eight-petalled flowers or leaves and many drilled as if they were intended to represent garlands of flowers. Scarcely less in number were flower shapes cut from gold or silver leaf, with the same gold and silver leaf being used for a remarkable variety of other tiny ornaments, which Willie Peppé began to list:

> an impression of a woman's figure, an inch long, on gold leaf, the upper part of her body being nude and the lower portion clothed; another small figure in gold leaf, nude; a large circular piece of rather thicker gold leaf, two inches in diameter, with scroll; an elephant stamped on gold leaf; several pieces in gold leaf stamped with the figure of a lion, having a trident over his back and the Buddhist cross (*svastika*) in front; several pieces with the impression of the Buddhist cross; one piece of solid gold, measuring ¾″ × ¼″ × ⅛″; pearls of various sizes …

Ella Peppé was the artist in the family and she now used her skills

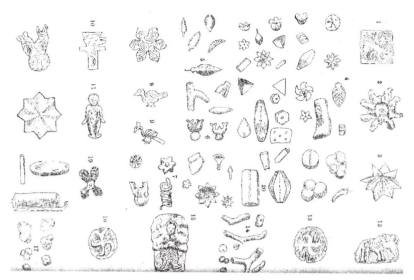

Mrs. Peppé's drawing of a selection of items from the Piprahwa stupa as published in the *Journal of the Royal Asiatic Society*. Her original drawing was subsequently lost.

to make drawings of a representative selection of what the family could only think of as buried treasure.

What was overlooked in all the excitement was that intermingled with all this 'treasure' were fragments of bone and ash which had originally been contained within one or more tiny wooden boxes. On exposure to the fresh air the box or boxes had simply crumbled into dust, scattering the contents, so that afterwards no one was quite sure where these contents had originally been placed or even if there had been one wooden box or several. However, a moment came when it dawned on all those gathered round the table that these fragmentary odds and ends must – could only be – human relics, and that the soapstone containers were actually reliquaries, the gold and gems and other precious objects no more than accompanying offerings. According to Willie Peppé, these bone fragments were 'quite recognisable, and might have been picked up a few days ago'.

The mood became more solemn as the latter were placed on one side so that what remained on the table could be gathered together and put in two stone jars. 'I hereby certify,' declared Willie Peppé afterwards in a signed deposition witnessed by members of his family –

> that these two jars contain all the bones and wood & dust that were found in the different urns and lying loose in the coffer excavated by me in the stupa at Piprawah on the B. E. B D N W P [Birdpore Estate, Basti District, North-Western Provinces] ... These bones[,] wood dust etc have been kept in these jars under our mutual care & they have not been tampered with in any way. No one has been allowed to see them except in my presence & I have every confidence in saying they are exactly as they were unearthed by me.

On the evening of that same day, 19 January, both Vincent Smith in Gorakhpur and Dr. Anton Führer at his excavation site fifteen miles away received Willie Peppé's letters informing them of his discovery of the Piprahwa treasure. They immediately wrote back, both congratulating him on his finds – and both urging him to look for an inscription.

'My dear Peppé,' wrote Vincent Smith from Gorakhpur, 'Your discoveries at Piprahwa are very interesting. I send you a volume of the new Archaeological Survey Reports which gives an account of similar finds in the Madras Presd. [Presidency]. The great size of your stone chest is remarkable, and I believe the relics were very highly esteemed ones. I suppose there is no trace of any inscriptions.' He went on to ask Peppé to write 'a detailed account of your explorations accompanied by plans, sections and elevations', accompanied by drawings and photographs, and warned him that under the Treasure Trove Act he was required to inform the Collector of Basti District, since the Government of India had a 'right of presumption to such finds'. In answer to Peppé's invitation to come over to inspect his excavation and finds, Smith explained that he was tied up in court, including judicial sessions which continued up to 25 January and possibly 26 January as well.

Willie Peppé did what Smith asked: he wrote to the acting Collector and Joint Magistrate of Basti District, Pandit Rama Shankar Misra, informing him that he had opened the stone coffer from the

Piprahwa stupa and had found 'two stone vases, one stone *lota*, one stone box, one crystal bowl: all contained boxes, stones of various kinds, gold leaf and ornaments'. In that same note he added that he had 'communicated' with Dr. Führer, Archaeological Surveyor to the Government of the NWP&O, about these finds. This last remark was afterwards to provide ammunition to the conspiracy theorists, proving as it did that Peppé had been in touch with the German archaeologist at about the time of the opening of the stupa.

As for Dr. Führer himself, his response to that communication was remarkably similar to Smith's, although in his case he wrote from his excavation site inside Nepal and gave his address as 'Camp Kapilavastu':

> Dear Mr Peppé,
>
> I am exceedingly obliged to you for your very kind letter of yesterday's date, and take this early opportunity of congratulating you most heartily to [*sic*] your great success in excavating part of Piprahwa-kot. Kindly see carefully whether the stone chest or any of the other stone bowls found do not contain inscriptions, anything may give a clue for the date of that stupa.
>
> I should be delighted to accept your kind invitation to come and see the excavation, but I cannot leave the excavations here, not even for a day, as the coolies, 200 at present on the work, would do a great deal of damage to the buildings now being unearthed, if not properly supervised.
>
> I shall, however, be glad to come on about the 15th February, when the Nepalese Government will close the work for the season here, but if you like I shall be glad to continue the excavations from about the 10th March, and make a determined survey of the buildings unearthed and careful drawings of the relic caskets unearthed and their contents.

Who first noticed the Piprahwa inscription and when is not known. But it must occurred on 19 January and before Willie Peppé received the two separate requests from Smith and Führer urging him to seek out just such an inscription. At some point on that day, and most probably as the family were sorting out the various finds,

(Above) Detail from a photograph taken by Willie Peppé, with the lid of the smaller soapstone reliquary removed and tilted to show the inscription it carried, probably chalked in. *(Courtesy of Neil Peppé)*

(Below) Part of the inscription on the 'back' of the Piprahwa reliquary casket, where the vase had suffered some damage and appears to have been patched up with wax. The two letters added above the line of script can just be made out. *(IOL, BL)*

someone spotted that the smaller of the two round soapstone jars with the decorated tops carried an inscription on its lid.

Inscribed all the way round the upper part of the lid in tiny scratches were thirty-six letters of an alphabet that looked to the Peppés like a crude form of Greek and quite different from the two sorts of writings they were familiar with locally: the Perso-Arabic script mainly used by Indian Muslims when writing Urdu and the Devanagri in which Hindi was written.

On the first scraps of paper that came to hand Willie Peppé painstakingly made no less than three copies of the inscription. One he sent that same day to Vincent Smith in Gorakhpur and the other two to Dr. Anton Führer at his excavation site in Nepal. The first has been preserved and it can be seen that Peppé first drew five parallel lines with a pencil and ruler and then painstakingly copied down the letters from the soapstone vase. Above it he added two lines in ink which he initialled and dated:

My dear Smith – this is some writing scratched round the top of one of the bowls – yours W. C. P. 19.1.98.

Vincent Smith's immediate response on receiving Peppé's scrap of paper was to attempt to transliterate and translate the inscription on that same bit of paper:

ya salîla nidhâne Budhasa bhagvatasu ki su ki ti bhû tî na m sa bhagi nî ka
This [is] the relic receptacle of the Blessed Buddha [a proper name?] sister

nam sap u tra da la nam
son

Although no serious Sanskritist, Smith had a good understanding of the Brahmi script and of the Prakrit language it contained. Although parts of the inscription defeated him he very quickly grasped its main import and its huge significance. His response was to turn over Peppé's scrap of paper and write a brief note, which he initialled and dated:

The relics appear to be those of the Buddha himself (i.e. believed to be his) as the beginning of its inscription proves. *Salîla* = Sanskrit *sarîram* 'body', the regular word for 'relics'.

I cannot at present make out the sense of the remainder – probably some of the letters are erroneously copied.

On that same day, 23 January 1898, Smith wrote a more formal letter to accompany his note:

My dear Peppé

Your find turns out to be of even greater interest than we thought as the bones were believed by their depositor to be those of Buddha himself. This explains the unusual size of the chest and the large number of precious articles accompanying the deposit. The characters may be as early as B. C. 300.

The exact dates of Buddha's birth and death are still disputed but you may take his *floruit* [when he flourished] as B. C. 500. Rhys Davids tried a later date but that won't wash [T. W. Rhys Davids was at this time Secretary of the Royal Asiatic Society. In his *Buddhism*, published in 1886, he had argued that 'the Buddha died within a few years of 412 B. C.' – an approximate date now supported by many students of Buddhist history].

With kind regards
Yours sincerely
V. A. Smith

Dr. Führer's reaction to the two copies of Peppé's inscription was equally enthusiastic. As well as the two hand-copies of the inscription Peppé had also sent him a photograph of the five reliquary vessels and a drawing of the Piprahwa site. 'Dear Mr. Peppé,' Führer replied on 26 January in a spidery, shaky hand that must have been as difficult to decipher then as it is today, 'I am exceedingly obliged to you for so kindly sending me a plan of your excavations, a photograph of the relic caskets and the copies of the inscription on the lid of one of the bowls. From a cursory glance at it, I can safely say that your shrine contains *real* relics of *Lord Buddha*, as the reading "Bhudasa Bhagavatasu" is quite clear. This is indeed a great find, and you have done a great service to ancient history by unearthing it.'

As the rest of his letter made clear, Dr. Führer's expert advice had evidently been sought, and Peppé had also suggested that he and Vincent Smith might come up to Führer's excavation site in Nepal to confer with him – something about which that the German archaeologist was not entirely happy:

I shall be glad to follow out the plan of the buildings [at the Piprahwa excavation site], when coming on the 15th inst, and if [illegible] to explore also the other mounds in the neighbourhood and the ancient road to Kapilavastu, you mention.

I shall be glad to see you and Mr. V. Smith, if you can arrange [the permission?]. But you will have a very trying ride, as the distance from here to Birdpur is certainly 18 or 20 miles if not more. Kindly let me know as soon as possible, when you intend to come, as it is very difficult to get provisions here and I [illegible] anything.

As soon as I can make out the whole inscription, I shall let you know.

Yours sincerely
A. Führer

Extraordinary as it now appears, when the young gentlemen who called themselves servants of the East India Company began to penetrate into what was then known to the British as Upper

Hindoostan in the late eighteenth century they knew nothing of Buddhism. The Mughals and the many dynasties of earlier Muslim invaders who had preceded them had set down extensive written accounts of the means by which they had conquered Hindustan and the manner in which they had ruled, yet very little appeared to have survived from pre-Muslim India. Superficially, there was nothing to show that northern India had once been the fountain-head of Buddhism, no records to suggest that the Dharma had flourished here for centuries. Thanks to the efforts of a devoted band of Orientalists – amateur savants, antiquarians, numismatists and epigraphists – led initially by the high court judge Sir William Jones and centred on the Asiatic Society of Bengal, that missing history was slowly pieced together. In the process it was discovered that Buddhism had its roots in India's Gangetic plain and that the Buddha himself, Gautama Sakyamuni, was no mythical figure but a real person who had lived, taught and died in that same region.

Playing an important but now largely forgotten pioneering role in this process was the surgeon and naturalist Francis Buchanan, who after observing practising Buddhists at first hand in Burma and Nepal was given the thankless task of surveying the 'history, antiquities, topography and statistics' of Eastern India for the East India Company. After seven lonely and debilitating years in the field he and his little team of intelligence-gathers and draftsmen returned to Calcutta in 1814 with a mass of new information, all of which was put to one side and forgotten when Buchanan abruptly resigned after failing to secure what he regarded as his reward: the long-coveted post of director of Calcutta's Botanic Garden.

In the last year of his great survey Buchanan explored the country round Gorakhpur just ceded to the East India Company and found it to be almost as well stocked with long-forgotten ruins as the landscape of southern Bihar he had surveyed six years earlier. Everywhere he went he was told that these were the work of the Tharus. Like so many of the foreigners who came after him, Buchanan was fascinated by the Tharus and speculated at length as to their possible origins:

The Thārūs pretend to be in fact the proper descendants of the sun … Their claims to rank however are treated with the utmost contempt, because they are an abomination to the Brahmans, and indulge in all the impurities of eating and drinking. This would to me prove very little, because I have little doubt, that the [Brahminical] rules of purity in eating and drinking were established after the time of the old Kasi Rajas, and the monuments of the Thārūs bear every mark of the most remote antiquity.

He considered the claims of the Tharus to be descended from the Rajput warrior caste groundless, chiefly because 'they retain in their features strong marks of a Chinese or Tartar origin, though it must be confessed, that these marks are somewhat softened, and that the faces of the men especially do not differ so much from those of Hindus, as those of a pure Chinese. Still however a difference is observed even in the men, and in the women and children is very clearly marked.' Buchanan also noted that while some of the Tharus had abandoned their traditional way of life to become boatmen, palanquin bearers and artisans, others 'scorn innovation and adhere, so far as they can, to their impure customs … rear and eat fowls and swine, and probably devour even the cow. The Hindus are very much afraid of them, especially of the women, who are considered formidable enchantresses.'

These unreconstructed Tharus 'reject the sacred order [of Hinduism], but have priests of their own, some of whom are called Guro'. They also claimed ancient loyalties to a ruling dynasty named Sen:

The only prince of the Tharus of whom tradition has preserved any knowledge, is Madana Sen, a perfect Hindu name, as is also that of his lady named Karnawati; so that if I am right in supposing him of a Chinese or mountain tribe, he must have adopted the language of his subjects. His chief priest, Rasu, is said to have been of the impure tribe called Musahar, and there can be no doubt, if the tradition which points out this priest's temple be correct, that he worshipped the Buddhas.

As Buchanan himself noted, Sen was a common enough

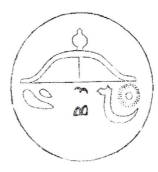

The seal of the Sen dynasty of Butwal and Palpa rajas, showing a Buddhist stupa complete with umbrella spire and inner axis.

surname among Hindus but it was also the family name of the very recently overthrown ruling house known as the Palpa rajas, who took that title from their summer seat at Palpa in the first range of the Himalayan foothills. The last ruling Palpa raja, Prithvi Pal Sen, had been overthrown by the Gorkhas in 1801, but his ancestors had ruled over a considerable tract of the Nepal Tarai for generations and their family seal bore a number of curious images.

The Sen seal showed that someone among their forebears was sufficiently acquainted with Buddhism to know that the complete Buddhist stupa not only bore an external *chattrayashti* or conical spire made up of discs and an umbrella but also contained at its core a central pole or pipe known in Sanskrit as a *yupa*, representing the cosmic axis linking heaven and earth. If the Sen rajas of Palpa were not themselves Tharu in origin they appeared to have had some role as protectors of Buddhism – or of Buddhist holy places – within their territory.

Francis Buchanan was the first Westerner to examine in some detail the extensive ruins near and round about Gorakhpur. Many of the sites he explored he found to have already been excavated for their bricks, such as the conical hill beside the River Rapti south of Gorakhpur said locally to have been 'a temple where Basu, the Musahar who was the family priest of Madaba Sen, was wont to pray'. On its summit Buchanan found a deep trench that had been made only twenty years earlier by a local official in search of building material:

When a good many bricks had been taken, several images were found, although the workmen had not penetrated into any chamber. On the images having been found, the work was abandoned as impious. Some of the images … have been removed by the Hindus to a small terrace at a little distance from the ruin, where one of them has become an object of worship. The image remaining near the trench represents a male with two arms. He has a male and female attendant, and on each side is supported by two Buddhas. The one which has become an object of worship, and has been placed on the terrace by the name of Hathi Bhawani, is evidently a Buddha with a triple umbrella over his head.

A larger complex of ruins known locally as the Rajdhani or 'royal city' was located by Buchanan seven kos or about sixteen miles to the south-east of Gorakhpur – 'a rampart of brick about a cose [kos] round, and … overwhelmed by forests'. Further east still was another complex near the village of Kasia:

About a mile west a little southerly from Kesiya is a conical mound of bricks, which in the neighbourhood is called Devisthan, or the place of the goddess, because under a large tree growing on the mound is a place where as usual in this district the natives attempt to gain the favour of the deity by offering rude images of elephants made of potters' ware. This mound, except in being covered in trees, and in wanting a modern building on its summit, has a strong resemblance to that at Nij Kasi [Sarnath] near Benares, and in the same manner as at the ancient temple of the Buddhas. There is here also, at about 400 yards west from the mound, the ruin of a solid temple, of a circular form, built indeed entirely of brick… The people have no tradition concerning the time when this building was erected but say that the Dewhara was the abode of Matakumar a person of the military order [i.e. a Hindu *kshatriya* or Rajput], and that, when he was flying from his enemies, he was converted into stone. What is shown as this miraculous stone, is a large image of a Buddha carved on a block of stone lying under a tree east from the ruin … The image … has under its feet a scrole, on which has been an inscription now very much defaced, so that only the first line is legible. It is said to be 180 Rama Rupa Ramu Ray. The figures probably refer to the year of some era, but of which it is impossible to say.

There were yet more ruins north-west of Gorakhpur, the most impressive of which was located 'at the west end of a marshy lake called Bhuila Tal … a heap of rubbish of a rounded form and about 1200 yards in circumference.' Here Buchanan was able to trace the walls of houses and a large tank or man-made reservoir, again, attributed to the Tharus. He was now in the district which took its name from the little town of Basti, forty miles due west of Gorakhpur. Here the ruins were smaller and more scattered:

About ¾ of a mile N.E. from Basti is another ruin attributed to the Tharus, and called Laknaura. It may be 300 yards in diameter, but of very little elevation … About 100 yards beyond this is another ruin attributed to the same people and called Barawa. Its diameter is smaller, but the elevation is more considerable … About 2 miles beyond this, north and east, is another ruin called Arel, and attributed to the Tharus. It is about 300 yards in diameter, but is higher than Laknaura. Some deep and large excavations have been made into it, probably by men in search of bricks. Besides these I heard of ruins attributed to the same Tharus at Naringaw NE from Basti 3 coses.

Buchanan never completed his survey of the border region but before returning to Calcutta he recorded the existence of a number of stone pillars, the most impressive of which he found 'near a village named Khangho.' It was attributed 'by some to Parasu Rama, and by others to Bhim, the son of Pandu; but most people call it merely the staff (*Lat*) and have no tradition whatever concerning the person by whom it was made.' It stood about twenty-four feet in height on a four-sided base, which carried a Buddha image:

The image is naked and stands before a large many headed serpent while there is a votary at each foot. The shaft for about 7 feet is octagonal, and on two of the faces has an inscription of 12 lines, tolerably perfect, which has been copied in the drawing. The character differs very much from the Devanagri [modern script] now in use, and has some resemblance to that in the ruins of Mahabalipur south from Madras. The upper part of the shaft has 16 sides, alternately wider and narrower. The capital is about 6 feet long, and is not easily described, but near its upper end is quadrangular, with the figure of a standing Buddha carved on each face. A large spike, apparently metallic, is inserted into the top of the pillar, and it probably supported an ornament of the same material.

The site of this pillar has never been identified. Buchanan's drawings were lost and the pillar itself was almost certainly broken up within a few years of Buchanan's visit to the area.

There were at this time three great stone pillars – two at Delhi and one at Allahabad – that were known and much discussed in antiquarian circles on account of the curious and indecipherable inscriptions they carried. The great breakthrough came in 1837 with James Prinsep's decipherment of the script known initially as 'Delhi No. 1', as inscribed on the stone column known as Feroze Shah's *lat* or staff outside Delhi. Prinsep's reading of what is today known as the Brahmi script and his discovery that its Prakrit language was the precursor to Pali and Sanskrit, combined with the realisation that the inscription carved on a fourth pillar newly discovered in northern Bihar was to all intents a copy of what was written on the pillars in Dalhi and Allahabad, led directly on to the revelation that all the edicts found carved on large boulders and smoothly polished pillars throughout the Indian sub-continent were the work of one man who called himself Piyadasi, or 'Beloved of the Gods'. In that same year of 1837 the civil servant George Turnour in Ceylon produced the first translation of in the ancient chronicle of the island known as the *Mahavamsa*, which revealed that Piyadasi was another name for India's first Buddhist Emperor, Asoka the Great.

It soon became clear that Asoka's pillar edicts had been erected at specific sites for specific purposes. Each carved from a single piece of sandstone up to fifty feet in length and weighing something like fifty tons, the pillars had all come from the same quarry

The Radhia Pillar
in zilla Sarun.

The Bakhra Pillar.
in Tirhut.

The Mound and Dehgope at Kesariah in Tirhut.

Mottrah Lath near Bettiah.
on the river Gunduk.

Brian Hodgson's drawings of the some of the antiquities seen by him in northern Bihar on the road from Patna to Kathmandu. He noted that one of the pillars had been used for artillery practice by a band of Muslim freebooters. (*Asiatick Researches*)

on the banks of the Ganges, from which they had been transported in some cases hundreds of miles before being erected and capped by variously carved statues in the shape of lions, bulls, elephants or horses.

Working in close partnership with Prinsep were a large circle of government officials such as Brian Hodgson in Kathmandu, who in his off-duty hours worked on ancient Sanskrit and Pali texts which revealed the full extent of Buddhism in ancient India. As secretary of the Asiatic Society of Bengal, editor of its journal *Asiatick Researches* (latterly spelt *Asiatic Researches*) and much else besides, James Prinsep was their lynch-pin, and with his sickness and premature death in 1838 Indian studies suffered a severe setback. However, one of Prinsep's helpers in Calcutta was a young engineer officer named Alexander Cunningham, who in the 1850s began a systematic search to rediscover the ancient Buddhist sacred sites, beginning with Sarnath, the scene of Buddha Sakyamuni's first sermon, known subsequently among Buddhists as the First Turning of the Wheel of the Dharma.

Cunningham's work was greatly assisted by the appearance of French translations from the Chinese of accounts of journeys into India made many centuries earlier by Chinese Buddhist monks. The first of these to become accessible in the West was written by the greatly revered scholar monk and collector of Buddhist texts who first became known in the West as Yiouen Tsang, Yuan Chwang or other variations of that name – now standardised as Xuanzang. The Orientalist Stanislas Julien's French translation of Xuanzang's journey appeared in 1853 as *Voyages du pelerin Hiouen-tsang*. The book set out in great detail how the Chinese monk had reached India in 631 CE after a long and perilous journey across central Asia. He had then spent some fifteen years on the sub-continent, travelling from one Buddhist location to another before settling at the great Buddhist monastic university of Nalanda, where he spent two years studying the sutras. Xuanzang had kept a detailed record of where he went and what he saw and, crucially, how he got there, which on his return to China he set down in his *Journey to the West in the Great Tang Dynasty*.

With Julien's French translation in his hands Alexander Cunningham was able to locate and excavate a great many ancient cities and locations associated with the Buddha, most notably at Rajgir, the ancient Rajagriha of Gautama Sakyamuni's royal patrons King Bimbisara and his cruel son Ajatashatru. Here the first Buddhist monastery had been built and the First Buddhist Council held after the Buddha's Maharaparinirvana. After his retirement from the Indian Army in 1861 as a Major-General, Cunningham returned to India to become Director-General of the newly established Archaeological Survey of India (ASI). In 1863 the directions supplied by Xuanzang led Cunningham to Sahet-Mahet, north-west of the town of Balrampur, in the Gonda District of Oude and just over sixty miles due west of Birdpore. Contained within a massive brick wall three miles in circumference were the ruins of what was clearly an ancient city now covered in dense forest. After cutting a series of tracks through the jungle Cunningham excavated some of the larger mounds, which revealed themselves to be the remains of stupas built of fired brick, together with attendant monasteries. A magnificent standing Buddha was also uncovered, with a damaged inscription at the base which included the word 'Sravasti'. More stupas and viharas were unearthed just south of the city walls, which Cunningham concluded had to be the Jetavana Garden, the monastic centre that had served the Buddha and his disciples for so many years as their summer rains retreat.

Indian archaeology then suffered a second setback in 1865 when the ASI was disbanded for financial reasons, but five years later Cunningham returned to India as Sir Alexander Cunningham, KCIE, to resume his work as the revived ASI's director. In 1873 he made a second visit to the Sahet-Mahet site which only strengthened his opinion that this important site had to be Sravasti and its associated monastery of Jetavana, as seen and described by Xuanzang more than fourteen centuries earlier.

Cunningham's main efforts thereafter were concentrated elsewhere, initially in the Sanchi area near Bhopal in central India and latterly at Bodhgaya, the seat of Sakyamuni's enlightenment, where he has to take some responsibility for the botched reconstruction of the Mahabodi temple we see today. The work of tracking down the remaining lost sites of Buddhism was now delegated to Cunningham's assistants, one of whom was the eccentric Archibald Carleyle, who soon after his arrival in India chose to add another 'l' to his name and spell it 'Carlleyle'. His main claim to fame today is his pioneering work on India's prehistory, but in the cold weather months of 1874–75 and 1875–76 Carlleyle travelling through northern Bihar and what had now become the united provinces of the North-Western Provinces and Oude (NWP&O). His first tour took him to the lake of Buila Tal, fifteen miles north-west of Gorakhpur, first noted by Buchanan in 1814. Here his exploration of the site was greatly impeded by the hostility of the local people who were determined to destroy whatever he uncovered. 'This,' he reported, 'is the invariable policy of the brutish, ignorant, and evil-disposed natives of this part of the country, who have, moreover, already destroyed some ancient monuments since I have been here, simply because they knew I wanted to preserve them'.

Despite the local hostility Archie Carlleyle was able to convince himself that what he saw beside the lake at Buila Tal matched the Chinese pilgrim Xuanzang's descriptions of Kapilavastu, the city in which the young prince Siddhartha had grown up. General Cunningham then visited the site himself. 'The result of my examination,' he concluded, 'was the most perfect conviction of the accuracy of Mr. Carlleyle's identification of Bhuila Tâl with the site of Kapilavastu, the famous birthplace of Sâkya Muni.'

A year later Carlleyle did even better when he located the ruins of Kushinagara, the scene of Sakyamuni's Maharaparinirvana and cremation, which he placed near Kasia, thirty-three miles due east of Gorakhpur in a 'great long mound of ruins called the *Matha Kunwar ka kot*' – in other words, the fort or abode of Matakumar, the chieftain or prince described to Buchanan in 1814 as 'a person of the military order'. Here Carlleyle had the enormous satisfaction of finding precisely what he was looking for: 'The famous colossal statue of the [Mahapari-] Nirvana of Buddha' – famous, because this was what the Chinese traveller Xuanzang had seen and described in the course of his visit to Kushinagara some twelve centuries earlier. 'After digging to a depth of about 10 feet,' wrote Carlleyle in his report to Cunningham, 'I came upon what appeared to be the upper part of the legs of a colossal recumbent statue of stone … I then hurried on the excavations, until I had uncovered the entire length of a colossal recumbent statue of Buddha, lying in a chamber'.

Much of the statue was damaged but further excavation uncovered most of the missing parts, which Carlleyle restored with the aid of Portland cement. In his enthusiasm for reconstruction, he went on to paint the statue as he thought it ought to be: 'I coloured the face, neck and hands, and feet a yellowish flesh colour, and I coloured the drapery white; and I also gave a black tint to the hair. Thus I really made the statue as good and as perfect as ever it was – or perhaps even better than it ever was.' Carlleyle then rebuilt the

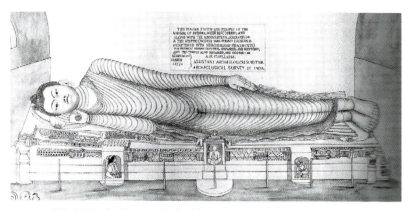

Archibald Carlleyle's rebuilt Buddha Maharaparinirvana statue at Kasia, the ancient Kushinagara, drawn by his draftsman Ram Narayan Bhaggat. *(IOL, BL)*

temple that had held the statue, adding a vaulted roof to his own design, after which he affixed a large notice above the Maharaparinirvana statue, proclaiming himself its finder and restorer. He concluded his report to Cunningham by explaining that all this had been done at his own expense and that he was now out of pocket to the tune of 1,200 rupees. 'And finally to all I would say,' he ended, 'Let those who cavil come and see the complete work with their own eyes, and then I shall be satisfied!'

But this was not the full extent of Carlleyle's triumphs. From Kushinagara he led his survey party eastwards across the Gandak River into northern Bihar and to the district town of Bettiah, not far from which stood the two inscribed Asokan pillars first observed and reported upon by Brian Hodgson some forty years earlier: one at Lauriya Araraj, twenty miles south east of Bettiah; the other at Lauriya Nandangarh, fifteen miles north-west of Bettiah. Here Carlleyle encountered a party of Tharu tribesmen who told him that in their home country to the north there was 'a stone sticking in the ground which they called Bhim's Lat, and which they said resembled the top or capital of the pillar at Laoriya'. Guided by the Tharus, Carlleyle hurried northwards some twenty miles, 'although I had heard that the locality was most unhealthy, and a most dangerous place for my native servants'. Half a mile outside the little village of Rampurva he came upon 'the upper portion, to about 3 feet in length, of the capital of a pillar ... sticking out of the ground in a slanting position, and pointing towards the north'. With the Tharus' help he managed to expose the upper part of the pillar to a length of about forty feet. The ground was too waterlogged and the stone column itself too heavy to be moved so he had to content himself with an imperfect impression of the Asokan edict it carried, achieved by his men 'standing up to their waists in water'.

The Rampurva edict turned out to be identical in lettering and content with the inscription carried on the Lauriya Nandangarh pillar, which led Carlleyle to propose that Emperor Asoka had erected these pillars to mark his royal pilgrimage:

> Four different pillars of Asoka are now known to be situated along the line of the old north road which led from Magadha to Nipâl, or from the Ganges opposite Pataliputra or Patna, through Besarh or Vaisali, in a northern or rather north-north-westerly direction, keeping at a moderate distance to the east of the Gandak, to the Tarai and hills of Nipâl ... The fourth pillar is the fallen and buried pillar discovered by me close to Rampurva, 21½ to the north-north-half-north-east from the pillar at Laoryia Naondangarh ... Now it is evident that the inscriptions on these pillars were intended to be read by passing travellers and pilgrims passing along the old north road from the Ganges opposite Pataliputra to Nipâl. I should therefore expect to find either another pillar, or else a rock-cut inscription, still further north somewhere in the Nipâl Tarai.

With the publication of the ASI's annual report for 1876 it seemed that all the major Buddhist sites had been satisfactorily located. Much of Carlleyle's field-work thereafter was taken up with palaeontology in the wild hill country known as Bundelkhand but already his behaviour had become increasingly irrational and in May 1885 Sir Alexander Cunningham ordered his compulsory retirement at the age of fifty-four. The General himself retired from the ASI in that same year, and with his departure

The Rampurva Asokan pillar, first uncovered close to the Nepali border by Archie Carlleyle in 1876, but not fully excavated until 1904, when its missing lion capital (upper left) was located – and when this photograph was taken by John Marshall. *(IOL, BL)*

Indian archaeology suffered yet another major setback when the organisation he had established was broken up into a number of provincial archaeological services each subordinate to their local Public Works Departments (PWD).

A year prior to General Cunningham's retirement Samuel Beal's English translation of Xuanzang's travels was published as *Si-Yu-Ki: Buddhist Records of the Western World by Hiuen Tsiang*. And a year after his retirement James Legge published *A Record of Buddhistic*

Kingdoms: Being an Account by the Chinese Monk Fa-Hiuen of his Travels in India and Ceylon (AD 399–414) in Search of the Buddhist Books of Discipline. This was a translation from a Korean text of the travels of an earlier Chinese traveller: Fa-Hiuen – today Faxian – who had entered India more than two and a quarter centuries before Xuanzang. Despite this difference Faxian and Xuanzang had covered very much the same ground in their journeys across India. Consequently, it now became possible to use the two accounts in tandem not only to confirm the validity of those Buddhist sites already discovered by Cunningham and Carlleyle – particularly in relation to their locating of ancient Sravasti, Kapilavastu and Kushinagara – but also to take the process of rediscovery a stage further.

That, at least, was the theory and in 1886 no one was better placed to take advantage of these new research tools than Dr. Anton Führer, Curator of Lucknow Museum and Assistant Architectural Surveyor to the Government of the NWP&O. Unfortunately for Führer the resources of the NWP&O's Archaeological Survey Department were so limited and its responsibilities so enormous – extending as they did to scores of major historic Hindu and Muslim sites such as Agra, Allahabad and Ayodya (to list only the more important of the 'A's) – that very little could be done beyond keeping records of what was already known. These records included the Museum's existing collection of inscriptions, and one side-effect of the lack of funding for excavation was that Anton Führer became a major contributor to *Epigraphica Indica*, a project set up by his old Sanskrit teacher Professor Georg Bühler to record and publish every known ancient and mediaeval inscription in India.

The situation improved in 1887 when Führer took over as the province's Archaeological Surveyor. At the start of the cold weather months of that year he accompanied, at the request of Professor Bühler, the eminent Dr. James Burgess, formerly Archaeological Surveyor for the Madras and Bombay Presidencies, in what was to be Dr. Burgess's last excavation before his retirement. It was under Dr. Burgess's brief and already outdated tutelage that Anton Führer acquired his skills as an archaeologist. Their dig took place on a large mound outside the ancient city of Mathura (which

69

the British authorities insisted on calling 'Muttra') known as the Kankali *Tila*, or 'hill', which had long served as a brick quarry. It had first attracted the attention of General Cunningham in the early 1870s and two British local magistrates had subsequently extracted some magnificent Buddhist and Jain statues carved out of the local red sandstone, along with stupa pillars and railings and a great many inscriptions. Burgess and Führer were no less successful and returned to Lucknow Museum at the end of their first season with a magnificent haul that, according to Dr. Führer's annual report, included:

> 10 inscribed statues of several Svetambara Jinas of the Indo-Scythian period, four inscriptions of which are most important for the history of the Jainas; 34 pieces of sculpture forming parts of a magnificent Svetambara Jaina temple of the time of the IndoScythian king Huvishka; a statue of Mahaviranatha surrounded by the remaining 23 Tirthamkaras; two colossal statues of the Jina Padmaprabhanatha, dated Samvat 1036 and 1134, respectively; a colossal pillar with the life-size figure of a dancing girl; an inscribed statue of the Bodhisattva Amogha Siddhartha of the first century A. D.; 10 inscribed Buddhist statues of the Indo-Scythian period; six bases of Buddha statues inscribed and dated in the regnal years of the Indo-Scythian rulers Huvishka, Kanishka, and Vasudeva; 19 pillars, 16 cross-bars and 12 pieces of copings of Buddhist railings, etc

This same dig produced the only certain surviving photograph of Anton Führer, then aged thirty-four, standing beside a newly-excavated Jain statue – one of the two 'colossal statues' listed above (more correctly of Prashvanath, dated to 981 CE; the statue now stands in pride of place in the foyer of Lucknow Museum). Close examination of this poor-quality photograph reveals the German archaeologist to have possessed a dark and bushy beard.

After the triumph of the 1887–88 season, Dr Führer obtained official sanction to return to the Kankali Tila to direct further excavations at the start of the next cold weather season – and again a year later. According to his annual report for 1890–91,

Dr. Anton Führer (to the right of the statue) at the Kankali Tila site in 1886–87. The original photograph was removed from the photographic records of his Archaeological Survey Department after his forced resignation (from the frontispiece of *The Jain Stupas and Other Antiquities of Mathura* by Vincent A. Smith, 1901).

this third season was the most fruitful of all, so much so that the extensive cellars of the Lucknow Museum became crammed with statuary and carved stone work almost to bursting point. 'The results of his work,' Führer wrote proudly of himself in his role as Curator of the Lucknow Museum, 'far surpass those of the previous two years, as the new finds form important additions to our knowledge of Indian history and art. He [i.e. Führer himself] forwarded to the Museum 737 fine pieces of sculpture, comprising beautifully-finished panels, doorways, *toranas*, columns, complete railings with copings and bars, statues of Tirthamkaras, etc.' Sixty-two of these pieces carried inscriptions and dates which, according to the Curator, ranged from 150 BCE to 123 CE. All had come from two Jain temples, one much older than the other and probably built before 150 BCE. With no one to challenge him, these and other claims went unquestioned.

Within the hierarchy of the NWP&O Dr. Führer remained a comparatively lowly and poorly-paid official in charge of a sub-department of the PWD on a fixed salary of 400 rupees a month and with no prospect of a pension. But in the field of Indology the Reverend Doctor's reputation as a leading authority in the field of Jain studies was now secured – in large part because his work dovetailed very neatly with the studies of his old mentor Professor Bühler, who had now extended his scholarship to Jain religious texts. 'Dr. Bühler'sservices to the cause of Jain religious history are immeasurable,' wrote another of Bühler's former students of his contributions at this time. 'By a systematic study of the famous Mathura Inscriptions and those of Karavela he successfully and incontrovertibly established the priority of Jainism over Buddhism.'

Although his work on the Mathura excavations took up most of his time Anton Führer found opportunities to make a number of brief forays into the field to document the province's antiquities, the fruits of which he published in two reports in 1889 and 1891. One early visit was to the supposed site of the ancient city of Sravasti and its famous Jetavana monastery, which Sir Alexander Cunningham had located a few miles to the north-west of the town of Balrampur. Führer first visited the site in the winter season of 1888–89, perhaps prompted by excavation work undertaken there by Dr. William Hoey four winters earlier. He found the ancient city covered in what he correctly termed 'jangal', the Hindi word for waste ground:

At the present day the whole area of the city, excepting a few clearances near the gateways, is a mass of almost impenetrable jangal, which is broken into a wavy surface by the remains of temples and palaces underneath. All the principal buildings were in the western half, and it is there that the undergrowth is the thickest, only ceasing along two or three broad streets which have been left bare and indicate the chief features of the old city ... At a distance of half a mile from the south-west gate, and separated from the main town by swamps, which probably mark the course of the old moat, is another considerable ruin, generally called *Jogimia bhariya*, or the 'witches' mound', identified by General Cunningham with the great monastery of Jêtavana, which was one of the eight most celebrated buildings in India.

His appetite whetted, Führer then travelled east to visit another of the sites promoted by Sir Alexander Cunningham: Buila Tal, which the General had confirmed as the ruins of Buddha Sakyamuni's Kapilavastu following its earlier identification by Archie Carlleyle. Führer criss-crossed the ruins twice, on the first occasion armed with a copy of Beal's *Si-Yu-Ki: Buddhist Records of the Western World by Hiuen Tsiang*. 'This place,' he wrote afterwards, 'has been identified by Mr. Carlleyle with Kapilavastu, the birthplace of Sakyamuni, which identification General Cunningham approves of. After careful inspection of all the places identified by Mr. Carlleyle, I have come to the conclusion that this spot cannot be the Kie-pi-lo-fa-su-tu (Kapilavastu) of Hiuen Tsiang.'

Führer returned again two years later, this time with a copy of Legge's *A Record of Buddhistic Kingdoms*, and again he was not impressed: 'Buila Dih,' he declared, 'cannot be the Kapilavastu of Fa Hian and Hiuen Tsiang on the following grounds'. He then listed his reasons, one of which was Carlleyle's identification of the large circular lake at Buila Tal as the hole made by a dead elephant which, according to Buddhist legend, had been thrown by Gautama Sakyamuni from Kapilavastu. Carlleyle had claimed that this lake was known to the local people as Hathikund, or 'elephant lake', but Führer learned from these same locals that it was Carlleyle himself who had given the lake that name.

Although now in retirement in England, General Sir Alexander Cunningham was still widely revered in antiquarian circles as the father of Indian archaeology. Dr. Führer's questioning of his judgement was not well received. However, this challenge, first made in print in 1889 and repeated two years later, had the effect of encouraging others to do the same.

The Expected Visit:

Birdpore House, 27 January 1898

Vincent Smith's first opportunity to see the Piprahwa reliquaries for himself came on Thursday 27 January, a public holiday. He caught the early morning train to Uska Bazaar railway station, where a pony trap sent down by Willie Peppé conveyed him over the twelve miles to Birdpore House. His first reaction to the stone coffer and its contents was one of amazement at the size of the coffer and the 'richness of the deposit of precious objects in the vases', which struck him as 'obvious proofs of the veneration attaching to the relics enshrined'. It was clear that 'the depositors believed the fragments of bone to be part of the sacred body (*śariram*) of Gautama Buddha himself. Whether or not the depositors' belief was actually well-founded no man can say. Mr. Peppé, unfortunately, omitted to take a note of the contents of each vase separately.'

A visit to the Piprahwa excavation site followed, allowing Smith the opportunity to examine the main stupa and the partial excavation Peppé had carried out, particularly on its eastern side, which Smith confirmed as a classic example of a large Buddhist *vihara*, with more than thirty individual monastic cells and an entrance opening directly on to the stupa. He suggested to Peppé that further excavation of the partially cleared area immediately north of the stupa would probably reveal a temple or shrine (which indeed proved to be the case).

What Smith also noted was that there were other mounds in the area: 'A group of *stūpas* lies about half a mile south-west of Piprāhwā *stūpa*, and there is another mound of ruins more than

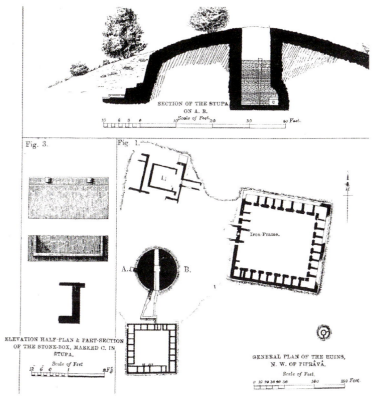

Plans of the Piprahwa excavations, drawn by Babu P. C. Mukherji and his draftsman Sohan Lal after their visit a year after W. C. Peppé's original excavation, during which Mukherji exposed more of the monastic buildings surrounding the relic stupa.

a quarter of a mile to the east. A fourth mound of ruins exists to the north-east near Siswā reservoir, and there are several mounds, probably *stūpas*, in the Dulha Grant [east of the Birdpore Grant]. It was quite clear that the area must at one time been a place of significance in the Buddhist world.

The Piprahwa stupa itself impressed Smith not so much by its size, which he thought placed it 'in the second class of monuments of the kind', as by its solid mass of brickwork: 'The bricks are of the large size specially characteristic of the Ásoka period, and are well made. Rice-straw has been freely used to strengthen the cohesion of the clay'. He calculated the height of the stupa in its present form to be just under twenty feet and its diameter at the base 116 feet: 'Though the original height must have been considerably greater it must have fallen far short of half a diameter. According to a well known rule this low ratio of height to diameter is a certain sign of high antiquity'. The whole thing reminded him of a slightly larger but badly-damaged stupa that Alexander Rea of the Madras Archaeological Survey had excavated at Bhattiprolu in the Madras Presidency six years earlier. At Bhattiprolu the stupa had been found to house three stone coffers, two of which were buried several feet below the first. All were much smaller that the Piprahwa coffer and much more crudely cut. The first contained a soapstone casket, globular in shape, containing a single bone fragment enshrined in a tiny crystal phial. The other two caskets were without relics but held between them a total of 194 pieces of gold leaf, all cut into flower shapes of six, eight or nine petals, and very similar in appearance to the gold flowers found at Piprahwa.

What was significantly different about the two excavations, however, was the sheer scale of the Piprahwa offerings and the exceptional quality of the lapidary work. The three Bhattiprolu coffers had together contained some 250 individual pieces of gold, pearl, crystal, gemstone, semi-precious stones and beads. The Piprahwa coffer contained almost eight times that number, the bulk of which the Peppés divided into various categories and placed in fourteen glass cases. Several lists of items in Smith's and Peppé's handwriting survive, showing that in addition to what was placed in the fourteen cases there was: 'One bottle containing gold stars – about 38 stars of gold & silver leaf & a few black bits'; a pen box with 'pieces of wood with metal through them' – pieces of silver vessel; a box of 'metal snakes etc'; a pill box with 64 rolls of gold; and a bag of pearls. There also appear to have been two further boxes of crystals, stones and beads which Smith did his best to sort: 100 small beads, 81 white cornelians, 67 cornelian bugle beads, 41 crystal beads, 33 long bugle cornelians, 30 purple amethysts, 28 crystal beads, 28 serrated white cornelian leaves, 20 red garnet stars, 14 coral beads, 13 small coral cups, 13 blue pyramids, 13 long beads, 13 crystal blocks, 11 white cornelian leaves with red tips, 11 yellow

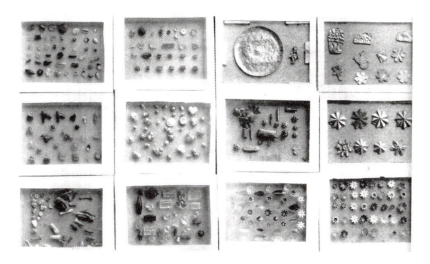

Willie Peppé's photographs of twelve of the fourteen glass cases containing items from the Piprahwa stone coffer. This did not represent the entire collection, the total number amounting to approximately 2,000 individual pieces. *(Courtesy of Neil Peppé)*

topazes, 11 topaz beads, 9 purple topazes, 8 pyramids, 8 transparent crystals, 8 topaz and cornelian beads, 8 lotus seed pods, 7 flat crystals, 6 pyramids, 6 red cornelians, 5 amethyst beads, 5 white crystals, 5 small amethysts, 4 blueish crystals, 4 topaz bugle heads, 3 amethyst leaves, 3 deep stars, 3 amethyst stars, 3 peppercorns, 2 pink amethysts, 2 yellow topazes, 2 amethysts, 2 small garnets, 2 pink and white cups, 2 amethyst drops, 2 long beads, 2 green topazes, 2 crystals, 2 coral cups, 2 drops, 2 lapis lazuli, 1 pendant, 1 white star, 1 white pyramid, 1 piece of ivory.

However, the most important item in the Peppés' collection had to be the inscribed vase. A meticulous examination by Smith showed him where he had gone wrong in his first reading based on Willie Peppé's eye copy. Peppé had missed the triangle of three dots before the first letter and the further dot after, so that Smith read it as *ya* rather than *iyam* – 'this is'. Smith had also failed to realise that the two genitive characters *ya nam* positioned above the first line in Peppé's rendering were not random scratches but had been set there deliberately: 'The characters *yanam* were accidentally omitted by the scribe and were then inserted above the line.' When inserted at the proper place they helped to make the key phrase *sakiyanam*, or 'of the Sakya'. But what Smith could still not make sense of were the next three letters, which spelled out *su ki ti*. This made no sense to Smith except as possibly as an honorific proper name, although, so far as he knew, 'Sukiti' held no significance in Buddhist literature. A tentative second reading, written in pencil in Smith's handwriting on a slip of paper, was probably made at this time: 'This is the relic receptacle (of the) Buddha (blessed) of the Sakyas and the brothers (noble) and the sisters people with the sons' [-] portion (virtuous offering)'.

Smith's conclusion was that his first impressions of the inscription's great antiquity had been sound: 'The exact age of the inscription cannot as yet be settled with certainty. The record is probably older than the reign of Asoka ... The Śākyas of Kapilavastu, "as the relations of Buddha", obtained a share of the relics of the master at the time of the cremation. It is possible that the Piprāhwa *stūpa* ... may be that erected by the Śākya brethren immediately after the death of Gautama'.

Since General Sir Alexander Cunningham's retirement in 1885 and the scaling down of the ASI a new generation of archaeologists and Sanskritists had come to the fore, many of them gentlemen amateurs drawn from the ranks of the ICS and the Indian Political Service. These were highly educated and motivated young men, the cream of Oxford, Cambridge and Trinity College, Dublin. Some preferred to spend their off-duty hours at the gymkhana club or out on *shikar*, or 'hunting', but a surprising number followed in the footsteps of their celebrated predecessors by to taking up antiquarian pursuits which the central and provincial governments were unable or unwilling to fund.

Among these Young Turks were Vincent Smith and William Hoey. For both of them Sravasti-Jetavana came to have a special resonance, for by the end of the 1880s it had become obvious that this was the key to Sakyamuni's lost homeland. Although neither may have cared to say so, it was Dr. Führer's public questioning of

General Cunningham's judgement that first led them to this view.

These two Indian civil servants had much more in common than membership of the same elite service. Smith was Hoey's senior by one year, but both men were Anglo-Irish, both had topped the ICS final examinations and both had elected to serve in the NWP&O. Remarkably, the study of Sanskrit was an integral part of the ICS training course at this time so that both men had come out to India well qualified to pursue antiquarian interests. As outlined earlier, Smith spent his early years in the NWP, whereas Hoey was initially attached to Oude, where he served as assistant commissioner and junior magistrate in a number of districts that included Sultanpur, Fyzabad, Gonda, Unao and Lucknow. During that time Hoey was encouraged to spend as much of the cold weather months as possible out in the field, a practice known as 'touring', its purpose to allow junior officers to get to know their district and its people. It also enabled Hoey to become something of an authority on the antiquities of every district he served in. After a decade of service Hoey went on 'furlough' or home leave, during which time he acquired a wife and, much more unusually, a doctorate, based in part on his translation into English of Oldenberg's *Buddha: His Life, Doctrine and Order.* Already proficient in Hindi, Urdu, Persian and Sanskrit, Dr. Hoey soon began to make a name for himself as an amateur Indologist.

In December 1884, shortly after the publication of Samuel Beal's *Si-Yu-Ki: Buddhist Records of the Western World by Hiuen Tsiang,* William Hoey was posted for a second time to Gonda District, within which lay the supposed remains of Sravasti and the Jetavana Garden at Sahet-Mahet. He at once applied to the Government of the NWP&O for permission to re-examine the ruins first brought to light by Cunningham in 1863. Two months of excavations added further weight to Cunningham's theory that these two linked sites were indeed the ruins of Sravasti and its associated garden monastery as seen and described by Xuanzang.

Next door in the NWP Division of Gorakhpur Vincent Smith shared with William Hoey the advantage of being on the spot at the right time. In 1883–84 he travelled the length and breadth of Basti District in the capacity of Settlement Officer, a post which required

Vincent Smith with fellow shikaris, probably photographed in Basti District in the late 1870s when Smith was assistant commissioner. It is presumed that Smith is the young man in the centre foreground but he could be any one of the Europeans present. He very soon abandoned shikar for more serious pursuits. The photograph is from an album of Smith's donated to the Indian Institute at Oxford and since lost. *(From Richard Symonds,* Oxford and Empire, *1986)*

land holdings and crop yields to be checked on the ground for taxation purposes. In 1885 he was appointed joint officiating magistrate of Basti District and it was while in that post that he first began to make himself an expert on the Indian travels of Faxian and Xuanzang.

Like Jones, Prinsep, Hodgson and Cunningham before him, Smith was a driven man when it came to the subject of India's early history. In 1878 he joined with a Hindu *pandit* to write a paper on two copper-plates of the Chandella period found at Nanaura in the Hamirpur District west of Banda. These were among the first such plates of that period found, and from this time onward Smith began to steep himself in the past to a degree that made him a formidable opponent in matters of dispute and perhaps a less than agreeable colleague. One of his first projects was the re-cataloguing of the many thousands of coins in the Indian Museum in Calcutta, which led him to become the leading authority on coinage of the Gupta period. At the same time he worked on the indexing of the twenty-three volumes of Sir Alexander Cunningham's monumental *Archaeological Survey of India Reports*, which gave him an unrivalled understanding of Indian archaeological work. This breadth of knowledge he put to good use, whether it was tracking the movements of Faxian and Xuanzang in the field or gathering material for what was to be the first biography of Asoka the Great. This last undertaking was only made possible by the fact that there now existed a wide circle of scholars, professional and amateur, whose published work Vincent Smith was able to draw upon. In the course of a quarter-century of lonely scholarship, Smith contributed dozens of scholarly articles on a wide range of historical topics to *Asiatic Researches*, the *Indian Antiquarian*, the *Journal of the Royal Asiatic Society* and other such periodicals, culminating in the writing of *Asoka: the Buddhist Emperor of India*, published in 1901, which itself became but a part of Smith's *Early History of India*, published three years later. This was, in Smith's words, 'the first attempt to present a narrative of the leading events in India history for eighteen centuries', drawing on all the epistemological, genealogical, numismatic and archaeological research available.

What made Smith's achievement all the more remarkable was that his research was unpaid and done outside his official duties – an undertaking that must surely have taxed his colleagues and made him a distant husband to his wife, and father to their four children. Yet it gave Smith a surer grasp of early Indian history than any of his contemporaries. 'He accomplished a great work that lay beyond the scope of the researches of other individuals,' was the judgement of a colleague, made possible because 'his knowledge of Indian history and art and all their connection was comprehensive and unrivalled'. It was Vincent Smith who first grasped the full impact of Emperor Asoka, who in his zeal to extend the Dharma throughout and beyond the borders of his empire introduced an entirely new concept of moral duty to much of Asia. 'In the space of two years,' wrote Smith –

between the emperor's entry into the Order in the eleventh year and the publication of his earliest inscriptions in the thirteenth year of his reign, missions charged with the preaching of the doctrine of the Sâkya sage had been despatched to Ceylon and the independent kingdoms in the south of the Peninsula, to Mysore and the Bombay coast, to the Maratta country, to the mountains of the Himâlayas and Kashmir, and to Pegu ... Prior to Asoka's conversion Buddhism had maintained its position in a portion of the valley of the Ganges as a sect of Hinduism ... The transformation of this local sect into a world religion is the work of Asoka alone. The romances written by monks naturally represent the king as a tool in the hands of his clerical advisers, to whom all the credit of the missionary enterprise is given. But the monuments do not support this view. Asoka claims all the credit for himself ... and he is fairly entitled to the credit of the measures taken in his name.

In the eleventh year of his reign, Emperor Asoka began the first of a series of royal tours devoted to pious purposes. According to Smith, one such tour in the twenty-first year of his reign followed the last journey taken by Sakyamuni Buddha:

The king started from his capital Pâtaliputra, crossed the Ganges, and entered the Vaisâli territory of the Lichchavi tribe, now known as the Muzaffarpur and Champaran districts. His line of march is marked by the ruins of Vaisâli (Basar), which include the Bakhira lion-pillar, by the stupa of Kesariya, and the lion-pillars of Lauriya Araraj and Lauriya Nandangarh. He may then have kept to the east, passing Rampurva, where another lion-pillar lies, and have then crossed the passes over the hills to Kusinagara, the scene of Gautama Buddha's death, or he may have turned westward, crossed the Gandak river, and proceeded direct through the Tarai to the Lumbini Garden, the reputed scene of the birth of Gautama Buddha.

What Smith also showed was that the Mauryan Empire had reached its zenith under Asoka, who ruled as a lay Buddhist for thirty-eight years before abdicating to become a monk, leaving his dynasty fatally vulnerable by the determination of his immediate descendants to enter the Buddhist church rather than rule. The best-known of these offspring were the son and daughter who helped establish the Dharma in Ceylon. Less well documented was the daughter who went north into the Himalayas. Local genealogies state that a King of Pataliputra came to 'Nevala' or Nepal in the reign of Raja Sthunko, fourteenth monarch of the Kirat dynasty. Smith believed that this could only have been Asoka, even though Nepal – meaning the Kathmandu Valley – is not mentioned on a rock edict listing all the places visited by Emperor Asoka. According to Nepalese legend, however, Asoka came to the Kathmandu Valley accompanied by the monk Upagupta and his daughter Princess Carumati, who married a local warrior named Devapala. The couple subsequently established two *viharas* or monastic centres, while Asoka himself is credited with founding the city of Deva-pattana, today Patan, where he built memorial stupas to honour Sakyamuni Buddha and the three earlier Buddhas. Sited at the four corners of the city, these 'Asokan' stupas survive almost unscathed to this day, although there is as yet no hard evidence that it was Asoka who ordered them built.

'How long the efforts of Asoka continued to bear fruit after the close of his protracted and brilliant reign we do not know,' wrote Smith in closing his chapter on Asoka's administration of his empire. 'Envious time has dropped an impenetrable veil over the deeds of his successors, and no man can tell the story of the decline and fall of the Mauryan empire'. What was known was that in about 185 BCE the ninth and last of the Mauryan line was assassinated by the commander of his army, Pusyamitra Sunga. The Buddhist chronicles portray the founder of the Sunga dynasty as a Brahmin Shaivite implacably hostile to Buddhism and a great persecutor of Buddhists. He was said to have raised a mighty army specifically to destroy all traces of Buddhism within the Magad-han empire and to have put a price on the head of every Buddhist monk. Yet Pusyamitra Sunga's son and subsequent successors may well have reversed his father's policy since the archaeological record revealed by Cunningham and his successors showed that Buddhism continued to receive royal patronage under the

One of the four 'Asokan' stupas which originally stood at the four corners of Patan in the Kathmandu Valley. The photo was taken by the court photographer Chitrakar in the 1940s before the stupas were swallowed up by the expanding city. *(Courtesy of Kiran Chitrakar)*

Sungas, particularly in Central India, where the Mauryan stupas at Sanchi and Barhut were restored and beautified to a new level of magnificence. In north-western India, too, Buddhism continued to prosper under Pusyamitra Sunga's contemporary, the Graeco-Bactrian ruler Menander.

The last of the Sungas was assassinated by a slave-girl in about 73 BCE, by which time the empire of Magadha was a mahajanapada in name only. In the middle of the first century of the Christian era a Jain king of Kalinga named Kharavera briefly occupied the Buddhist heartland and became known as another 'dharma raja' very much in the mould of Asoka the Great, ruling wisely and protecting Buddhism. However, the centre of power had by then shifted to Gandhara in the north-west, where the Bactrians gave way to the Shakas, who in turn were dispersed by the Kushan nomads from central Asia. In the second and third centuries CE the Kushan summer and winter capitals at Kapisha (Kabul) and Purushapura (Peshawar) became the central axis of a thriving east-west trade linking Rome and China.

Under the great Kushan emperor King Kanishka, who ruled from about 127 CE to 150 CE, raiding parties ravaged the Gangetic plain as far east as Pataliputra (today Patna), returning to Purushapura laden with Buddhist trophies by way of booty. These included relics of Sakyamuni Buddha taken from Pataliputra and Rajgir, which were then interred in a enormous stupa at Purushapura afterwards visited by the Chinese monks Faxian and Xuanzang. According to Buddhist texts, King Kanishka was converted to Buddhism by the Buddhist scholar Ashvaghosa and subsequently convened the Fourth Buddhist Council in Kashmir. He became, at the very least, a protector of Buddhism and under his patronage a syncretic Graeco-Buddhist art developed whose influence extended across northern India and deep into the Gangetic plain. As well as being the first ruler to show images of Sakyamuni Buddha on his coins King Kanishka and his immediate successors presided over the restoration and enlargement of Buddhist monasteries, temples and stupas in what amounted to a second golden age of Buddhism that continued well into the third century CE.

The usual dynastic decline and fragmentation followed. In the Magadhan country the Bharshivas seized power in what appears to have been a violent overthrow of the old Buddhist-dominated order, accompanied by the burning of monasteries. After a period of political confusion a powerful new dynasty emerged: the Guptas, originating most probably from Bengal. In about 320 CE Chandragupta – not to be confused with his namesake who had founded the Mauryan dynasty – formed an alliance with the much-weakened Licchhavis of Vaisali through marriage and restored Magadha to something like its former glory. His son Samudragupta continued the expansion of the revived mahajanapada in a series of brilliant military campaigns that added twenty kingdoms to what was now the Gupta empire. In Smith's estimation, Samudragupta was the 'Indian Napoleon', whose 'lost fame has been slowly recovered by the minute and laborious study of inscriptions and coins during the last eighty years ... The fact that it is now possible to write a long narrative of the events of his memorable reign is perhaps the most conspicuous illustration of the success gained by patient archaeological research in piecing together the fragments from which alone the chart of the authentic early history of India can be reconstructed.'

But it was not only Samudragupta whom Smith and his con-temporaries rescued from obscurity. Samudragupta's second son Chandragupta the Second built on his father's successes by extending the Gupta empire from coast to coast. In the process he 'unburdened the sacred earth of the Mlecchas [barbarians without caste].. and by so doing annihilated these sinful Mlecchas completely'. A forty-year reign gave Chandragupta the Second the time to move on from the consolidation of his empire to its just government. A third golden age followed which saw a flowering in literature, mathematics, science and astronomy, centred on the royal court at Pataliputra. Although himself a Vaisnava Hindu, the emperor added to the lustre of his name with his support for both the Buddhist and Jain communities and his patronage of religious art in general.

Emperor Chandragupta had been on the throne for more than a quarter of a century when the Chinese pilgrim Faxian entered the western borders of his empire through Gandhara. He and his travelling companion Tao-chin entered the great northern plain of India in the year 401 CE. As they made their way across the Land of the Five Rivers they were suitably impressed by the order prevailing throughout the country. This they attributed to the lasting effects of the Dharma of the Buddha as propagated by Asoka:

> The people are numerous and happy; they have not to register their households, or attend to any magistrates and their rules; only those who cultivate the royal land have to pay (a portion of) the grain from it. If they want to go, they go; if they want to stay on, they stay. The king governs without decapitation or (other) corporal punishments. Criminals are simply fined, lightly or heavily, accord-ing to the circumstances (of each case). Even in cases of repeated attempts at wicked rebellion, they only have their right hands cut off. Throughout the whole country the people do not kill any living creature, nor drink intoxicating liquor, nor eat onions or garlic.

What also impressed Faxian was the prevailing atmosphere of religious tolerance and the respect shown by the local rulers to the Buddhist religious communities:

> In all the countries of India, the kings had been firm believers
> in that Law. When they make their offerings to a community of
> monks, they take off their royal caps, and along with their relatives
> and ministers, supply them with food with their own hands. That
> done, (the king) has a carpet spread for himself on the ground, and
> sits down in front of the chairman – they dare not presume to sit
> on couches in front of the community. The laws and ways, accord-
> ing to which the kings presented their offerings when Buddha was
> in the world, have been handed down to the present day. ... From
> the nirvana of Buddha, the forms of ceremony, laws, and rules,
> practised by the sacred communities, have been handed down
> from one generation to another without interruption.

Faxian and his companion passed the summer monsoon of 404 CE
in Mathura, the 'peacock city' on the banks of the River Yamuna
(Jumna), where Hindu, Jain and Buddhist communities lived side
by side in apparent harmony. From Mathura they followed the
River Ganga down to the city of Kannauj, where they stayed in a
monastery belonging to the Theravada school of Buddhism. They
then crossed the great river and, according to Beal's translation,
travelled south for a distance of eight *yojanas* to reach the city of
Sravasti, former capital of the kingdom of Kosala.

In setting down his account of his travels Faxian used two units
of measurement: *li* and *yojana*. He began with the Chinese *li*, a unit
of measurement representing a set number of paces, possibly as few
as 360 (in modern China the li has been standardised at 500 metres
but it seems to have been much less in ancient times). Later Faxian
included the Sanskrit *yojana*, representing the distance covered in
a day's march by a royal army. Based on his measurements in the
field, General Sir Alexander Cunningham worked out that there
were just less than six li to one mile and 6.71 miles to one yojana.
For want of anything better, Anton Führer and his contemporaries
followed Cunningham's conversion chart (as will this writer).

But, of course, both Faxian and Xuanzang were scholar monks
and not geographers, and the distances and directions they gave
were rudimentary and even arbitrary. Both they and the scribes
who afterwards made copies of their accounts made mistakes – as,

indeed, did the European scholars who made the first translations. Faxian's directions in describing how he travelled from Kanauj to Sravasti is a case in point. He wrote: '*Going on from this* [Kanauj] *to the south, for eight yojanas, (the travellers) came to the city of Sravasti in the kingdom of Kosala*'.* In fact, Sravasti lies *east* of Kanauj, and the distance between the two is more than twice that given, however one cares to measure a yojana. To treat as gospel Faxian's and Xuanzang's distances and directions as they survive today was bound to lead to confusion and dispute – and it did.

So far in their travels Faxian and his companion had seen plenty of evidence of the continuing success of Buddhism, but when they reached Sravasti, where Buddha Sakyamuni had spent so many summers teaching, they were dismayed to find a city in decline, its inhabitants '*few and far between, amounting in all (only) to a few more than two hundred families*'. Even more disconcerting was the fact that Buddhism was in retreat, and the local Hindu priests hostile – '*the Brahmans, with their contrary doctrine … full of hatred and envy in their hearts*'. However, their main concern was to reach the great monastic complex at the Jetavana Garden south of Sravasti, the grounds of which had originally been donated to the Sakyamuni by the wealthy tradesman Sudatta, and where he and many of his followers had spent so many summers during the months of the rains. Here, at least, they were made welcome:

> *When Fa-hien and Tao-ching first arrived at the Jetavana mon-astery, and thought how the World-honoured one* [Sakyamuni Buddha] *had formerly resided there for twenty-five years, painful reflections arose in their minds. Born in a border-land, along with their like-minded friends, they had travelled through so many kingdoms; some of those friends had returned (to their own land), and some had (died), proving the impermanence and uncertainty of life; and to-day they saw the place where Buddha had lived now unoccupied by him. They were melancholy through their pain of heart, and the crowd of monks came out, and asked them from what*

---

*For reasons that will become clear, extracts from the accounts of Faxian and Xuanzang are set in italics from this point onwards.

The building of the great vihara at the Jetavana Garden, the gift of a devotee who paid for the land with gold laid over the ground. A bas-relief from the so-called 'Prasenajit Pillar' of the Bharhut stupa, excavated by Sir Alexander Cunningham and his assistant J. D. Beglar in 1874.

kingdom they were come. 'We are come,' they replied, 'from the land of Han.' 'Strange,' said the monks with a sigh, 'that men of a border country should be able to come here in search of our Law!'

Guided by the Buddhist monks in residence, the Chinese travellers were able to visit and venerate the many places associated with Sakyamuni Buddha:

The park was the space of ground which the head Sudatta purchased by covering it with gold coins. The vihara was exactly in the centre. Here Buddha lived for a longer time than at any other place, preaching his Law and converting men. At the places where he walked and sat they also (subsequently) reared topes [stupas], each having its particular name ... Outside the east gate of the Jetavana, at a distance of seventy paces to the north, on the west of the road, Buddha held a discussion with the (advocates of the) ninety-six schemes of erroneous doctrine, when the king and his great officers, the householders, and people were all assembled in crowds to hear it ... Further, at the place where the discussion took place, they reared a vihara rather more than sixty cubits high, having in it an image of Buddha in a sitting posture. ... It has been handed down, that, near the time when these things occurred, around the Jetavana vihara there were ninety-eight monasteries, in all of which there were monks residing, excepting only in one place which was vacant. ... Four le [li] south-east from the city of Sravasti, a tope has been erected at the place where the World-honoured One encountered king Virudhaha [Vidudhaba], when he wished to attack the kingdom of Shay-e [Sakya, thus Kapilavastu], and took his stand before him at the side of the road.

From Sravasti Faxian and his companion set out for Kapilavastu, the homeland of Sakyamuni Buddha. To get there they first journeyed south-east to a town that Faxian's English translator set down as Na-pei-kea:

Going on south-east from the city of Sravasti for twelve yojanas, (the travellers) came to a town named Na-pei-kea, the birthplace of Krakuchanda Buddha. At the place where he and his father met, and at that [place] where he attained to pari-nirvana, topes were erected. Going north from here less than a yojana, they came to a town which had been the birthplace of Kanakamuni Buddha. At the place where he and his father met, and where he attained to pari-nirvana, topes were erected. Less than a yojana to the east from this brought them to the city of Kapilavastu.

Although greatly moved to find themselves at last in the hallowed country of the Sakyamuni's birth and early years, the two Chinese pilgrims were shocked by what they found there:

> In it there was neither king nor people. All was mound and desola-
> tion. Of inhabitants there were only some monks and a score or two
> of families of the common people. ... The country of Kapilavastu is
> a great scene of empty desolation. The inhabitants are few and far
> between. On the roads people have to be on their guard against
> white elephants and lions, and should not travel incautiously.

Fortunately for posterity – and to the great confusion of archaeologists – both Faxian and Xuanzang left detailed accounts of
their impressions of the city in which Prince Siddhartha grew to
manhood in the confines of the palace of his father King Suddhodana, albeit, as filtered through the religious sensibilities of two
devout Buddhists. First Faxian:

> At the spot where stood the old palace of king Suddhodana there
> have been made images of the prince (his eldest son) and his mother;
> and at the places where that son appeared mounted on a white
> elephant when he entered his mother's womb, and where he turned
> his carriage round on seeing the sick man after he had gone out
> of the city by the eastern gate, topes have been erected. The places
> (were also pointed out) where (the rishi [ascetic]) A-e inspected the
> marks (of Buddhaship on the body) of the heir-apparent (when an
> infant); where, when he was in company with Nanda and others,
> on the elephant being struck down and drawn to one side, he tossed
> it away; where he shot an arrow to the south-east, and it went a
> distance of thirty le [li], then entering the ground and making a
> spring to come forth, which men subsequently fashioned into a well
> from which travellers might drink; where, after he had attained to
> Wisdom, Buddha returned and saw the king, his father; where five
> hundred Sakyas quitted their families and did reverence to Upali
> ... where Buddha preached his Law to the devas ... ; where Buddha
> sat under a nyagrodha [Ficus religiosa or pipal] tree, which is still
> standing, with his face to the east, and (his aunt) Maja-prajapati
> presented him with a Sanghali [robe]; and (where) king Vaidurya
> [Vidudhaba] slew the seed of Sakya, and they all in dying became

Srotapannas [saints]. A tope was erected at this last place, which is still existing ...

From Kapilavastu Faxian went on to the Lumbini Garden, the scene of Queen Mayadevi's delivery of the baby Prince Siddhartha. To get there he walked east:

Fifty le east from the city [of Kapilavastu] was a garden, named Lumbini, where the queen entered the pond and bathed. Having come forth from the pond on the northern bank, after (walking) twenty paces, she lifted up her hand, laid hold of a branch of a tree, and, with her face to the east, gave birth to the heir-apparent. When he fell to the ground, he (immediately) walked seven paces. Two dragon-kings (appeared) and washed his body. At the place where they did so, there was immediately formed a well, and from it, as well as from the above pond, where (the queen) bathed, the monks (even) now constantly take the water, and drink it.

From Lumbini Faxian continued eastward, travelling through country even more desolate than before. He soon entered the country that in the days of the Sakyas had been known as Koliya-grama, but which had since come to be known as Ramagrama, after the place where the Koliyas' share of the Sakyamuni's relics had been interred: '*East from Buddha's birthplace, and at a distance of five yojanas, there is a kingdom called Rama. The king of this country, having obtained one portion of the relics of Buddha's body, returned with it and built over it a tope, named the Rama tope.*' Having located the Ramagrama stupa without apparent difficulty, Faxian was unusually forthcoming about its history:

By the side of it there was a pool, and in the pool a dragon, which constantly kept watch over (the tope), and presented offerings to it day and night. When king Asoka came forth into the world, he wished to destroy the eight topes (over the relics), and to build (instead of them) 84,000 topes. After he had thrown down the seven (others), he wished next to destroy this tope. But then the dragon showed itself, took the king into its palace; and when he had seen all the things provided for offerings, it said to him, 'If you are able with your offerings to exceed these, you can destroy the tope, and take it all away. I will not contend with you.' The king, however, knew that such appliances for offerings were not to be had anywhere in the world, and thereupon returned (without carrying out his purpose). (Afterwards), the ground all about became overgrown with vegetation, and there was nobody to sprinkle and sweep (about the tope); but a herd of elephants came regularly, which brought water with their trunks to water the ground, and various kinds of flowers and incense, which they presented at the tope.

This period of neglect had apparently ended when a Buddhist ascetic came to worship at the Ramagrama stupa and found it venerated only by elephants: *'He prevailed on the king of the country to form a residence for monks; and when that was done, he became head of the monastery. At the present day there are monks residing in it. This event is of recent occurrence.'*

From Ramagrama Faxian's pilgrimage took him to Kushinagara, the scene of the Maharaparinirvana. To get there he apparently went east:

East from here four yojanas, there is the place where the heir-apparent [Prince Siddhartha after quitting his father's palace in the Great Renunciation] *sent back Chandaka* [his groom], *with his white horse; and there also a tope was erected. Four yojanas to the east from this, (the travellers) came to the Charcoal tope* [the Sakyamuni's cremation site], *where there is also a monastery. Going on twelve yojanas, still to the east, they came to the city of Kusanagara, on the north of which, between two trees, on the bank of the Nairanjana river, is the place where the World-honoured one, with his head to the north, attained to pari-nirvana (and died). There also are the places where … in his coffin of gold they made offerings to the World-honoured one for seven days … and where the eight kings divided the relics (of the burnt body). At all these places were built topes and monasteries, all of which are now existing. In the city the inhabitants are few and far between, comprising only the families belonging to the (different) societies of monks.*

From Kushinagara Faxian went south to Vaisali and crossed the Ganges to enter the city of Pataliputra, where the magnificent palace, pillared halls and other Buddhist edifices erected by Emperor Asoka were still standing – works so magnificent that Faxian judged them to be the work of spirits employed by the emperor.

Approximately 216 years after Faxian's departure from India (in about 415 CE) the Chinese scholar-monk Xuanzang arrived on the north-western border of the Indian sub-continent (in about 631 CE). During the intervening centuries northern India had undergone a series of major upheavals in which Buddhism had been one of the main losers. Of these the most devastating was the eruption onto the plains of India of a new wave of Mleccha from central Asia who called themselves the *Huna*, known to the Greeks as the Hephthalites or 'White Huns'. They first appeared at a time when the Gupta empire was being threatened on his southern borders by the growing power of the Pushyamitras. In about 475 CE Kumaragupta the Second defeated the Pushyamitras and repulsed the first wave of the Huns. But his empire's defences had been fatally weakened and when the Huna warlord Toramana launched a second assault in about 480 CE the Gupta armies were forced into retreat. More attacks followed under Toramana's successor Mihirakula, whose name is forever blackened in Buddhist eyes by his relentless persecution of Buddhists and his destruction of Buddhist monasteries. The Hunas were eventually broken up but not before the Guptas had been forced back to their original mahajanapada of Magadha, which they managed to cling on to until the last significant ruler of their line, Vishnugupta, was ousted in about 550 CE.

The years that followed saw the rise of militant Shaivism, with King Sassanka of Karansuvara in Bengal leading an assault on Buddhist centres in Bihar in which the revered pipal tree at Bodgaya was cut down, its roots dug out and burnt and the ground soaked with sugar-cane juice to ensure that nothing would ever grow there again. Over this same period the various *Prakrit* or 'vulgar' languages, including Pali, derived from the original speech introduced into India by the Aryans, was formalised into *Sanskrit* or 'pure' language, which became the dominant literary language of northern India and of Mahayana Buddhism.

Northern India was now divided among a number of independent rulers, with bands of Hunas vying with other invaders from the north to establish strongholds in the wild country south of the Jamuna River – a process that eventually led to the emergence of the Rajputs of Rajputana and Central India. Out of this struggle there also emerged the Vardhana dynasty, whose third in line, Harsha Vardhana, killed the last of the Guptas in battle at the age of sixteen and added Magadha to his family's fast-expanding mahajanapada. Having established his capital at Kannauj, Harsha Vardhana marched against the anti-Buddhist King Sassanka and defeated him to bring Bengal, Bihar and Orissa under his authority. Raised by his father as a worshipper of the sun-god Surya, King Harsha was nominally a Shaivite for most of his adult life but may well have converted to Buddhism before his death. Like Asoka, Kharavera, Kanishka and Chandragupta the Second before him, he extended his royal patronage to all the faiths within his empire, and he, too, was fortunate to live long enough to ensure the consolidation of his rule.

It was during the latter years of King Harsha's reign that the great scholar-monk Xuanzang travelled through India.

When Xuanzang entered the Gangetic plain towards the end of the year 634 CE he was as impressed as his predecessor had been two centuries earlier. The city of Mathura was now dominated by Hindu temples to Shiva and Vishnu, but the two main Buddhist schools of the Mahayanas and Theravadas he found there were well supported, with more than 2,000 monks enrolled in their monasteries. Like Faxian before him, Xuanzang continued on to Kannauj, now thriving as a centre of religion and culture. Here Xuanzang reported the existence of a hundred Buddhist monasteries supporting 10,000 monks. He also spent some months studying the Pali scriptures in a Theravada monastery before moving on to Sravasti.

At this point in his travels Faxian had proceeded directly to Sravasti. The more determined Xuanzang wanted to take in every scene associated with Sakyamuni Buddha and his three predecessors. From Kannauj he went downstream to the confluence of the Jamuna and Ganga Rivers at Prayag (afterwards Allahabad), from

The seventh-century Buddhist scholar-monk Xuanzang returns from India laden with precious texts. From a tenth-century coloured woodcut from Tun-huang on the Silk Road, now in the Bibliothéque National in Paris.

where he made an excursion to the ancient city of Kosambi, only to find the Buddhist monasteries in ruins and the number of Hindu devotees 'enormous'. He then re-crossed the Ganges to make his way northwards towards Sravasti, travelling by way of Kasapur (Sultanpur) and the ancient Hindu town of Saketa (Ayodhya). To get from Saketa to Sravasti he went north-east for '500 li or so'.

Although thoroughly conversant with Faxian's account of his travels, Xuanzang was as shaken as his predecessor had been by what he found at Sravasti. Of the few active Buddhist foundations that Faxian had noted nearly every one was in ruins, including the great monastery of Jetavana:

> The kingdom of Sravasti (Shi-lo-fu-shi-ti) is about 6,000 li in circuit. The chief town is desert and ruined. ... There are several hundreds of sangharamas [Buddhist monasteries], mostly in ruin, with very few religious followers. ... There are too Deva [i.e. Hindu] temples with very many heretics. ... Within the old precincts of the royal city are some ancient foundations; these are the remains of the palace. ... To the south of the city 5 or 6 li is the Jetavana. This is where Anathapindada (Ki-ku-to) (otherwise called) Sudatta, the chief minister of Prasenajita-raja, built for Buddha a vihara. There was a sangharama here formerly, but now all is in ruins. On the left and right of the eastern gate has been built a pillar about 70 feet high; on the left-hand pillar is engraved on the base a wheel; on the right-hand pillar the figure of an ox is on the top. Both columns were erected by Asoka-raja. The residences (of the priests) are wholly destroyed; the foundations only remain, with the exception of one solitary brick building, which stands alone in the midst of the ruins, and contains an image of Buddha.

The reader will have observed that at the Jetavana Garden Xuanzang saw two Asokan pillars which Faxian failed to mention in his account. Faxian seemed to hold no particular regard for these columns and tended to overlook them. Another significant difference between the two pilgrims' accounts is that (despite the impression given by the abbreviated version set down here) Xuanzang's is the more detailed, chiefly because he set down whatever he heard or already knew by way of associated Buddhist legends – as, for example, in his explanation of Sakyamuni Buddha's attempts to prevent King Virudhaba from slaughtering his Sakya kinfolk: '*After King Virudhaka* [Virudhaba] *had succeeded to the throne, stirred up to hatred by his former disgrace, he equipped an army and moved forward with a great force. The summer heat being ended and everything arranged, he commanded all advance.*' One of the Sakyamuni's followers got to hear of the king's plans and went to warn him. Meanwhile, King Virudhaba let his army towards Kapilavastu – only to see the sage of the Sakyas seated beside the road under a withered tree:

> *Virudhaka-raja, seeing him thus seated some way off, alighted from his chariot and paid him reverence. Then as he stood up he said, 'There are plenty of green and umbrageous trees; why do you not sit beneath one of these, instead of under this withered one with dried leaves, where you walk and sit?' The Lord said, 'My honourable tribe is like branches and leaves; these being about to perish, what shade can there be for one belonging to it?' The king said, 'The Lord of the World by his honourable regard for his family is able to turn my chariot.' Then looking at him with emotion, he disbanded his army and returned to his country.*

From Sravasti Xuanzang continued on to Kapilavastu. Faxian at this stage in his journey had first gone south to Na-pei-kea, the birthplace of the earlier Buddha Krakuchanda, and then north from Na-pei-kea to a town which was the birthplace of another earlier Buddha, Kanakamuni. Xuanzang initially ignored these two sites associated with Buddhas Krakuchanda and Kanakamuni and instead made an excursion to the north-west of Sravasti to honour the memorials of the early Buddha, Kasyapa: *To the north-west of the capital 16 li or so, there is an old town … in which Kasyapa Buddha was born. To the south of the town there is a stupa. This is the place where he first met his father after arriving at enlightenment. To the north of the town is a stupa, which contains relics of the entire body of Kasyapa Buddha. Both these stupas were built by Asoka-raja.*

From this relic stupa a short distance north-west of Sravasti Xuanzang went directly to the country of Kapilavastu: '*From this point going south-east 500 li or so, we come to the country of Kie-pilo-fa-sse-ti (Kapilavastu).*' Like Faxian before him, Xuanzang found everything in ruins: *This country is about 4,000 li in circuit. There are some ten desert cities in this country, wholly desolate and ruined. The capital is overthrown and in ruins. Its circuit cannot be accurately measured. The royal precincts within the city measure 14 or 15 li round. They are all built of brick. The foundation walls are still strong and high. It has been long deserted. The peopled villages are few and wasted.*

In describing Kapilavastu Xuanzang drew freely on his predecessor's account but added more detail (only the bones of which can be given here for reasons of space):

Within the royal precincts are some ruined foundation walls; these are the remains of the proper palace of Suddhodana-raja; above is built a vihara in which is a statue of the king. Not far from this is a ruined foundation, which represents the sleeping palace of Mahamaya [Great Maya, Mayadevi], *the queen. Above they have erected a vihara in which is a figure of the queen. By the side of this is a vihara; this is where Bodhisattva descended spiritually into the womb of his mother. ... To the north-east of the palace of the spiritual conception is a stupa; this is the place where Atisha the rishi prognosticated the fortune of the royal prince. ... At the south gate of the city is a stupa. This is where the royal prince, when contending the Sakya princes, cast the elephant away. ... At the south-east angle of the city is a vihara in which is the figure of the royal prince riding a white and high-prancing horse. ... Outside each of the four gates of the city there is a vihara in which there are respectively figures of an old man, a diseased man, a dead man, and a sramana* [ascetic]. ...

To the north-east of the city [of Kapilavastu] *about 40 li is a stupa. This is the spot where the prince* [Siddhartha] *sat in the shade of a tree to watch the ploughing festival. ... To the north-west of the capital there are several hundreds and thousands of stupas, indicating the spot where the members of the Sakya tribe were slaughtered. Virudhaka-raja having subdued the Sakyas, and captured the members of their tribe to the number of 9,990 myriads of people, then ordered them to be slaughtered. They piled their bodies like straw, and their blood was collected in lakes. ... To the south-west of the place of massacre are four little stupas. This is the place where the four Sakyas withstood an army. ...*

To the south of the city 3 or 4 li is a grove of Nyagrodha trees in which is a stupa built by Asoka-raja. This is the place where Sakya Tathagata, having returned to his country after his enlightenment, met his father and preached the law. ... By the side of the sanghar-ama and not far from it, is a stupa; this is the spot where Tathagata sat beneath a great tree with his face to the east and received from his aunt a golden-tissued kashaya garment. A little farther on is another stupa; this is the place where Tathagata converted eight king's sons and 500 Sakyas. ...

Within the eastern gate of the city, on the left of the road, is a stupa; this is where the Prince Siddhartha practised (athletic) arts. Outside the gate is the temple of Isvara-deva. In the temple is a figure of the deva [deity] made of stone, which has the appearance of rising in a bent position. This is the temple which the royal prince when an infant entered. ... The nurse, carrying the child in her arms, entered the temple; then the stone image raised itself and saluted the prince.

Crucially, Xuanzang saw and described two Asokan pillars associated with the early Buddhas Krakuchanda and Kanakamuni, located south and south-east of the city of Kapilavastu:

To the south of the city going 50 li or so, we come to an old town where there is a stupa. This is the place where Krakuchanda Buddha was born. ... To the south of the city [of Buddha Krakuchanda], not far, there is a stupa; this is the place where, having arrived at complete enlightenment, he met his father. To the south-east of the city is a stupa where are that Tathagata's relics [i.e. Krakuchanda's]; before it is erected a stone pillar about 30 feet high, on the top of which is carved a lion. By its side (or, on its side) is a record relating the circumstances of his Nirvana. It was erected by Asoka-raja.

To the north-east of the town of Krakuchanda Buddha, going

Devotees worship 'Bodhi' trees under which earlier Buddhas achieved enlightenment, offering garlands of flowers; the Buddhas here being Buddha Krakuchanda *(left)* and his Bodhi tree the *sirisa (Acacia sirisa)*, and Buddha Kanakamuni *(right)* and his Bodhi tree the *udambara (Ficus glomerata)*. Buddha Sakyamuni's tree was, of course, the *pipal (Ficus religiosa)*. Bas-reliefs from the Barhut stupa.

> *about 30 li, we come to an old capital (or, great city) in which there is a stupa. This is to commemorate the spot where ... Kanakamuni Buddha was born. To the north-east of the city, not far, is a stupa; it was here, having arrived at complete enlightenment, he met his father. Farther north there is a stupa containing the relics of his bequeathed body; in front of it is a stone pillar with a lion on the top, and about 20 feet high; on this is inscribed a record of the events connected with his Nirvana; this was built by Asoka-raja.*

The reader will recall that Faxian also visited memorials to Buddhas Krakuchanda and Kanakamuni on the way to Kapilavastu, but made no reference to any Asokan pillars. Both pilgrims placed these memorials on the southern side of Kapilavastu – but in different places. Faxian linked Krakuchanda Buddha with the town of Na-pei-kea, which he sited twelve yojanas south-east of Sravasti and one yojana south of an unnamed town associated with Kanakamuni Buddha, itself less than one yojana west of Kapilavastu city. Xuanzang, however, placed Krakuchanda's memorials fifty li south of Kapilavastu and Kanakamuni's memorials a lesser distance south-east of Kapilavastu.

On applying Cunningham's conversion table of just under six li to one mile and 6.71 miles to one yojana (thus 40 li to one yojana), the following chart of these conflicting positionings emerges:

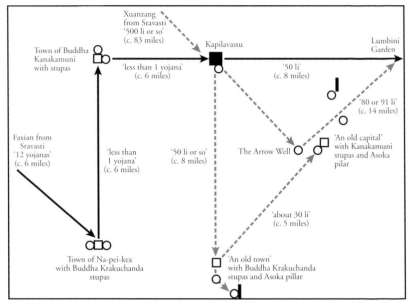

--→ = Xuanzang's journey

—→ = Faxian's journey

From Kapilavastu Faxian had travelled directly to Lumbini, whereas Xuanzang chose to proceed indirectly, by way of a sacred spring south-east of Kapilavastu known as the Arrow Well, where a stupa marked the spot where an arrow fired by Prince Siddhartha had landed: '*Outside the south gate of the city* [of Kapilavastu], *on the left of the road, is a stupa; it was here the royal prince contended with the Sakyas in athletic sports … From this 30 li south-east is a small stupa … Here it was, during the athletic contest, that the arrow of the prince, after penetrating the targets, fell and buried itself up to the feather in the ground, causing a clear spring of water to flow forth.*'

From the Arrow Well stupa Xuanzang continued on to Lumbini:

To the north-east of the arrow well about 80 or 90 li, we come to the Lumbini garden. Here is the bathing tank of the Sakyas. ... To the north of this 24 or 25 paces there is an Asoka-flower tree, which is now decayed; this is the place where Bodhisattva was born. ... East from this is a stupa built by Asoka-raja. ... To the east of this stupa are two fountains of pure water, by the side of which have been built two stupas. ... To the south of this is a stupa ... Close to this there are four stupas. ... By the side of these stupas and not far from them is a great stone pillar, on the top of which is the figure of a horse, which was built by Asoka-raja. Afterwards, by the contrivance of a wicked dragon, it was broken off in the middle and fell to the ground. By the side of it is a little river which flows to the south east. The people of the place call it the river of oil. This is the stream which the Devas caused to appear. ... Now it is changed and become a river, the stream of which is still unctuous.

From Lumbini Xuanzang followed the same eastward course to Ramagrama as Faxian, experiencing the same difficulties: '*From this going east 300 li or so, across a wild and deserted jungle, we arrive at the kingdom of Lan-mo (Ramagrama). The kingdom of Lan-mo has been waste and desolate for many years. There is no account of its extent. The towns are decayed and the inhabitants few. To the south-east of the old capital (town) there is an old stupa, in height less than a hundred feet.*' This was the stupa containing the Koliya's eighth share of the Sakyamuni's relics, with the attendant monastery seen by Faxian now on the verge of collapse, but still surrounded with all the old stories of attentive elephants and the dragon guardian who had prevented Emperor Asoka from removing the relics.

Still following the same course as Faxian, Xuanzang continued east again from Ramagrama: first, through a great forest for more than a hundred li to reach an Asokan stupa marking the place of the groom Chandaka's return; then east again to the Head-Shaving stupa, where Prince Siddhartha had shaved off his hair; then southeast, going 180–190 li to reach the Embers stupa; and then northeast, '*along a dangerous and difficult road, where wild oxen and herds of elephants and robbers and hunters caused incessant trouble to travellers'*, to reach the ruined and deserted city of Kushinagara itself. Here at the site of the Sakyamuni's Maharaparinirvana, Xuanzang found a grove of sal trees, noting four of particular size. Nearby was a large stupa built by Emperor Asoka, a stone pillar recording the circumstances of the Buddha's decease and a brick temple containing a giant statue: *'an image (or presentation) of Ju-lai-nie-pan (that is, of the Buddha dead) lying with his head to the north'.*

Xuanzang then crossed the Ganges to the country of Magadha and settled at the great Buddhist monastery-cum-university of Nalanda, where he spent several years studying before returning to China laden with more than a thousand precious Buddhist texts. As a direct result of his sojourn in India Emperor Harsha sent an embassy to China which established the first diplomatic links between the two countries. According to the Tibetan chronicle known as *The White Annals* the Chinese responded with their own mission, which reached India through Nepal only to find Harsha dead and his throne occupied by his chief minister Arjuna, who attacked the Chinese envoy and forced him and his escort to flee to Tibet. A combined Tibetan and Nepalese army then invaded India, defeated Arjuna in battle and sent him and his family to the Chinese emperor in chains. Harsha's empire then disintegrated and another 'dark age' followed in which the Gangetic valley reverted to the old pattern of warring states. In the words of Vincent Smith: 'The partial unity of India vanishes with Harsha and is not restored in any considerable measure until the closing years of the twelfth century, when the extensive conquest of Muhammad of Ghori brought the most important provinces under the sway of the Sultans of Delhi'.

Buddhism in India was now threatened with extinction as Hinduism underwent a spiritual revival beginning in the ninth century spearheaded by the Brahmin reformer Adi Shankara, in the course of which Sakyamuni Buddha was absorbed into the Hindu pantheon as the ninth *avatar* or incarnation of Vishnu. Only in Bengal and Bihar did Buddhism survive and even prosper, thanks to the Pala kings, who took their dynastic name from the word *pal* or 'protector'. The founder of their dynasty, Gopala, came to power in

Gaur, in West Bengal, in about 755 CE by the remarkable process of democratic election. His Buddhist successors Dharmapala and Devapala expended their empire up the Gangetic valley as far west as Mathura and in the process helped to spread the esoteric practices of Tantric Buddhism into the Kathmandu Valley and beyond. Under Pala patronage Eastern Indian forms of Buddhist practice underwent a revival based on the great centres of learning at Nalanda in southern Bihar and Vikramshala in eastern Bihar, from which missionaries and students took the Dharma as far afield as the spice islands of south-east Asia.

In the final decade of the eleventh century the last of the Pala kings was overthrown by the orthodox Hindu founder of the Sena dynasty, and from that moment Buddhism in India went into rapid and terminal decline, helped along by the arrival of Muslim Sufi refugees from Afghanistan and Central Asia fleeing from the Mongols. There is some evidence that the religious orthodoxy of the Senas led to mass conversions of Buddhists to the Islam propagated by Sufi missionaries but Muslim iconoclasts also played their part, culminating in the bigotry of the Turkish warlord Qutb-ud-Din, who took Delhi in 1193 and set the pattern by building Delhi's first mosque, the Qubbat al-Islam, over the Hindu temple built by the conquered Rajput leader Prithvi Raj. His leading general, Muhammad bin Bakhtiyar Khilji, then put fire and sword not only to Nalanda and Vikramshila but virtually every other Buddhist monastery in the Gangetic plain. By the end of the twelfth century Buddhism had to all intents been eradicated from the country of its birth. Within the space of another two or three centuries all its great monuments had been reclaimed by nature where they had not been plundered by builders or treasure-seekers.

So it came about that when Dr. Anton Alois Führer came to tour the tarai country east of Lucknow in the winter of 1889–90 he found much of it to be a wilderness. 'Nowhere,' he wrote, 'is there any trace of genuine continuous tradition handed down from the times of Buddhist ascendancy and civilisation. So far as it appears, Gorakhpur and Basti Districts lapsed into jungle during the disturbances which accompanied the extinction of Buddhism, and remained for centuries unoccupied by settled or civilised inhabitants.' What traces there were to be seen of the past were in the form of large mounds:

> Nothing is known of the history of these ruined mounds. The villagers, as a rule, ascribe them to the forest tribe of Thârûs … due to the fact that when the ancestors of the present inhabitants immigrated, they found the country, as far as it was peopled at all, in the possession of the Thârûs. The immigrants knew nothing of an earlier and vanished civilisation, and naturally ascribed all ruins to the people whom they found in occupation of the country.

The Unannounced Visit

'Camp Kapilavastu', 28 January 1898

On Friday 28 January, the day after Vincent Smith's arrival in Birdpore, he made what he afterwards described as an 'unannounced visit' to the site of Dr. Anton Führer's excavation in the Nepal Tarai, accompanied by Willie Peppé. Smith provided no explanation for this visit, which has allowed conspiracy theorists to propose that collusion took place between Führer, Smith and Peppé – some sort of conspiracy involving the removal of objects from one excavation site to another and the forging of an inscription. A more straightforward motive was that Smith had long been convinced that Kapilavastu was to be found in Nepal and wanted to see for himself what Führer had found there. Another, was that he and Peppé wished to seek the professional opinion of the Archaeological Surveyor of the province in which they lived and worked. Smith said nothing about it at the time for the very good reason that he had not sought the permission of the Government of Nepal to enter Nepalese territory. This might not have mattered in Peppé's case but Smith was a senior official of the British administration and such persons only entered Nepal by permission of the Nepal Durbar. In fact, the Government of Nepal *did* get to hear of his intrusion and complained to the British Resident, resulting in Smith receiving a rap over the knuckles for his improper conduct.

Smith and Peppé left the Birdpore bungalow at dawn and made their way on horseback to Border Post 44 on the Nepal border, where the *pukka* road built by the Peppés terminated in a rice field. As Smith afterwards remarked, 'The Nepalese Government does not encourage the construction of roads, and leaves its subjects to make their way as best they can along rough tracks, or, when the crops are off the ground, across the fields'. Fortunately, two elephants were waiting for them at the border, on loan from Smith's friend, the local zamindar Babu Shobrat Singh. 'We crossed the frontier north of Birdpur close to pillar No. 44, and advanced a little west of north through the villages of Siswa [Sisawa], Bankasia, Kuangawan [Kurwagaon], Dhani [Dohani], Ramsahai, Dhamauli and Simri [Semari]. Beyond Simri we passed some ancient mounds and tanks, and then for 14 minutes crossed a belt of jungle.' This itinerary shows that they steered well clear of the district town of Taulihawa.

Once through the stretch of jungle north of Taulihawa they passed by the little settlement of Srinagar, and about half a mile beyond reached the Tharu hamlet of Sagarwa, situated on the eastern bank of the Banganga. This was where Dr. Führer had set up his camp. Sagarwa village took its name from a nearby lake, known locally as *lambu sagar* or 'the long lake', which was roughly oval in shape and about a quarter of a mile in length. At the western end of this lake they found Dr. Führer and no less than 200 Tharu coolies, all hard at work removing earth from a rectangular pit running north and south for about 250 feet. Watching over the proceedings was a Nepali officer in military uniform whom they came to know as 'the Nepalese Captain': Captain Bir Jang, deputed by General Khadga Shumsher Rana to 'superintend the excavations on behalf of his Government'.

As the two Britons approached the pit Dr. Führer emerged holding five small copper caskets, which were immediately taken from him by the Nepalese Captain. The German archaeologist welcomed them to his excavation and declared the caskets to be nothing less than the ashes of some of the thousands of Sakya warriors massacred here by King Prasenajit of Kosala. He explained that he was in the process of excavating the fifth of a series of small stupas covering the remains of these Sakyas, having been guided to this spot by Xuanzang. The Chinese traveller's account of the ruins of Kapilavastu had, he claimed, been proved to be correct in every detail:

According to his *Si-Yu-Ki*, the 'place of massacre' of the Sakyas, who fell in battle with the Kosalan army of the king of 'Sravasti' shortly before the demise of the Buddha, was situated to the north-west of the capital. Following this direction, we dug into the vast brick ruins, skirting the eastern bank of the Banganga, and stretching far away between the Tharu villages of Sagrava [Sagarwa] and Bandhauli, and were rewarded by finding a great number of small square relic-stûpas, built of well-burnt bricks, and varying in size from 19´ by 19´ to 7´ by 9´ and in height from 12 feet to 5 feet. These square relic-stûpas are the oldest monuments ever unearthed in India. ... Exactly in the true centre of each shrine, at the level of the foundations, we discovered the relic chamber, built up in some instances of nine, seven and five bricks, respectively, impressed with well-executed designs of a full blown lotus flower or a *svas tika*, under which the relic caskets were buried in the soil. The remaining bricks, forming the relic chambers, bore representations of the arms and instruments used by the Sakya in the battle, such as daggers, swords of different sorts, javelins, battle-axes, tridents, thunderbolts, shields and standards.

What Smith and Peppé saw for themselves was very much in accordance with what Führer claimed. What they also observed was the manner in which the Nepalese Captain moved in to remove every item as it was recovered. 'When Mr William Peppé and I rode up unannounced on the morning of 28 January 1898,' reported Smith, 'we happened to find Dr. Führer and the Nepalese Captain, who watched him, in the act of taking out the deposit from one of the seventeen stupas ... The little caskets lay immediately under the bricks – one in the centre and one at each corner – five in all. They were small, shallow, circular, metal vessels with lids crushed and thickly coated with verdigris ... They contained a few gold stars, etc., and probably fragments of bone.' But it was what happened next that stayed in Smith's mind:

They were instantly taken possession of by the Nepalese Captain, who stood over Dr. Führer, and were opened by the Captain who then laid them aside. I doubt greatly if Dr. Führer was ever allowed

The decorated brick layer from one of the seventeen small stupas excavated by Dr. Führer at Sagarwa, showing the symbols which he identified as memorials to the slain Sakya warriors. The copper relic caskets were found under the central and corner bricks. From P. C. Mukherji's *Report*.

> to touch them again, and he certainly never got the chance of cleaning them. ... Dr. Führer complained to me that he was hardly allowed to look at what he found, and was not permitted to remove even a brick. He also told me that no inscriptions had been found.

The Nepalese Captain's behaviour did not surprise Smith in the least. 'Nothing,' he had written a year earlier with characteristic bluntness, 'will persuade the Nepalese that Englishmen, digging among old ruins, can really want anything but treasure. All our protestations of interest in ancient history and so forth, though they may be listened to with politeness, are regarded as mere lies to cover the real object of these explorers.' What Smith was more concerned about was Dr. Führer's archaeological method, which appeared to consist of digging away until nothing was left. Being a visitor and a gentleman, he said nothing about his reservation, but quietly observed.

In 1885 – the same year in which Anton Führer joined the
Archaeological Department of the Government of the NWP&O,
that Vincent Smith was appointed joint officiating magistrate of
Basti District, and that William Hoey next door in Gonda District
completed his two-month dig at Sahet-Mahet – an Englishman
named Duncan Ricketts got to hear of a standing stone pillar just
inside Nepalese territory. Ricketts was at that time the assistant
manager of the Dulha Estate, adjoining Birdpore Estate to the east
and situated in the extreme north-east corner of Basti District. He
slipped across the border and found the pillar protruding from the
side of a tree-covered mound near the village of Paderiya, about
five miles north-east of his estate in the Nepalese district of Rummindei. There was an inscription cut into 'the exposed parts of the
pillar'. Ricketts took a rubbing and showed it to Vincent Smith, who
dismissed the writing as 'mediaeval scribblings' – a hasty verdict
he lived to regret.

Smith spent almost four years in Basti District and by the end of
his time there had come to the conclusion that Cunningham, Carl-
lyle, and, indeed, his ICS colleague William Hoey had got it wrong:
that Sravasti and Kushinagar, as well as Kapilavastu, Lumbini and
Ramagrama, were all still waiting to be rediscovered; and that, if
the routes provided by Faxian and Xuanzang were to be believed,
the real location of these five sites must lie across the border in the
Nepal Tarai. His reasoning was based entirely on the directions
and distances given by the Chinese travellers. If they were correct
the site of Sravasti and the Jetavana Garden had to lie somewhere
in the Nepal Tarai just north of Basti District. And since both the
Chinese pilgrims had then gone on from Sravasti in a predominantly easterly direction, it followed that Kapilavastu, Lumbini,
Ramagrama and even Kushinagar must all lie north of the border.

This reading put Smith at intellectual odds with William Hoey,
who in 1889 took up a new appointment on the other side of Oude,
initially as joint magistrate of Banda District, south of the River
Jumna, and then as Collector of Banda. Sakyamuni Buddha was
said to have twice visited the Banda region and both Faxian and
Xuanzang had passed through on their travels, the latter spending
some months studying Pali texts in the ancient city of Kannauj.

'Committee of Hoey Park, Gorakhpur', February 1894. Dr. William Hoey, Collector of Gorakhpur, seated in the centre flanked by Muslim and Hindu worthies. The park (now 'Government Gardens') in the centre of Gorakhpur town was created as the result of Dr. Hoey's initiative. It is said that he used to sit in the park's raised bandstand in the evenings to survey the rose gardens and to smoke a cigar. *(Courtesy of the Hoey family)*

During his time in Banda District Hoey purchased a number of finds, mostly gold coins but also an inscribed copper plate and three small bronze statuettes. These important statuettes had been found in the ruins of Dhanesar Khera and all three were Buddha figures: one, seated in the classic lotus position, is now in the British Museum; another, a very fine standing figure, is in the Nelson-Atkins Museum, Kansas City; but the whereabouts of the third and smallest Buddha, also a standing figure, is unknown – although a statuette which appears identical and which has the same damage is now in the Bangkok Museum.

For Hoey, a second period of home leave followed the Banda tour, and on his return to India in 1892 he was transferred from Oude to the NWP, taking up the post of Magistrate and Collector of Gorakhpur Division, based in the town of Gorakhpur.

Hoey's transfer brought him right back into the Sravasti-Kushinagar debate. One of his first known forays out from Gorakhpur, made in about December 1892, took him about eighteen

The Sohgaura plate, possibly the earliest discovered in India, presented by Dr. Hoey to the Asiatic Society of Bengal and since lost or stolen.

miles south-south-east of the town to a big bend in the Rapti River covered in a 'series of mounds', seemingly the remains of an ancient city. His explorations led him to a hamlet named Sohgaura in 'the middle of the long mound of remains'. Here he got talking with an old man who recalled how when laying down the foundations of his house many decades earlier he had dug up a small copper plate covered in strange writing. This he had presented to the local *zamindar* or landowner, who had since died. Hoey made enquiries, which ended some months later when the son of the dead zamindar turned up with the plate and presented it to him.

Although scarcely more than 2½ inches wide and 1½ inches in height, the plate was in astonishingly good condition and covered in symbols and lettering that had been cast in such high relief that they were easy to make out. The writing consisted in four lines of the script that Hoey recognised as the Brahmi of the Asokan columns. But above the lettering was one line made up of seven distinct symbols representing what appeared to be two trees in railings, two buildings, a spear, a central image of three domes topped by a sun and moon and beside it a globe topped by what appeared to be a pair of horns, a familiar symbol known as a *taurine*. This was beyond Hoey's expertise and he turned to his colleague for help.

By a stroke of luck, Hoey's move to Gorakhpur had put him in close touch with Vincent Smith, by now acknowledged as India's leading authority both on copper plates and Gupta coinage. Indeed, his work on Gupta gold coins had more or less filled two entire issues of the *Journal of the Asiatic Society of Bengal* in 1884 and 1889, and he was about to continue the process in a third issue. Smith and Hoey now began the first of a number of collaborations with a joint presentation on the Sohgaura copper-plate, which was read on their behalf at a meeting of the Asiatic Society of Bengal (ASB) in Park Street, Calcutta, in May 1894. It was Smith's view that no plate of such antiquity had ever been found in India – and in this surmise he was subsequently proved correct. He declared the characters of the writing to be 'ancient Nagari of the Maurya period' but confessed himself unable to make sense of the text because its language appeared to be Pali rather than Sanskrit. Dr. Rudolf Hoernle, principal of the Calcutta Madrassa College and a leading light of both the ASB and the Indian Museum, was then brought in and fared little better. The meanings of the seven symbols were equally mystifying, although the central image of three linked domes topped by a sun and moon struck Smith as undoubtedly 'Buddhistic' and probably represented a memorial stupa. The two structures of wooden posts and thatch roofs obviously represented three-storied buildings of some sort but perhaps the most intriguing element were the two trees, each set behind railings but distinctively different from one another. Smith thought the tree on the left was meant to represent a sal tree but offered no opinion as to what the other might be.

Dr. Hoey presented the plate to the ASB – a misplaced act of generosity, as it turned out, for so chaotic was the Society's curating in the years that followed that it was some decades before it could be officially admitted that the Sohgaura plate was missing believed stolen. The loss is incalculable, for the plate may well be the earliest copper plate ever found in India, very likely made at the time of Asoka himself – whose personal seal may well be represented by the central stupa image – if not earlier.

Fortunately, a photograph of the plate was taken and a copy sent to Prof. Bühler, who published the first tentative translation in his own journal, the *Vienna Oriental Journal*: 'The order of the great official of Sravasti (issued) from (their camp at) Man-avasitikata: These two storehouses with three partitions (which are situated) even in famous Vamsagrama, require the storage of loads of Black Panicum, parched grain, cumin-seed and Amba for (times of) urgent (need). One should not take (any thing from the grain stored).' In fact, Bühler was uncharacteristically wide of the mark here, except in so far as he identified the plate as being some form of order about the storage of food supplies. He was equally uncertain about the significance of the line of images above the inscription, five of which he took to be *mangala* or auspicious symbols. He thought the railings round the two trees identified them as *chaitya* or sacred trees, 'such as are often mentioned in the Buddhist Canon, the Brahminical books and elsewhere – the second of them without leaves being probably one of the so-called "shameless" trees which shed their leaves in winter'. The spear-like object, which Vincent Smith had thought resembled a long-handled spoon, he identified as a 'toilet mirror, as the mirror is one of the auspicious symbols and is depicted as such, together with other symbols, above the entrance of the Jaina cave at Junagadh, called Bawa Pyari's Math'. As for the supposed Buddhist symbol of combined stupas at the centre, this Bühler thought 'may be meant for a rude representation of Mount Meru'–the mountain at the centre of the cosmos in Hindu, Jain and Buddhist cosmography. Lastly, there was that curious symbol of the orb linked to the pair of horns, which Vincent Smith had described as the sun and moon. This, according to Bühler, was 'a *nandipada*, the footmark of Shiva's bull Nandin'.

It was more than a decade before the puzzle of the Sohgaura plate was partially solved. Even then, the idea that these symbols might be pictographs and the plate a combination of two forms of communication, one old and one new, rather in the manner of the Rosetta Stone, was not entertained (this was, after all, still four decades away from the discovery of Mohenjo-Daro and the re-emergence of the Indus-Harappa civilisation). Hoey's Sohgaura plate may be the only one of its kind, a unique representation of the transition from pictographs and hieroglyphs to a proper written language – a quantum shift that (however much modern Hindu nationalists may wish it otherwise) almost certainly came about in the early Mauryan period as a result of Chandragupta's contacts with the Graeco-Persians and his realisation that the efficient administration of the Magadhan empire required proper written communications.

This first collaboration led Hoey to work with Smith on his third paper on Gupta coinage, read at the ASB in December 1894. 'Since I have been stationed in Gorakhpur,' Smith wrote in that paper, 'I have had the opportunity of examining the large and varied collection of coins formed by my friend, Mr. William Hoey, I. C. S. The most remarkable coins of the Gupta Period in his cabinet are noticed in this paper. On other occasions I hope to publish some of the novelties in other departments which he possesses.' The 'novelties' that had particularly excited Vincent Smith's interest were the three bronze statuettes that his colleague had purchased during his posting in Banda District some years earlier. These now became the subject of 'Ancient Buddhist Statuettes and a Candella Copperplate from the Banda District' read at the ASB and published by Smith and Hoey in the *JASB* in 1895. The two largest statuettes carried inscriptions on their bases which enabled the authors to determine that both were donations by devotees and early Gupta bronzes from the third and fifth centuries CE.

Further collaboration followed, most notably a joint article on some bricks from the village of Gopalpur on the north bank of the Gogra River twenty-eight miles due south of Gorakhpur. A local zamindar building some indigo pits had raided a large mound for its bricks and having exhausted the surface supply had dug deeper. A Hindu pandit from the village had spotted writing on some of the bricks from this deeper level, one of which he secured and sent to Vincent Smith. The latter knew of the site as the place where a hoard of twenty gold coins from the Gupta period had been found four decades earlier. He 'gave a high price' for the brick and showed it to his ICS colleague, who himself owned a terracotta plaque found at Gopalpur showing an archer hunting a wild boar and two deer. Hoey then visited the site and persuaded the builders to reopen the pit from which they had extracted the bricks. All had come from a small underground chamber about eight feet square. However, two of the inscribed bricks had been overlooked by the builders and Hoey afterwards recovered another two from the newly-built indigo vats. The bricks did indeed carry inscriptions, cut into the clay before baking – a find which the joint authors considered of 'much interest and importance', since 'no similar discovery has ever before been made in India, and it is startling to find the Indian Buddhists using brick, as the Assyrians did, to preserve long documents'. From the character of the inscriptions, Smith and Hoey ascribed them to 'the Northern alphabet of the third or fourth century' written in 'good grammatical Sanskrit prose'. As to their contents, while the authors were in no position to offer complete translations 'and must leave that task to professed scholars', they were in no doubt that they were Buddhist sutras: 'They all deal with Buddhist ontology, and specially with the doctrine of the twelve *nidanas*, or "causes" which connect *Avidya*, or Blind Ignorance, with *Jara-marana*, Decay and Death, and thus form the *Bhava-cakra*, or Cycle of Existence.'

The authors concluded that the 'earliest possible date should be assigned to the inscriptions', and here they were greatly helped by William Hoey's discovery in the same underground chamber of a small earthenware saucer containing eleven copper coins. These he and Smith had no difficulty in identifying as Kushan: 'The coins belong to the reigns of the great Kusan kings, Hima Kadphises, Kaniska and Huviska, and therefore range in date from about A. D. 40 to about A. D. 150, according to the chronology generally accepted'. It followed that the brick sutras must also have been baked at the end of that same period.

Despite their alliance, Hoey and Smith continued to differ over Cunningham's and Hoey's identification of Sahet-Mahet as Sravasti-Jetavana – and whenever the opportunity arose Hoey sought to confirm the correctness of that identification by looking for Kapilavastu within the Gorakhpur Division, taking his lead from the Chinese travellers' directions. The reader will recall that Faxian had proceeded from Sravasti to Kapilavastu indirectly by way of the town of Na-pe-kea, a journey of twelve yojanas, which by the Cunningham rule placed Na-pe-kea about eighty-four miles to the south-east of Sravasti. Then from Na-pe-kea Faxian had moved on to the birthplace of Kanakamuni Buddha, some six miles north of Na-pe-kea, after which he had gone another six miles east to reach the city of Kapilavastu. Thus, if Faxian's directions were transferred to a modern map, the city of Kapilavastu ought to be found a few miles north-east of Basti town not far from the Rapti River and more or less on the border between Basti District and Gorakhpur District. As for Xuanzang, from the relic-stupa of Kasyapa Buddha north-west of Sravasti he had gone directly to the country of Kapilavastu. Thus, approximately eighty-seven miles in a south-easterly direction. '*From this point going south-east 500 li or so, we come to the country of Kie-pilo-fa-sse-ti (Kapilavastu)*.' This also placed Kapilavastu beside the Rapti River and no more than a mile or two north-west of Gorakhpur town. In fact, both the Chinese had placed Kapilavastu uncomfortably close to Archibald Carlleyle's discredited Kapilavastu site at Buila Tal.

Hoey went over the ground again. 'I began researches as to Buddhist sites,' he afterwards wrote. 'I observed in the north-east of Basti [town] many villages called Kapid, which suggested the Kapilavastu kingdom.' Further north-east again and near the town of Bansi, Hoey noted a number of scattered mounds but none extensive enough to match the Chinese travellers' accounts. This left him with no option but to follow Smith's lead, so that he too began to cast his eyes further north, even going so far as to employ a local agent who could cross the border into Nepal without restriction. This agent brought back news of what sounded like a second inscribed pillar in the Nepal Tarai, as well as other possible archaeological remains, as a result of which Hoey contacted the Governor of the Western Tarai, General Khadga Shumsher Rana, exiled from Kathmandu Valley and with his summer and winter headquarters at Palpa and Butwal.

'In 1893,' continued Hoey, 'I came to know Kharga [*sic.* Khadga]

General Khadga Shumsher Rana at about the time of his exile to the Western Tarai. In 1887 he would have been aged 26. *(Courtesy of Deepak Shumsher Rana)*

Shamsher Jang, Governor of Tausem [Tamsem], and he corresponded with me about Buddhism in Nepal, and he even sent me rubbings from pillars, but these were not of Asoka lettering. I did nothing, as I could not go to the places, but I had supplied Kharga Shamsher with heel-ball, and instructed him how to take rubbings. The rubbings he sent were taken under my direction'.

The General's rubbings turned out to be of inscriptions carved on two different pillars by the same man: Raja Ripu Malla, a fourteenth-century ruler of Western Nepal. Like Smith before him, Hoey failed to consider the fact that where there was one inscription visible on a pillar, there might well be others hidden from view.

In March of that same year, 1893, a zamindar named Major Jaskaran Singh of Balrampur, who owned estates on both sides of the border, reported the existence of an inscribed stone pillar inside Nepalese territory at a place called Bairat in the district of Kolhuwa near the border town of Nepalganj, some distance to the north-west of Balrampur beyond Sahet-Mahet. Among those who took note of the report was Dr. Anton Führer in Lucknow, by now a leading figure in the world of Indian archaeology and epigraphy. On 15 September 1893 Dr. Führer published a brief 'Note' in what was then India's leading English-language newspaper, the *Pioneer* of Allahabad, giving details of the several reports of Asokan pillars and inscriptions in the Nepal Tarai. He also applied to the Government of the NWP&O for permission to visit the Nepal Tarai 'in order to take estampages of the new Asoka edicts'. His request was passed on to the Government of Nepal through the British Resident in Kathmandu, Colonel H. Wylie.

The policy of the Durbar – as the Government of Nepal termed itself – had always been to discourage outsiders from entering Nepal. By the terms of its treaty with the British the Durbar was required to host a British Resident and a small staff in Kathmandu but every effort was made to confine his movements and to prevent other British officials from entering the country. However, the Durbar was less fussy when it came to the Nepal Tarai. British officials were regularly invited to join the Ranas in their cold weather tiger hunts and the British Resident was himself allowed to invite guests for his own annual shoot in the Tarai provided their names were submitted in advance. So there was a precedent for Dr. Führer's application for permission, but one complicated by the fact that the governor of the region in question was Prime Minister Maharaja Bir Shumsher Rana's younger brother and exiled rival General Khadga Shumsher Rana. Dr. Führer's application reached the desk of the Prime Minister and stayed there, presumably in the 'Decisions Pending' tray.

Meanwhile, a new contender for the discovery of Kapilavastu had entered the lists: Major Lawrence Austine Waddell, MD, of the Indian Medical Service (IMS). Dr. Waddell had been born in Scotland in 1854, which made him two years younger than Willie Peppé and one year younger than the man he came to regard as his greatest rival, Dr. Anton Führer. Raised in a strict Presbyterian household and trained as an MD at the University of Glasgow, Waddell had come out to Calcutta at the age of twenty-six to join the IMS. His first six years in India had been spent as an assistant sanitary commissioner in Bengal, during which time he had travelled widely through what he referred to as 'the greater part of the Buddhist Holy Land'. He had then been attached as a medical officer to the expeditionary force which brought about the deposition of the last king of Ava and the acquisition of Upper Burma. This was his first contact with a Buddhist culture and was followed by seven lonely years in the hill-station of Darjeeling, during which time he made himself an authority on Indian venomous snakes, the birds of Sikkim – and what he called 'Lamaism'. What he discovered in Darjeeling was 'the most depraved yet interesting form of Buddhism' in the form of Tibetan Vajrayana, which both fascinated and repelled him. He got to know some Tibetan exiles and with their sometimes reluctant assistance made at least two bold but unsuccessful attempts to penetrate Tibet in disguise. Finding Tibet closed to him he began to look elsewhere.

Armed with a Tibetan pilgrimage guide to the sacred places of Buddhism, L. A. Waddell took to spending his leaves trying to locate those same ancient sites that Führer, Smith, Hoey and others were looking for. A fruitless foray up the Brahmaputra River in search of the Buddha's Maharaparinirvana site in Upper Assam led Waddell to set aside his Tibetan pilgrim's guide in favour of the newly-available translations of Faxian and Xuanzang. He soon came to share Vincent Smith's belief that the Nepal Tarai was where Sravasti, Kushinagar, Ramagrama and Kapilavastu were to be found – and he also became increasingly determined that he should be the man to do the finding. 'For many years past,' Waddell afterwards wrote –

I had been devoting a portion of my holidays to a search for this celebrated site – Kapilavastu, the birthplace of Prince Gautama Siddharta, the Buddha Sakya Muni – as well as for that of the Buddha's death – Kusinagara – ever since I had realised that General Cunningham's identification of the villages of Bhuila and Kasia with these sites was clearly altogether false. ... Pursuing my search for these two famous lost sites, and attempting to trace the itineraries thither of the Chinese pilgrims, I cross-quartered the greater part of the country in question which lay within British territory, traversing in this search some thousands of miles, of which several hundreds had to be done on foot. ... In addition to accumulating much minor archaeological information, I formed the opinion, from a close study of the locality, that the line of the Asoka edict pillars which runs northwards from Pataliputra seemed intended to mark the route of Buddha's last journey to Kusinagara, where he died; also that ... the birthplace of the Buddha seemed to lie either in the extreme north-west of the modern Gorakhpur district, where I had not visited, or in the Nepalese Terai, where a Tibetan manuscript of mine had placed it.

In the early spring of 1893 Dr. Waddell believed he had achieved an archaeological coup with his exploration of the ruins at Rajdhani at the junction of the Rapti and Paren rivers south-east of Gorakhpur, a site first noted by Francis Buchanan (see p. 56) back in 1813–14. As he went over the ground he became increasingly convinced that he could trace among the ruins at the centre of the complex King Suddodhana's palace, Queen Maya's chamber and Prince Siddhartha's residence, and in its north-west corner the scores of little stupas marking the site of the massacre of the Sakyas. In April 1893, as he was about to make his way to Europe on sick leave, he wrote from Patna to William Hoey in Gorakhpur what reads today like a frantic letter written in great haste, full of scratchings out and heavily overwritten or underscored words. He informed Hoey of his conviction that he had found 'no less an important place than Kapilavastu, for such I fully believe it to be', and he more or less demanded that Hoey, as Collector of Gorakhpur District, take action to secure the site:

My now offering what I believe to be the real site within your district feasibly reachable from Gorakhpur, I trust you may take an active interest in probing this question now raised to the bottom; and the matter is of much urgency on account of the well known fact that the vestiges of these sites are yearly disappearing & becoming irredeemably lost – and from this particular site all the superficial images have been removed within the last two years. ... At present I cannot enter into many details as my health has for the present broken down & I am just going on sick leave for 2 yrs.; but I appeal to you to lose no time in visiting Rajdhani in view of this identification & especially to recover the images which have been removed thence within the past two years. ... I trust you will lose no time in instituting a search for them. They must be found, and also further excavating for bricks in three places which even now is going on should not be permitted.

Waddell wrote again a month later enclosing a sketch map of the Rajdhani site, showing how neatly it matched with Xuanzang's account of Kapilavastu. We do not know whether Hoey was able to act on Waddell's requests but he would have sympathised with the point Waddell had had made on the need for action before more archaeological sites and artefacts were destroyed beyond recovery. The ever increasing pace of human settlement of the tarai, north and south of the border, was having a devastating effect on the ancient landscape. The problem, as elsewhere in India, was not so much a lack of will as of funds and manpower. Men like Smith and Hoey were already doing the best they could with what they had.

Dr. Waddell's search may have begun as a hobby but by the mid 1890s it had become something more serious. He corresponded regularly with his fellow Indologists but came increasingly to see them either as adversaries or as inferiors who lacked his expertise. He was greatly frustrated by the fact that Messrs. Smith and Hoey, besides being among the 'Heaven-Born', with all the privileges that membership of the ICS conferred, were on the spot and had plenty of opportunities to get out and about – and that Dr. Führer had even greater opportunities. Whereas he, Lawrence Austine Waddell, had to suffer the indignity of being at the beck and call

Dr. L. A. Waddell, photographed in 1903 after he had joined the Younghusband Mission to Tibet as the expedition's archaeologist. (*National Army Museum*)

of both the civil or military authorities. His career had so far been littered with lost opportunities, not the least of which were his frustrated attempts to enter Tibet. In 1892 he had been forced to hand over a most promising archaeological dig at Patna to a PWD engineer, so that when remains from what were almost certainly Emperor Asoka's palace at Pataliputra were uncovered it was the local man and not he who got the plaudits. Then after returning from his sick leave in 1895 he was again prevented from conducting further excavations at Patna by being ordered to the North-West Frontier to join the military column that force-marched into the high Pamirs to relieve the beleaguered garrison at Chitral. On his return he had been appointed to the post of Professor of Chemistry and Pathology at Calcutta Medical College where, to his disappointment, he discovered that his new teaching and administrative duties gave him even less opportunity to follow the Chinese pilgrims' trails than before.

In late February 1895 the Government of the NWP&O received word from Col. Wylie in Kathmandu that the Durbar had at last granted permission for the Archaeological Surveyor of the NWP&O to enter the Nepal Tarai to conduct a search for the reported Asokan pillars. This was late in the season as far as safe travelling in the tarai was concerned but Anton Führer was determined to seize the opportunity. He lost no time in setting out from Lucknow for the Nepal border and in early March met up with his Nepalese military escort at the frontier.

After following a couple of false trails Führer was redirected east to the district centre of Taulihawa, a little township lying eight miles inside Nepalese territory due north of the Birdpore Estate. This was in response to a report of a large stone pillar in that region known locally as *Bhimasenaki nigali* or 'the smoking pipe of Bhim Sen'. The source of this report, never acknowledged by Dr. Führer, was almost certainly General Khadga Shumsher Rana, who was well aware of the pillar's location, having previously sent a rubbing of its inscription across the border to Dr. Hoey.

Although large stretches of the Nepal Tarai had by now been cleared for cultivation there remained numerous swamps, large swathes of high elephant grass and patches of thick jungle, all divided by numerous rivers and streams, and nearly all running from north to south. As a result, the Archaeological Surveyor's progress was extremely slow and arduous until he secured the services of two elephants from a local landowner through the offices of Vincent Smith in Basti. 'After experiencing many difficulties,' as Führer put it in his report, he found – or, more accurately, was directed to – Bhim Sen's smoking pipe.

The stem of this 'pipe' turned out to be a large pillar with a smooth-polished surface measuring some ten feet six inches and broken at both ends. It was lying just above the water's edge of a small tank or reservoir known locally as Nigliva Sagar, not far from the hamlet of Nigliva.

The pillar carried an inscription in the form of two lines of mediaeval Sanskrit, the first carrying the well-known Mahayana

Dr. Führer's photograph of the longer section of pillar lying above the water at Nigliva Sagar. *(IOL, BL)*

Buddhist mantra *Om mane padme hum*, the second reading *Sri Ripu Malla chiram jayatu*, indicating that a king named Raja Ripu Malla had visited the site as a Buddhist pilgrim. The inscription had been cut round and not down the pillar, which showed that the pillar had been standing upright at that time. What was also apparent was that it had been moved relatively recently, since it had only been prevented from rolling into the lake by two young trees that could not have been more than fifteen years old.

Further up the bank and about twenty feet from this fallen column was the 'bowl' of Bhim Sen's smoking pipe: a second section of pillar showing as a badly damaged stump sticking about a foot out of the ground. This appeared to be the base of the pillar and did not show any sort of inscription – until the surrounding undergrowth and debris was cleared away.

It must have been a very special moment for Anton Führer when the previously hidden lower part of the stone stump was exposed to reveal four neatly inscribed lines of Brahmi, the ancient script of the Asokan edicts. 'The new edict of Asoka,' he afterwards reported, 'is incised in four beautifully engraved lines on the lower

The cleared stump of the Asokan pillar at Nigliva Sagar showing part of its damaged inscription. *(IOL, BL)*

half of the mutilated lion pillar, just 10' 6" above its base, and has suffered by its fracture a great deal on its left side in losing the first five letters of the third as well as the first seven of the fourth line'. But what he failed to report was that his Nepalese escort had then refused him permission to excavate the pillar to its base, so that his reference to its inscription being 'just 10' 6" above its base' was, to put it bluntly, a fib. Forbidden to dig, he had to content himself making ink impressions and paper moulds of the inscription and taking photographs. He took just three such photographs, all of the two sections of pillar beside the lake, after which he and his party turned about and headed back to the Indian border.

The discovery of the Nigliva Sagar Asoka edict was, by any account, a triumph. Führer's language skills enabled him to make a fair translation but his interpretation had to be confirmed, and immediately upon his return to Lucknow in March 1895 he posted his rubbing of the inscription to his old Sanskrit mentor at the University of Vienna, Professor Georg Bühler – who very promptly published his translation in the April issue of the *Academy* journal:

> When the god-beloved king Piyadasi had been anointed 14 years, he increased the stupa of Buddha Konakamana for the second time; and when he had been anointed [damaged section] years, he himself came and worshipped it, caused to obtain [damaged].

The opening phrase of the inscription was the familiar royal refrain first identified by James Prinsep and George Turnour almost sixty years earlier as belonging to Emperor Asoka. The rest made it clear not only that the stupa had been enlarged by Asoka's orders but that the emperor had himself come to this site to honour this early Buddha. The name of the Buddha on the inscription, Konakamana, was a Pali version of the more familiar Sanskrit Kanakamuni, the second of the five Buddhas of our age – and the very same Buddha Kanakamuni whose memorial stupas had been seen and venerated by both Faxian and Xuanzang in close proximity to Kapilavastu.

Faxian, it will be recalled (see p. 90), had visited these memorials while proceeding from Sravasti to Kapilavastu:

> *Going on south-east from the city of Sravasti for twelve yojanas, (the travellers) came to a town named Na-pei-kea, the birthplace of Krakuchanda Buddha. At the place where he and his father met, and at that where he attained to pari-nirvana, topes were erected. Going north from here less than a yojana, they came to a town which had been the birthplace of Kanakamuni Buddha. At the place where he and his father met, and where he attained to pari-nirvana, topes were erected.*

According to Faxian's account, these last two memorials to Buddha Kanakamuni lay '*Less than a yojana*' west of the city of Kapilavastu.

Xuanzang, in his account (see p. 101), had even gone so far as to describe an Asokan pillar seen by him at the site of Buddha Kanakamuni's Nirvana stupa: '*Farther north there is a stupa containing the relics of his bequeathed body; in front of it is a stone pillar with a lion on the top, and about 20 feet high; on this is inscribed a record of the events connected with his Nirvana; this was built by Asoka-raja.*' This pillar Xuanzang had placed a few miles to the south-east of Kapilavastu, having first walked south *'about 50 li'* from Kapil-avastu to the Krakuchanda stupas, then north-east *'about 30 li'*. Thus both Chinese pilgrims had placed their respective Buddha Kanakamuni stupas roughly the same distance from Kapilavastu – about six miles, according to the Cunningham reckoning – but on opposite sides of the city: Faxian to the west, Xuanzang to the south-east. Either way, the positive identification of an Asokan pillar dedicated to Buddha Kanakamuni at Nigliva Sagar by Anton Führer could only mean one thing: that the city of Kapilavastu lay close by.

It is clear from Dr. Anton Führer's subsequent actions that he immediately grasped this fact. But what is equally clear is that he knew he had run out of time. Realising that Kapilavastu was close at hand but having no time left to actually locate it, he did the next best thing, which was to anticipate its discovery – and claim it for himself.

In the preliminary version of his report of his discovery of the Nigliva Sagar Asokan pillar Führer chose to state quite categorically: 'The Capital of the Sakyas [i.e. Kapilavastu] is situated just five miles north-west of Asoka's broken lion pillar lying on the west bank of the Nigali Sagar'; and 'A short distance from the western embank-ment of the lake (Nigali [Nighira] Sagar) on which the mutilated portion of the edict pillar stands are vast brick ruins stretching far away in the direction of the south gate of Kapilavastu'.

Not content with these two bold statements, he went on to describe in detail what remained of the great stupa of Buddha Kanakamuni seen and described by Faxian and Xuanzang:

The great Nirvana-stûpa of Konagamana [Buddha Kanakamuni] is despite its great age still fairly well preserved and rears its imposing pile close to Asoka's Edict Pillar. ... Among the heaps of ruins, the Nirvana-stûpa of Konagamana is clearly discernible, *the base of its hemispherical dome being about 101 feet in diameter, and its present height still about 30 feet.* The dome seems to have been constructed of solid brick to a depth of about 20 feet, while the interior is filled up with earth packing. This dome rests of a great circular mass, 109 feet in diameter, built in the shape of a huge brick drum, about 6 feet high, cased with solid bricks of a very great size, 16" by 11" by 3", thus leaving a procession-path round the exterior of about 8 feet in breadth. About 10 feet beyond the great circular base all round was apparently a stone railing with gateways, the position of which can still be traced. It is thus abundantly evident that the corporeal relics of Konagamana, collected from his funeral pyre, were carefully and securely interred in this stupa, and that his Nirvana stupa is undoubtedly one of the oldest Buddhist monuments still existing in India. On all sides around this interesting monument are *ruined monasteries, fallen columns, and broken sculptures.*

When Vincent Smith came to read Dr. Führer's final report on behalf of the Government of the NWP&O he was sufficiently impressed to declare that 'There cannot be any doubt that the site [of Kapilavastu] has been correctly identified'. What he overlooked was the lack of any supporting evidence to support Führer's claims other than his three photographs of the Nigliva Sagar pillar. Where were the photographs of the 'vast brick ruins stretching far away in the direction of the south gate of Kapilavastu' or of the 'great Nirvana-stupa of Konagamana' that reared 'its imposing pile close to Asoka's Edict Pillar'? Not until three years later did it become clear why there were no other photographs.

It was also some time before anyone – and, unfortunately for the German archaeologist, it happened to be Vincent Smith – noticed the remarkable similarities between Dr. Führer's description of the Buddha Kanakamuni stupa and its surrounds and General Cunningham's account of the stupa of Satdára given in his book *The Bhilsa Topes*, beginning 'The base of the dome is 101 feet in diameter; but its present height is only 30 feet' (p. 321). Elsewhere (p.183) Cunningham had written of 'ruined monasteries, fallen columns, and broken sculptures' (compare these two quoted excerpts with my *italicised passages* above).

This was by no means the first of Anton Führer's deceptions – nor was it to be his last. At about this same time the first accusations of plagiarism by Dr Führer began to surface. One concerned the incorporation into his *Report on the Moghal Architecture of Fatehpur Sikri* of details on the life of Emperor Akbar lifted directly from the British Museum's catalogue of Mughal coins written by the numismatist Stanley Lane-Poole, who then complained in a letter to the *Athenaeum* that all Dr. Führer had done was to 'interpolate a couple of paragraphs, add a word here and omit one there'. Although Führer afterwards claimed that the plagiarism was inadvertent and due to an error by a member of his staff, there were those who thought that his explanation did not, as Vincent Smith might have put it, wash.

This habit of 'borrowing' passages from other people's writing had probably begun as early as 1892 when in writing about his excavation work at Ramnagar in his annual progress reports on archaeology in the NWP&O Dr. Führer had recycled an analysis on the inscriptions at Sanchi by none other than his old mentor Professor Georg Bühler, something that the latter either failed to spot or kept quiet about.

Following on from his indisputably important discovery in the Nepal Tarai Dr. Führer returned in the cold-weather season of 1895–96 to Mathura, the site of his early and highly productive excavations of 1888–89, 1889–90 and 1890–91. But this fourth season did not go nearly as well, largely because he dug at a new mound some distance away from his earlier excavations and was hampered throughout by a local landowner who claimed the land belonged to him and took possession of whatever the excavators dug up. The best that the Archaeological Surveyor could come up with was a Buddhist processional path carrying an inscription stating that that it had been repaired in Samvat 76 by the Kushan king Vasishka (i.e. in the 76th year of the Kushan dynasty, *samvat* being the word for a dynastic calendar). Unfortunately, no rubbing or photograph of the inscription was taken, leading its finder's chief prosecutor, Vincent Smith, to afterwards declare that 'there can be no doubt that the Vasuska [*sic*. Vasishka] inscription can only be a product of his [Führer's] imagination'.

Eventually Führer was forced to abandon the disputed site and return to the Kankali Tila digs which he had excavated so successfully in earlier years. Even so, when he got back to Lucknow at the end of March 1896 he was still able to declare in his Museum Report that, for all his difficulties, he had returned with '57 ornamental slabs of great finish and artistic merit and 15 inscribed bases of images'. According to Führer, one of the latter was particularly noteworthy:

> One inscription especially, dated Samvat 299, and inscribed on the base of a life-sized statue of Arhat Mahâvîra [the founder of Jainism] possesses, in spite of the omission of the reigning king's name, a considerable interest, and, in all probability, indicates that the dates of the Kushana kings of Mathurâ must be interpreted otherwise than is usually done. Hitherto the dates of the Kushanas have been taken to be years of the Śaka era of 78 A. D., supposed to have been established by king Kanishka; but on the strength of this inscription it would seem that the beginning of this northern era must fall in the first half of the first century B. C.

Here, it seemed, was evidence that the Kushan dynasty of Gandharan kings had become established a full century earlier than previously supposed. It was some years before anyone thought to question that claim, or to examine the sculptures and inscriptions in question.

In the meantime, Dr. Führer's discovery of the Asokan pillar in the Nepal Tarai was causing considerable excitement among the small band of Kapilavastu seekers. From Calcutta Dr. L. A. Waddell wrote to Lucknow for a copy of Führer's report and received no reply, so it was not until very late in 1895 that he finally saw a copy of the article containing Professor Bühler's translation of the Nigliva Sagar inscription published some months earlier. No sooner had he read it than he realised that the Kanakamuni Asokan pillar found by Führer at Nigliva Sagar could only be the one described by Xuanzang – which meant that Kapilavastu was waiting to be discovered just a few miles away. Furthermore, the Lumbini Garden where Queen Mayadevi had given birth to the future Buddha must also lie close at hand, since both the Chinese travellers had gone on to Lumbini from Kapilavastu.

Dr. Waddell now believed himself to be the only man who knew where Kapilavastu and Lumbini were to be found. He wrote again to Dr. Führer, and again received no reply. He then wrote to the

Secretary of the Asiatic Society of Bengal and received nothing more than a formal acknowledgement to his letter, which so irritated him that he wrote to the Calcutta *Englishman*, informing its readers that they stood 'on the verge of one of the most important Indian archaeological finds of the century', for –

> the long-lost birthplace of Sakya Muni, with its magnificent monuments, certainly lies at a spot in the Nepalese Tarai, about seven miles to the north-west of the Nepalese village of Nigliva . . The Lumbini or Lumbana grove (the actual birthplace) will be found three or four miles to the north of the village of Nigliva, and the old town of 'Na-pi-kia' with its relic-mound and its inscribed Asōka's pillar, should be found about five miles to the south-west of that village.

Waddell's bold forecast, published on 1 June 1896, was immediately picked up by the other Indian newspapers and excited official as well as public interest. As he had hoped, the Government of Bengal came forward with an offer to bear all the costs of a six-week exploration, provided the Nepalese Durbar was agreeable and provided Dr. Waddell's employers would give him the necessary leave. To Waddell's fury, the Director of the Calcutta Medical College refused to grant him time off. Then in February 1897 he received a letter from the Under-Secretary of the Bengal Secretariat, General Department, informing him that since 'the Government of India could not undertake to find a substitute to act for you' it had decided 'to allow Dr. Führer, Archaeological Surveyor, NWP&O, to carry out the work'.

To be prevented from putting his hypothesis to the test in the field was bad enough but to find his place taken by the man who, as it seemed to him, had deliberately kept him in the dark, was a bitter pill to swallow. Dr. Waddell was, by all accounts, a disagreeable and peevish character with a very high opinion of himself. He was not a man to bear grudges lightly and he continued to nurse this particular grudge for many months, choosing to believe that Dr. Führer had somehow cheated him. In fact, the record shows that the German archaeologist asked the Government of the NWP&O

to apply to the Government of Nepal for permission for a second and more detailed exploration of the area round Nigliva Sagar well before the publication of Dr. Waddell's letter in the *Englishman*. Führer was desperate to get back to Nigliva Sagar, and not simply because he had worked out for himself from the Chinese pilgrims' accounts where Kapilavastu ought to be. He had to get back, having already committed himself by stating in his presented but not yet published report that he had seen the lost city of the Sakyas in the form of 'vast brick ruins stretching far away in the direction of the south gate of Kapilavastu'. It was most likely for this reason that he had failed to respond to Dr. Waddell's pleas for information. Anton Führer needed Kapilavastu for himself.

In mid-September 1896 notice was received from Colonel Wylie in Kathmandu that Prime Minister Bir Shumsher Rana had directed his brother General Khadga Shumsher Rana to meet Dr. Führer at Nigliva Sagar, where the Governor would be ready 'to receive suggestions from him regarding the contemplated excavation among the ruins of Buddha Konagrama's Nirvana Stupa'. The implication was that the General would provide a labour force and the Archaeological Surveyor of the NWP&O direct the excavations.

In late November 1896, armed with his permit to enter Nepal and a gift of 800 rupees towards his expenses from his patron Professor Bühler, and once more riding on elephants supplied to him by Babu Shohrat Singh of Chandapur and Shohratganj, Dr. Führer again crossed the border into Nepal. But to his surprise, when he reached Nigliva Sagar and the two sections of Asokan pillar he was met by a messenger from General Khadga Rana telling him to proceed directly to the general's camp at the village of Padariya, some twenty-one miles away to the south-east.

Padariya village lay five miles short of the Indian frontier at a point where the border line bulged south into the plains. It was about thirteen miles north-east of Birdpore House and seven miles from the house of the Peppé's neighbour Duncan Ricketts, assistant manager of the Dulha Estate and the man who had first reported the existence of a stone pillar sticking out of a mound back in 1893. The village itself was surrounded by open fields which had been cleared of jungle a generation earlier. But less than half a mile north-east of the village and the General's tented encampment was a 'five-acre thicket of trees breaking the flat level of the surrounding plough-land', bounded by a small, meandering stream on its eastern side and a small pond on the south. As a subsequent visitor saw it, 'practically the whole extent of what I have described as a thicket is raised from ten to twenty feet above the surface of the surrounding country. It is, in fact, a huge mass of debris.'

Within this great thicket Dr. Führer was able to make out four mounds, on the largest of which stood a small, box-like brick temple. It had been built only very recently and was dedicated to the river goddess Rupa-devi: 'A small modern mean-looking temple, dedicated to that goddess, was about four years ago erected by a Saiva ascetic on the top of one of the ruined stupas'. Peering into this crude little structure Führer saw in a dark recess at the back 'an interesting nearly life-size stone image'. This, he learned, had been extracted from the ruins below and set up by the Hindu hermit in occupation as its 'tutelary deity for the worship of the purely Hindu population'. From its appearance Führer concluded that it was in fact a Buddhist sculpture, and one of enormous significance:

> The sculpture represents Mahamaya [Great Maya, thus Mayadevi, mother of Sakyamuni Buddha] in a standing position, bringing forth the infant Buddha from her right side; the child being received by the four guardian gods of the quarters. Unfortunately the free application of oil and *sindur* by worshippers has almost destroyed all minor details, and as the image is kept in a dark *cella*, it was impossible to prepare a photograph or even a drawing of it.

Less than forty feet away from the little temple, sticking out about half-way up the slope on the western side of the mound, was a 'slightly mutilated pillar rising about 10 feet above ground'. It had lost its capital and appeared to have suffered a lightning strike which had split what was left of the column all the way down to the ground. Only the inscriptions that Vincent Smith had earlier dismissed as 'mediaeval scribblings' were visible.

Anton Führer afterwards claimed the discovery of the Lumbini pillar and inscription for himself, and in this was supported by his patron Professor Bühler. But given that the pillar had been known and written about for some years, if anyone had a right to make such a claim it was General Khadga Shumsher Rana, who had previously taken rubbings of the inscriptions on the exposed section of the pillar for Dr. Hoey. On receiving his elder brother's instructions to meet with Führer at Nigliva the General had at once written back 'to report the existence of the Padariya monolith which had already struck me very much for [sic] its unique shape and surroundings characteristic of Ashoka-pillars'. He had duly been given permission by his brother to investigate the Padariya pillar, and it was to this end that he had asked Führer to meet him there rather than at Nigliva Sagar. He had wanted to draw on Führer's expertise but, with the example of the Nigliva Sagar stump fresh in his mind, he had come expecting to dig for an Asokan inscription, and to this end had brought with him a team of military sappers. 'It is only needless for me to remark,' he wrote afterwards, 'that I had a mind to clear the debris round it for finding out any inscriptions[,] the existence of which to me had seemed very probable.'

On his arrival at Padariya on 1 December 1896 Führer was immediately taken to see the unexcavated pillar by the General. He then told him that an Asokan inscription would be found 'if a search was made below the surface of the ground'. But what his subsequent report did not say was that he then left the site, most probably returning to his own camp. When he returned later in the day General Khadga's sappers had already dug away the ground on the southern side of the slope on which the pillar stood to a depth of about ten feet.

What the sappers' excavation had also exposed on that same, outer side of the pillar was what Führer afterwards described as 'a well-preserved inscription of the Maurya period in five lines', and Vincent Smith, more precisely, as 'four and a half lines of beautifully incised and well-preserved characters, averaging about 30 millimeters, or little over an inch in height.'

If Dr. Führer made an on-the-spot translation of the inscription,

The central stupa and 'bathing pool' at Lumbini *(above)*, photographed from the south by Babu P. C. Mukherji in March 1899 and *(below)* a detail from his map of the same area. In the photograph the top of the Asokan pillar can just be made out half-way down the slope left of the mound topped by the little Shaiva temple. A trial trench dug by Babu Mukherji can also be seen. *(Both photo and map are from P. C. Mukherji's Report)*

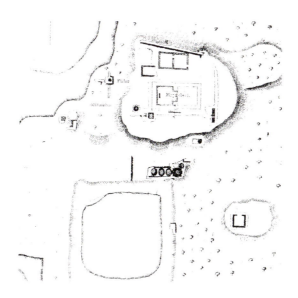

The newly-exposed lower section of the Asokan pillar at Lumbini, photographed by Anton Führer on 1 December 1896; in attendance, the Hindu ascetic from the nearby temple and one of General Khadga Shumsher Rana's Gorkha soldiers. The newly-revealed Asokan inscription is not visible here but begins about four feet below the end of the split in the column. *(IOL, BL)*

he failed to communicate it either to General Khadga or to the other European present, Duncan Ricketts from Dulha Estate. What is certain is that the General took two rubbings of the inscription which he gave to Führer, who in turn despatched them to Georg Bühler in Vienna for expert translation. However, a Sanskritist of Führer's ability familiar with the Brahmi script and the already-published Asokan edicts could have had no difficulty in working out the meaning of the first two lines:

Devānapiyena piyadasina lājina vīsativasābhisitena
Beloved of the gods, King Piyadasi [Asoka] when twenty years consecrated

atana āgāca mahīte hidabudhejate sakyamunīti
came to worship saying here the Buddha was born Sakyamuni

Those last two words of the second line, *hidabudhejate sakyamunīti*, must surely have jumped out at Anton Führer when he read them – to say nothing the phrase *lumminigāme* in the fourth line of the inscription, which could only have meant 'Lumbini village'. He knew then exactly who the emperor had come here to venerate – and why.

Hitherto in his search for Kapilavastu Anton Führer had only had the clues contained in the Buddha Kanakamuni inscription on the Asokan pillar at Nigliva Sagar and the contradictory accounts of the location of Kapilavastu in relation to the Kanakamuni relic stupa provided by the Chinese pilgrims. Dr. Waddell had, of course, very obligingly published his belief that Kapilavastu was to be found seven miles to the north-west of Nigliva but Dr. Führer had no wish to be seen to have acted on his rival's lead. Now, however, with the unambiguous identification of Lumbini Garden he now had two further sets of directions from the Chinese pilgrims to go on. Indeed, he would afterwards claim that 'the discovery of the Asoka Edict pillar in the Lumbini Grove enabled me to fix also, with absolute certainty, the site of Kapilavastu and of the sanctuaries in its neighbourhood. Thanks to the exact notes left by the two Chinese travellers I discovered its extensive ruins about eighteen miles north-west of the Lumbini pillar, and about six miles north-west of the Nigali [Nigliva] Sagar.'

But, of course, the Chinese did not leave exact notes, only conflicting ones. The reader will recall (see p. 92) that to get from Kapilavastu to Lumbini, Faxian had walked east: '*Fifty le east from the city was a garden, named Lumbini*'. By Cunningham's method that would place Kapilavastu about eight miles west of Lumbini. Xuanzang (see p. 102) had reached Lumbini indirectly by way of the sacred spring south-east of Kapilavastu known as the Arrow Well, first walking south-east for 30 li and then north-east for '*about 80 or 90 li*'. These directions placed Kapilavastu approximately fourteen miles west-south-west of Lumbini. Dr. Führer's subsequent actions show that when faced by four sets of contradictory directions from the Chinese travellers he plumped for Dr. Waddell's advice, which was to look for Kapilavastu 'about seven miles to the north-west of the Nepalese village of Nigliva'.

Before being summoned to Padariya by General Khadga, Dr Führer had planned to excavate at and around the site of the Buddha Kanakamuni pillars using the General's Nepali sappers. Indeed, he afterwards reported that he had done so, excavating down to the base of the pillar carrying the Asokan Kanakamuni inscription, which 'was found to measure 10 feet 6 inches in depth and its base 8 feet 2 inches in circumference', and 'still fixed *in situ*, resting on a square masonry foundation 7 feet by 7 feet by 1 foot'. But Führer had come to Nigliva Sagar expecting to add real bricks to his so far imagined Kapilavastu and the equally imaginary Kanakamuni stupa – instead of which he had been summoned to Padariya to witness General Khadga's momentous discovery of the Lumbini inscription. All might have been well if Anton Führer had been allowed to return to Nigliva Sagar to do his excavating. But then the General dropped what amounted to a bombshell by announcing that he 'did not think any other operations feasible on account of the severe famine'.

There had indeed been very severe famine throughout the tarai country that summer and autumn, when the initial failure of the summer monsoon had been followed by the failure of the lesser October rains known as the *hatiya*. General Khadga was directing relief operations in the Western Tarai, for which he needed all the manpower he could get. It meant that he was removing the sappers that Dr. Führer needed to make his case.

This was an awful blow to Dr. Führer – and not just because of his extravagant claims about Kapilavastu and the Kanakamuni stupa. The fact was that the very existence of the Archaeological Department of the Government of the NWP&O – and, with it, his own post as Archaeological Surveyor – was under threat, with rumours of severe cuts in the funding of the PWD circulating. Furthermore, after ten years of loyal service he was still on the same salary at which he had started: 400 rupees a month or about £400 per annum. A striking example of the value of his department and of his own worth was required – which he duly provided.

On or about 20 December Führer emerged from the Nepal Tarai to despatch a telegram to the *Pioneer* newspaper in Allahabad announcing a double discovery: he, Dr. Anton Alois Führer, had found Lumbini, the birthplace of the Buddha, and he had found Kapilavastu, too, the city where Prince Siddhartha had been raised. The *Pioneer* ran its exclusive on 23 December 1896 and other newspapers quickly picked up the story, which was reported in the London *Times* on 28 December.

Five weeks later Professor Bühler gave his public support to Führer's claims in a letter entitled 'The Discovery of Buddha's Birthplace' published in the *Journal of the Royal Asiatic Society*: 'Dr. Führer's discoveries are the most important which have been made for many years,' he declared. 'They will be hailed with enthusiasm by the Buddhists of India, Ceylon and the Far East. ... The [Lumbini] edict leaves no doubt that Dr. Führer has accomplished all the telegram [first published in the *Pioneer*] claimed for him. He has found the Lumbini garden, the spot where the founder of Buddhism was born.'

Professor Bühler went on to give his translation of the Lumbini inscription:

The decisive passages of the Paderia Edict are as follows:- 'King Piyadasi (or Ashoka), beloved of the gods, having been anointed twenty years, himself came and worshipped, saying, "Here

> Buddha Shakyamuni was born" ... and he caused a stone pillar to be erected, which declares, "Here the worshipful one was born."' Immediately afterwards the edict mentions the village of Lummini (Lumminagama), and adds, according to my interpretation of the rather difficult new words, that Ashoka appointed there two officials.

Since then innumerable attempts have been made to clarify the second half of Asoka's Lumbini edict, within which two phrases still continue to puzzle the world's leading Sanskritists. But over the first two sentences there has never been any dispute: Emperor Asoka had come to Lumbini after the twentieth year of his consecration as ruler; he had paid reverence there, because this was where Sakyamuni Buddha was born, at Lumbini village; and he had caused a stone pillar to be erected to mark that birth.

But it was not just the discovery of Lumbini that Prof. Bühler celebrated. The two inscriptions discovered by his protégée were very important pieces in the still far from incomplete jigsaw of Asokan inscriptions: 'The characters of the two edicts,' wrote Bühler in a longer follow-up article for *Epigraphica Indica*,

> agree exactly with those of the north-eastern pillar-edicts of Radhia, Mathia and Râmpurvâ. And their language is the Mâgadhi of the third century B. C., which is found also in the other two Bairât and Sahasrâm edicts, in the cave-inscription of Barâbar, and in the Sôhgaurâ copper-plate. ... The wording of the two inscriptions agrees very closely, and leaves no doubt that they were incised at the same time. It makes also the restoration of the lost portions of the Niglîva edict easy and absolutely certain.

And, of course, there was also the finding of the long-lost city of Kapilavastu, which Anton Führer had located with absolute precision. 'The Padêriya [i.e. Lumbini] edict, of course, fixes also the site of Kapilavastu,' added Bühler:

> Fahien says that the Lumbini garden lies 50 *li* or, adopting Sir A. Cunningham's reckoning, 8⅓ miles east of the capital of the Śâkyas,

and Dr. Führer has found its extensive ruins eighteen miles north-west of Padêriya 'between the villages of Amauli and Bikuli (north-east) and Râmghât on the Bangangâ (south-west),' covering a space seven miles long and from three to four miles broad. The country of the Śâkyas, it now appears, has been looked for too far south by Sir A. Cunningham and his assistants. Sir A. Cunningham's errors have been caused by the vague statements of the Chinese pilgrims, who both say that in travelling from Śrâvastî to Kapilavastu they went south-east. ... Nevertheless, the town lay much further north, and it may be pointed out that its real position agrees with the hints given in the Ceylonese canonical books. According to the *Ambattha-Sutta* the banished sons of Ikshvâku or Okkâka settled *yattha Himavantapassê pôkharaniyâ tire mahâ sâkasandô;* 'where there was a great grove of *śâka* trees on the bank of a lake in the slopes of the Himâlaya'. This description fits the Nepal Terai better than the absolutely flat districts of Basti and Gorakhpur.

The Return

Birdpore House, 29 January 1898

The two British visitors Smith and Peppé stayed the night of 28 January at Sagarwa. Whether this was in the Archaeological Surveyor's camp or in their own tents elsewhere is a matter for conjecture, since none of the three left any further account of what passed between them at Sagarwa. But given that Vincent Smith had spent the best part of a decade arguing that Kapilavastu was to be found in the Nepal Tarai and that Anton Führer had publicly claimed to have found Kapilavastu in the Nepal Tarai, it is hard to believe that there was not some enquiry made along the lines of: 'If this, my dear Doctor, is the site of the massacre of the Sakyas then where exactly is the city of Kapilavastu?' It may be that both men were keeping their cards close to their chests yet the amateur and the professional were equally aware that the Chinese pilgrim Xuanzang had given a specific site for the massacre of the Sakyas when he had written:

> To the north-west of the capital [Kapilavastu] there are several hundreds and thousands of stupas, indicating the spot where the members of the Sakya tribe were slaughtered. Virudhaka-raja having subdued the Sakyas, and captured the members of their tribe to the number of 9,990 myriads of people, then ordered them to be slaughtered. They piled their bodies like straw, and their blood was collected in lakes.

If the site that Dr. Führer was excavating was indeed the site of the massacre, which appeared to be the case from the evidence emerging from the stupas, then Kapilavastu city itself was close by to the south-east. Yet, bizarrely, there seems to have been no mention from either party of a most promising archaeological site, well known locally as Tilaura Kot, less than five miles away to the south and concealed in the same patch of forest through which the two Britons had crossed on their elephants the previous day. Had Führer brought up the subject of a great walled enclosure at Tilaura Kot, Smith would surely have demanded at least a cursory look at it – instead of which he and Peppé set off back to the Indian border at first light on the morning of 29 January.

However, the two gentlemen did make one diversion on this return journey – to the lake at Nigliva Sagar to see 'Bhim Sen's smoking pipe': the stump of the Asokan pillar and its Buddha Kanakamuni edict. 'We returned from the camp,' wrote Smith, 'in a south-easterly direction (I cannot give exact bearings) and after passing some ruins and going about a mile and a half, we reached the west end of the Niglîvâ lake, where the Asoka Pillar lies.' They saw no signs of recent excavation. Führer was to assert that his dig at Sagarwa lay four miles north-west of Nigliva Sagar, but modern satellite mapping shows that Smith's estimate of a mile and a half to be more accurate: Sagarwa lake is two miles north-west of the much smaller lake at Nigliva Sagar.

Once back at Birdpore House, Vincent Smith sat down with Willie Peppé to help him plan out a report on his excavation, which they agreed should go to the Royal Asiatic Society in London together with an introductory note from Smith. Willie would draw up plans and cross-sections of the excavation while Mrs Peppé would employ her artistic skills to provide drawings of the reliquary vases and a representative selection of the offerings they contained. On the afternoon of Sunday 30 January Vincent Smith left for Gorakhpur, where he was due back in his magistrate's court next morning.

The Peppés' next important visitor seems to have been Dr. William Hoey, now promoted to Commissioner of Gorakhpur Division, who must have been following events with the greatest interest ever since being officially notified of Peppé's discoveries by the Indian magistrate at Basti. His main focus of interest was evidently the inscription on the Piprahwa vase, which he subjected to a careful examination before making his own copy in the form of a pencil rubbing. He then returned to Gorakhpur to work on a translation, published in the Allahabad *Pioneer* on 27 February. Since Dr. Hoey was a servant of Government his notice could not be attributed to him but was ascribed to 'a correspondent':

I have seen the objects recovered by Mr Peppé in his excavation of a stupa at Piprahwa Kot on his estate on the north of the Basti district, which you noticed in your column about a month ago. A Pali inscription on one of the steatite urns is of great interest. It runs:

Yam salilanidanam Budhasa Bhagavato Sakiyanam sukitti-bhattinam sabhaginikanam saputadalinam.

Which may be translated:
'This relic deposit of the Lord Buddha is the share of (i.e. the share allotted at the division of his ashes after cremation to) his renowned Sakya brethren, his own sister's children and his own son.'

Hoey's notice was the first to alert the general public that what had been interred in the stone coffer of the Piprahwa stupa appeared to be no less than the Sakya clan's portion of Buddha Sakyamuni's ashes.

Dr. Führer's proclaimed double discovery of Kapilavastu and Lumbini in the Nepal Tarai was received by the local Indologists with mixed feelings. The first to react was Dr. William Hoey. Immediately after reading Dr. Bühler's account in the April 1897 issue of the *Journal of the Royal Asiatic Society* he contrived to slip over the border into Nepal in what was afterwards described as 'a hasty visit to Rumminidei'. He took with him his junior colleague Walter Lupton, the Joint Magistrate of Gorakhpur, in what was probably an unofficial visit made with the approval of his old acquaintance General Khadga Shumsher Rana. As well as inspecting the Asokan column and confirming the general accuracy of Bühler's reading of its inscription the two officials also 'had the good fortune to discover in the main shrine close to the pillar … a statue of Maya giving birth to the Buddha. … The image is of nearly life-size, and the infant is represented, according to the legend, as emerging from the right side of his mother, and being received by attendants'. This was, of course, the same nativity sculpture first identified by Anton Führer five months earlier.

No less exercised by Führer's triumph was Vincent Smith, for it appeared to vindicate his theory that Sravasti-Jetavana had to lie north of the position ascribed to it at Sahet-Mahet. In order to put that theory to the test he took some weeks' local leave at the start of the cold weather of 1897, having secured permission from the Kathmandu Durbar to make a couple of brief forays into the Nepal Tarai. His expedition took him in mid-October first to Birdpore House, where he advised Willie Peppé on how best to proceed with the excavation of what was at that time the only partly-revealed Piprahwa Kot stupa, and then to Lumbini. He made what must have been a very hurried inspection of the Asokan column before returning to Indian territory and travelling by rail to Gonda in Oude. Here he met up with the civil surgeon of the district, Dr. Vost, a fellow numismatist and an authority on coins of the Muslim period.

On 28 October the two men took another train to the border town of Nepalganj in the Western Tarai, approximately ninety miles east-north-east of Taulihawa. Vost had arranged for elephants to meet them and they lost no time in mounting their beasts and directing their *mahouts* to take them in a generally easterly direction for about six miles, which brought them to the edge of a broad expanse of sal forest. Here they made camp in a grove of trees near the village of Balapur. The next morning they pushed deep into the jungle until they came across 'a very extensive area of low mounds … covered with forest in many places all but impenetrable, and deeply scored by watercourses'. They gathered up some 'small and much defaced fragments of terra-cotta figures' before forging on through jungle cut with deep ravines to emerge on the western bank of the River Rapti at 'a spot known as Intawa (i.e. brick ruins)', where they found two small brick stupas, one 'opened on the south side down to ground level by treasure seekers'. From the local Tharu jungle dwellers they learned that the ruins here had formerly been much more extensive but had been washed away by the river. Gathering darkness forced them to return to their camp and it was dark by the time they reached their tents.

'The people of Nepal are very timid about giving information to Europeans,' grumbled Smith afterwards in an article bearing the uncompromising title of 'The Discovery of Sravasti' –

> and we were consequently unable to extend our researches. Enough, however, was learned to prove beyond doubt that Intawa marks the site of an extremely ancient and considerable settlement on the west bank of the Rapti. From native information we gathered that very extensive remains exist buried in the forest north-west of Balapur and west of Intawa. ... The indications point to the existence of an extensive city with outlying towns and villages. ... We are of opinion that the remains in that tract which we saw and heard of are certainly the remains of the great city of Sravasti, which was already in ruins when Fa-hian visited in or about A. D. 406.

Smith's report of his foray was duly published in the *Journal of the Royal Asiatic Society* but gained no acceptance. His supposed Sravasti on the western bank of the Rapti lies a few miles northeast of what is now the bustling border town of Nepalganj and what remains of it still awaits the archaeologist. From the evidence of a surviving letter from Col. Wylie, British Resident in Kathmandu, it is apparent that Smith also hoped to find Kushinagar in the Eastern Nepal Tarai. Having learned there was a village in the foothills of Eastern Nepal called Kusina he wrote seeking permission to visit it. Wylie's reply, dated 1 November 1897 and enclosing a tracing of a map showing where Kusina was located, told him his quest was pointless: 'From this [map] you will see where Kusina is situated, and, as it is far in the hills, I fear there is no chance of the Durbar's allowing any of us to visit it.' That was the last anyone heard of Kusina.

The upper left corner of Mrs Elfie Peppé's map of the Birdpore Estate, drawn in 1930. At the top the boundary markers, with Nepal and the Annapurna/Dhaulagiri Range beyond. At top left corner is the Piprahwa stupa, with Birdpore House (and tennis court) at bottom centre. The canals and reservoirs built by the two William Peppés, father and son, are much in evidence (Courtesy of Neil Peppé).

(Left) Worshippers at the modern structure enclosing the temple of Mayadevi, Lumbini Garden, in winter morning mist.
(Below) Emperor Asoka's inscription honouring the birthplace of Buddha Sakyamuni, with the crack in the column clearly visible (Photos: Binod Rai).

(Right) The Gotihawa pillar, probably erected by Emperor Asoka to honour Buddha Krakuchanda, examined by the author and Gyanin Rai of the LDT. *(Below)* The great stupa at Lori Kudan, believed to mark the place where the returning Sakyamuni was met by his father King Suddhodana (Photos: Binod Rai).

(Left) Sagarwa lake, believed to be the site of the massacre of the Sakyas, at evening. *(Below)* The pit at Sagarwa, first excavated by General Khadga Shumsher Rana and afterwards by Anton Führer. The site of the latter's main excavation lies between the pit and the lake, just visible at upper left (Photos: Binod Rai).

(Right) The Ramagrama stupa, said to be the only stupa containing the undisturbed remains of Buddha Sakyamuni. *(Below)* The temple at the heart of Tilaurakot, with animal offerings left by Tharu worshippers, said to be built over the remains of Queen Mayadevi's palace at Kapilavastu (Photos: Binod Rai).

(Above) Part of the city walls of Kapilavastu at Tilaurakot. (Below) The eastern gate at Tilaurakot, said to be that by which Prince Siddhartha left the city of Kapilavastu and by which he re-entered as Buddha Sakyamuni (Photos: Binod Rai).

(Right) The Ramagrama stupa, said to be the only stupa containing the undisturbed remains of Buddha Sakyamuni. *(Below)* The temple at the heart of Tilaurakot, with animal offerings left by Tharu worshippers, said to be built over the remains of Queen Mayadevi's palace at Kapilavastu (Photos: Binod Rai).

(Above) Part of the city walls of Kapilavastu at Tilaurakot. *(Below)* The eastern gate at Tilaurakot, said to be that by which Prince Siddhartha left the city of Kapilavastu and by which he re-entered as Buddha Sakyamuni (Photos: Binod Rai).

(Above) The Piprahwa stupa after restoration by the Archaeological Survey of India, seen from the east; in the foreground part of the great monastery where the 'Kapilavastu' sealings were found in 1972. *(Below)* The Piprahwa stupa from the west, with the western monastery in the foreground. The low ground immediately west of the stupa has never been excavated and may well contain an Asokan pillar (Photos: Liz Allen).

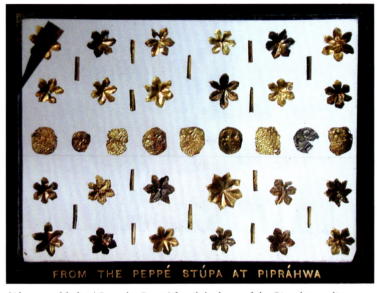

FROM THE PEPPÉ STÚPA AT PIPRÁHWA

(Above and below) Part the Peppé family's share of the Piprahwa reliquary jewels in their original display cases (Courtesy of Neil Peppé).

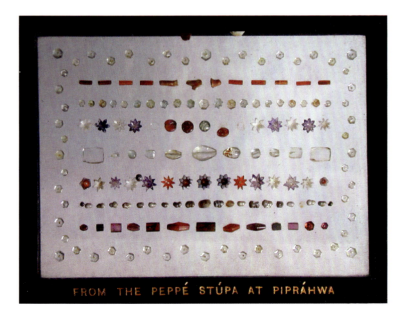

FROM THE PEPPÉ STÚPA AT PIPRÁHWA

A year after the publication of Prof. Georg Bühler's laudatory article Dr. Führer's star as the discoverer of Lumbini and Kapilavastu still appeared to be very much in the ascendant. Scores of articles about the twin discoveries had appeared in newspapers, periodicals and learned journals in Asia, Europe and America, all naming their discoverer. True, there had been some mutterings following the publication on 22 September 1897 in the *Pioneer* of a letter accusing the Archaeological Surveyor of the NWP&O of further plagiarism in reproducing without acknowledgement in his *Monograph on Christian Tombs in the North-Western Provinces* passages from an earlier source. And a bad-tempered argument was also being played out in the Indian papers, with Dr. Waddell of the IMS complaining to anyone who would listen that 'the entire credit' for the discovery of the Buddha's birthplace had been given to the German archaeologist when it should have gone to him, since 'it was I who first pointed out the clue which the Niglivi Pillar gave us for fixing with absolute certainty the place of Buddha's birth' – and with Dr. Führer responding by accusing the other of making 'egotistical statements', but also pointing out that what Waddell had actually said was that 'The Lumbini Grove (the actual birthplace) will be found three or four miles to the *north* of the village of Nigliva', whereas he, Dr. Führer, had actually found Lumbini thirteen miles to the *south-east* of Nigliva. Their quarrel spilled over onto the letters pages of the *Journal of the Royal Asiatic Society* in London before the Council of that august body stepped in to declare the correspondence closed.

But it was not closed as far as Dr. Waddell was concerned. Convinced that his reputation had been besmirched, he continued to harry Dr. Führer, intent on securing a full retraction of his claims and an apology.

And then there was also the small matter of the growing complaints of a venerable Buddhist monk from Burma, one U Ma, concerning Buddha relics sent to him by Dr. Führer from Kapilavastu – complaints which at this time must have seemed no more threatening than the proverbial few tiny black clouds on the distant horizon.

Following the triumph of December 1896 Führer had applied for permission to return to Nepal in the cold weather season of 1897–98, in order to conduct a full excavation of 'the ancient sites of Kapilavastu and the Lumbini Grove' and also to explore the Tarai further 'to determine the ancient sites of Sravasti, Ramagrama and Kusinara [Kusinagara], three famous pages in Buddhist literature, and described by the Chinese Buddhist pilgrims Fa Hien and Huien Tsiang'. He had succeeded in staving off the closure of his Archaeological Department for another year but his own position as Archaeological Surveyor was still under threat and the vultures of the PWD still circled. The lost city which he had already claimed to have located was still waiting to be revealed in all its glory and he knew exactly where it would be: six or seven miles to the north-west of Nigliva Sagar.

In late November 1897 the permission Führer had been waiting for finally came through, but with the proviso that he was not to enter the Nepal Tarai before 20 December and then only under the strictest conditions: 'The Darbar [Durbar] wish it to be clearly understood that Dr. Führer will have no authority to make excavations on his own account or to issue any orders. He should merely suggest to the Nepalese officials the best course to be followed, and they on their part will allow him to make casts of any objects of interest.'

These conditions were far from ideal but Führer had no alternative but to accept. He crossed into Nepal on the appointed day to find waiting for him a supervising officer in the person of Captain Bir Jang, the 'Nepalese Captain', and a labour force of 200 Tharus, rounded up from nearby villages and quite unaccustomed to working with picks and shovels.

What he did not know was that someone – almost certainly General Khadga Shumsher Rana – had beaten him to it. The General was no fool. He had kept himself fully abreast of what was going on south of his territory and was bound to have learned of Dr. Waddell's prediction published in the Calcutta *Englishman* on 1 June 1896 that Kapilavastu was to be found 'about seven miles to the north-west of the village of Nigliva'. There is strong circumstantial evidence to show that General Khadga made his own bid to find Kapilavastu, either in the weeks following his discovery of the Lumbini inscription in December 1896, after he had warned off Dr. Führer with the remark that he 'did not think any other operations feasible on account of the severe famine', or in the first weeks of December 1897 before Führer's arrival. It is more than likely that, taking Dr. Waddell's cue, the General started at the Asoka pillar beside the lake at Nigliva Sagar and proceeded in a north-westerly direction for seven miles. The only problem would have been that before three miles were up he and his party would have arrived at the River Banganga and the large oval-shaped lake beside it called Sagarwa. Between the river and the lake stood a large mound. What is beyond dispute is that someone or some persons took a great chunk out of this mound. It could have been the people of the new township of Taulihawa springing up five miles to the south, who used it as a quarry for bricks which they extracted and then shipped down river – or it may have been General Khadga Shumsher Rana.

The strongest piece of evidence that the first excavator of Sagarwa was the General was provided by the distinguished French linguist Dr. Silvain Lévi, who happened to be in Kathmandu Valley at this time, doing his best to decipher ancient inscriptions in the face of the hostility of just about everyone except the Prime Minister, Maharaja Dir Shumsher Rana. In an entry to his diary made on 27 January 1898 Lévi noted the belief widespread in Kathmandu that all such inscriptions denoted hidden treasure, adding that 'it is due to such belief that Khadga Shumsher, the brother, has dug out the great stupa of Kapilavastu in order to hunt out the large sum, and they take leave of me with the resonant hope that all this epigraphical treasure will end in treasures of resonant money.'

When it came to Anton Führer's turn to seek out Kapilavastu, it seems that having met his 'Nepalese Captain' at the border on 20 December he did exactly what General Khadga had done before him. That is to say, he returned to Nigliva Sagar and then set off in a north-westerly direction, convinced that after seven miles he would come upon the no-longer-imagined ruins of Kapilavastu. This would be the great prize he could carry back to Lucknow as his own, unshared discovery. It would save his department, his job and his reputation. But, like the General before him, the German archaeologist found himself on the eastern bank of the Banganga well short of his prize.

Führer's preliminary report suggests that his march took him to the banks of the Banganga upstream of Sagarwa and that, determined to go the full distance, he decided to follow the river upstream for another four miles. A four-mile march north brought him nothing, but a mile to the east was the little Tharu village of Bikuli (today Biduli). Here he discovered that the villagers had built their own dwellings of wattle-and-daub and thatch beside a much earlier settlement. Digging into the ruins of what he decided was a Shaiva temple, he uncovered what he described as 'a stone image of Abhaya-devi, the tutular goddess of the Sakyas, sculptured as if "rising in a bent position", as described by Huien Tsiang'. By a further leap of faith, the Doctor recognised this statue as the pre-Buddhist deity Isvara-deva seen by Xuanzang outside the eastern gate of Kapilavastu city, when he had written: '*Outside the* [eastern] *gate is the temple of Isvara-deva. In the temple is a figure of the deva made of stone, which has the appearance of rising in a bent position. This is the temple which the royal prince when an infant entered.*'

All Anton Führer's subsequent movements stemmed from this piece of self-deception. 'In order to test in another instance the accuracy of Huien Tsiang's description of Kapilavastu,' he afterwards wrote, 'we examined the ruins of the ancient Siva temple, which was situated outside the eastern gate of the city.'

Convinced that he was now close to the eastern gate of Kapilavastu Führer turned about and followed the Banganga back down river until he came to the lake of Sagarwa. But he had, of course, been preceded by General Khadga and he must immediately have seen that the great stupa between the river and the lake had already been brutally excavated. Putting this unfortunate fact to one side, he set his 200 Tharus to excavate what could only be Kapilavastu. It was from here that he wrote to Willie Peppé on 19 January (see p. 50), heading his notepaper 'Camp Kapilavastu'.

Führer's first area of excavation was the land between the damaged stupa and the western end of the lake. Here a line of small square stupas soon began to reveal themselves. Not until the dig was well under way could he accept the fact that there was nothing here to match the Chinese pilgrims' descriptions of the city of Kapilavastu, and that the only reference to a lake near Kapilavastu was to found in Xuanzang's description of the site of the massacre of the Sakyas:

> To the north-west of the capital there are several hundreds and thousands of stupas, indicating the spot where the members of the Sakya tribe were slaughtered. Virudhaka-raja having subdued the Sakyas, and captured the members of their tribe to the number of 9,990 myriads of people, then ordered them to be slaughtered. They piled their bodies like straw, and their blood was collected in lakes.

Xuanzang's predecessor Faxian had said very little about the Sakya massacre site beyond providing one snippet of information: 'A tope [stupa] *was erected at this last place, which is still existing.*' Xuanzang's lake, Faxian's stupa and the series of small stupas now being revealed forced Dr. Führer to abandon his first assumption that this was Kapilavastu and conclude instead that Sagarwa could only be the site of the Sakya massacre. This change of heart appears to have taken place just before the unexpected arrival in his camp of Vincent Smith and Willie Peppé on 28 January. In subsequent letters written in February his camp site was referred to simply as 'Camp Sagrawah'.

Shortly after the departure of his two British visitors Dr. Führer moved his workmen from the excavation site seen by Smith and Peppé to two other sites close by. One of these was the great stupa already wrecked by General Khadga or persons unknown, where his Tharu coolies dug down to its foundations to uncover an unusual floor-plan made up of fifteen square chambers. Exactly at the centre they found a cylindrical red earthenware casket covered by a copper lid containing 'several pieces of human bone … two heavy triangular bits of gold and silver, two figures of Nagas worked in gold, pieces of a pale greenish crystal, a garnet and a ruby, besides some grains of rice and pieces of black and white talc'.

Drawings of these relics and relic offerings were made by Führer's draftsman and afterwards logged in Lucknow. But then Dr. Führer

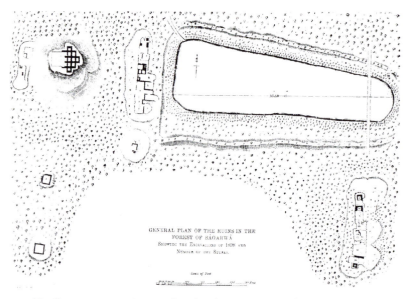

GENERAL PLAN OF THE RUINS IN THE
FOREST OF SAGARWA
SHOWING THE EXCAVATIONS OF 1898 AND
NUMBER OF THE STUPAS

The Sagarwa excavations undertaken by Dr. Anton Führer, as mapped by
Babu P. C. Mukherji a year later. The much damaged 'great stupa' with its
exposed foundations is shown in the top left. The initial excavations of the
'massacred Sakya' stupas lie between the great stupa and Sagarwa lake. The
second group of Sakya stupas were uncovered in the excavated area shown
in the bottom right corner, with Führer's excavated 'lion temple' in the
bottom left.

chose to add to his preliminary report by stating that the great
stupa 'on excavation turned out to be the relic-stupá of the Sakya
Mahanaman, the successor of King Suddhodana of Kapilavastu'.
He could say this because on the copper lid of the reliquary he
had found 'incised the following:- "Relics of the Sakya Mahanama"'.
This was a detail that his draftsman Bhairava Baksh somehow
overlooked in making his drawing of that same reliquary.

The next site excavated by Führer was about 350 yards to the
south-east and close to the village of Sagarwa. What he hoped to
find here was the northern gate of Kapilavastu. Instead his Tharus
uncovered yet more small stupas similar to the ten already uncovered on the western side of the lake. Not until he had uncovered
another seven did he call a halt and move on.

On 3 February Dr. Führer wrote to the Peppés at Birdpore to thank them for a shirt he had just received, and to tell them that he was still working on a translation of the inscription from the Piprahwa relic casket based on Willie Peppé's imperfect copy: 'I am reluctant to give you at present a complete translation of the inscription on the shrine relic casket, as I cannot yet make out the meaning of the last word of it'. His Tharu labourers were by now working on a fourth site, which Führer's draftsman, Bhairava Baksh, afterwards remembered as being about a quarter of a mile south of the despoiled great stupa. 'At present,' he continued in his letter, 'I have commenced excavating a very old lion temple which existed [illegible] at the home of Buddha Gautama and as the foundations are just being exposed I am afraid to leave the coolies here alone.' Führer closed his letter with the hope that he would be able to arrive at Willie Peppé's excavation at Piprahwa on 22 February 'as Captain Bir Jung says we cannot stay any longer here'.

February 22nd came and went at Birdpore House with no sign of the Archaeological Surveyor. Two day's later a messenger brought a letter from Dr. Führer at 'Camp Sagrawah' containing news that his excavations at that site were at last completed and that he was now moving south:

We have only just [brought to an end?] our work, and I am going tomorrow to Lori Kudan near Taulihava, where there had [been reported?] another broken pillar. I hope to arrive at Piprawa-kot on Friday evening at about six o'clock, and shall be glad to see you on Saturday morning, in order to see what is to be done next season, as I fear it will be almost impossible for me to commence the work this season, as I have to go to [Khajnapore?] in Bundelkhand on some urgent work. Of course, my draftsman will prepare drawings of the places [excavated?] by you and also to do photos [etc?] of all the relic caskets, and their contents, if you will so kindly permit it.

Believe me,
Yours sincerely
A. Führer

Dr. Führer finally struck camp at Sagarwa on 24 February and proceeded south with his labour force to the district headquarters of Taulihawa eight miles away. To get there he, his Nepali escort and the 200 Tharus had to pass through the stretch of dense sal forest extending eastwards from the banks of the Banganga for four or five miles. Had he travelled in a more or less straight line, he must have passed within a mile of the kot at the heart of this forest – no insignificant mound but a rectangular enclosure complete with walls and moat extending for almost two miles in circumference. Inexplicably, Führer by-passed Tilaura Kot as though unaware of its existence, seemingly intent only on reaching the site of the second broken pillar. Yet someone must have told him of the existence of this kot in the forest, because it is there marked in a crude map drawn up after his expedition to Lumbini the year before.

Dr. Führer's attention was quite evidently focused on finding the 'broken pillar' he had spoken of in his letter to the Peppés sent from 'Camp Sagrawah' on 23 February. His locating of this third Asokan pillar at the village of Gotihawa, three and a half miles south-west of Taulihawa, he represented as further vindication of the accuracy of Xuanzang's description of Kapilavastu and its surrounds:

> In yet a third instance Hiuen Tsiang's account proved to be correct. According to his itinerary Krakusandha Buddha's relic stupa, with its Asoka Edict pillar, stood about six miles south of Kapilavastu. This direction pointed to the modern village of Gotihva [Gotihawa], just 2½ miles south-west of Taulihava, where a high conical-shaped brick mound still exists. On excavating the western side of this mound, we alighted upon a broken Asoka column, still 10' 9" high, standing *in situ* upon a masonry basement being one solid block of stone measuring 7' by 7' by 1' … As the season had already far advanced, we were unable to continue our researches, in order to trace the missing portions of the pillar.

The Gotihawa pillar was indeed an Asokan column and its base was indeed firmly set in rock foundations. But, of course, Führer had been led to the site not by Xuanzang's directions but by local information, as stated in the Peppé letter. The fact remained that it was an extremely important archaeological find even without an Asokan inscription and it led Führer to deduce that since the Nigliva Sagar pillar was dedicated to Buddha Kanakamuni, the Gotihawa pillar had to be the other Asokan pillar seen by Xuanzang near Kapilavastu, of which he had written:

> To the south of the city [of Kapilavastu] *going 50 li or so, we come to an old town where there is a stupa. This is the place where Krakuchanda Buddha was born. ... To the south of the city, not far, there is a stupa; this is the place where, having arrived at complete enlightenment, he met his father. To the south-east of the city is a stupa where are that Tathagata's relics (of his bequeathed body); before it is erected a stone pillar about 30 feet high, on the top of which is carved a lion. By its side (or, on its side) is a record relating the circumstances of his Nirvana. It was erected by Asoka-raja.*

By the Cunningham rule this placed Kapilavastu city some nine miles north-west of the Krakuchanda pillar. Dr. Führer's Sagarwa site was some twelve and a half miles to the north-east; the overlooked Tilaura Kot site in the jungle six and a half miles away and almost due north. However, there was no question of going back to take another look. Once again the Archaeological Surveyor had run out of time.

Dr. Führer finally turned up at Birdpore House on the evening of Friday 26 February, having come on directly from Gotihawa. Here to his disappointment he learned that Willie Peppé intended to continue the excavation of the Piprahwa stupa and its surrounding monasteries – but under the direction of Vincent Smith. Nor was Peppé prepared to co-operate with him in preparing a joint article for publication in an academic journal, since he and Smith were already doing just that for the *Journal of the Royal Asiatic Society*. Führer's remaining hopes rested on securing the Piprahwa stone coffer and its contents for the Lucknow Museum, but here too he found Peppé strangely reluctant to do his duty. He had done all that was required of him, which was to inform the acting Collector and Joint Magistrate of Basti District, Pandit Misra, who had duly informed the Commissioner of Gorakhpur Division, Dr. Hoey. As far as Peppé was concerned, what happened next was up to the Commissioner.

So in the end Dr. Führer had had to content himself with a cursory inspection of the excavation site (see photo on p. 26) and the contents of the coffer lodged at Birdpore House. Meanwhile his draftsman, Bhairav Bhaksh, made three somewhat rushed drawings and took four photographs: one of the Piprahwa stupa, one of the five reliquary caskets and two of the inscribed reliquary vase, back and front. In his subsequent report Führer restricted himself to a summary of Peppé's excavation and his professional opinion that the Piprahwa stupa was indeed 'the identical one which the Sakyas of Kapilavastu erected over their share of the relics, received at the time of the partition [division of the relics], and which was built for the express purpose of spreading the belief in the Buddha'.

No one at the time could have imagined how this brief visit to Piprahwa Kot and Birdpore House by the Archaeological Surveyor of the NWP&O would cast such a long shadow – over the finds themselves and over the lives of their finder and his descendants.

Less than a week after Dr. Führer's visit to Birdpore Willie Peppé received an extraordinarily frank letter from Vincent Smith in Gorakhpur, dated 3 March. It began calmly enough, with thanks for the plans of the excavation that Peppé had made and what was probably a pencil-rubbing of the Piprahwa inscription, but then it developed into an extraordinary outburst against the Lieutenant-Governor of the NWP and Chief Commissioner of Oude (to give him his full title), Sir Antony MacDonnell. 'I am compelled to retire earlier than I had intended,' Smith wrote, 'The Lieut. Gov. by a D.O.[demi-official, meaning off the public record] letter to me dated the 23rd instant inflicted on me the public affront of cancelling my nomination to the Lucknow Bench, solely on the grounds that the Allahabad High Court wrote an angry letter objecting to my appointment.' The High Court judge Sir John Edge had, it seems, written to the Lieutenant-Governor 'in a rage' because some months earlier Smith had gone against him and his fellow judges in a judgement on a matter of Hindu Law where Smith had followed a Privy Council ruling which Edge and his colleagues had chosen to ignore. For Smith his resignation was a matter of principle:

I have nothing to be ashamed of or retract, and I will not give way. I at once intimated to Govt that I should resign the service. Not a word of explanation was asked for, and I consider myself grossly insulted. The L. G. is full of expressions of personal regret but I have told him that these do not alter the fact that he has inflicted on me a public indignity which I will not submit to. He says that my retirement will be very inconvenient. I tell him I know it will but that the responsibility for this inconvenience does not rest with me. I have also told him that I intend to appeal to the Viceroy, and to press my resignation which he says he will oppose. I expect the L. G.'s final answer in a day or two – so far all the correspondence is D. O.. I am angry at my treatment but for many private reasons glad to go. We are selling off all we can. With our kindest regards to you both.

It was a most indiscreet letter for a senior government official to have written, even if addressed to someone with whom he had evidently become quite close. But it also revealed Smith's volatile nature and the stress he was evidently under at the time. He had done more than his share of bread-and-butter district postings and felt he had earned his promotion to the Lucknow judicial bench as a senior judge. But there were also other issues on his mind, not the least of which were growing concerns about Dr. Anton Alois Führer and some of his actions.

About a month earlier, in early February 1898, Hofrat Doktor Johann Georg Bühler, Professor of Indian Philology and Archaeology at the University of Vienna, had received a package from India. It was from his former student and close collaborator on early Indian texts, Dr. Führer, and contained a somewhat crude hand-copy on a scrap of paper of an inscription found on the cover of a steatite vase, recovered from a stupa excavated by an 'English' planter in British territory close to the Nepalese border.

Unsatisfactory though this copy was, Bühler felt confident enough to attempt a preliminary reading until such time as a more accurate copy of the inscription could be obtained. Like so many epigraphists since, he was baffled by the three letters that spelled out *su ki ti* or *su kri ti*. Nevertheless, his was a reading that has stood the test of time:

> This relic shrine of the divine Buddha (is the donation) of the Sakya
> Sukiti-brothers, associated with their sisters, sons and wives.

On 21 February Bühler sent copies of his translation to Führer and
Peppé, together with a letter to the latter giving his assessment
of the significance of the Piprahwa inscription. He considered it
to be 'the first historical document found which proves that the
Sakyas, men belonging to the Buddha's tribe of Rajputs, resided in
the neighbourhood of Kapilavastu after his death'. He went on:

> It is not improbable that the stupa excavated by you, as the relic vase
> was dedicated by the Shakyas, belongs to those erected soon after
> the Nirvana [Maharaparinirvana]. If that is the case the inscription
> is the earliest document yet found in India. And it is remarkable
> that its alphabet differs from that used in the edicts of Asoka by the
> absence of the signs of the long medial vowels, though the letters
> agree in other respects.

As might be expected, Prof. Bühler had noticed that something
was wrong with Peppé's hand-copy and he went on to ask him to
check the inscription again for 'any traces of the required i in the
first word, of the medial i in the second and a vowel mark in the
last syllable of Bhagavata'. As mentioned earlier, Peppé had indeed
missed the triangle of three dots representing the sound 'i' at the
very beginning and a second dot over the second letter. However,
the inscription bore no vowel mark over the symbol representing
the sound 'ta' in *bhagavata* (divine or blessed), an absence that
suggested to the Professor that this was a very early inscription
predating the Asokan edicts. He said as much in his 'Preliminary
Note on a Recently Discovered Sakya Inscription', which he posted
in mid-March to the Pali scholar T. W. Rhys Davids, Secretary of the
Royal Asiatic Society in London, who arranged for it to be added to
the April issue of the *Journal of the Royal Asiatic Society*.

Exactly what communications Bühler subsequently received
from India over the next few weeks are largely a matter for conjecture. However, the following sequence events appear to have
taken place.

On 24 February the *Pioneer* published Dr. Hoey's translation of the Piprahwa inscription based on his own pencil rubbing. This was not radically different from Bühler's own reading, except in the matter of the rendering of *su-ki-ti*, so even if the Professor saw the notice he would have had no reason to feel he had been upstaged.

Far more relevant is the fact that on 23 March Dr. Führer sent to the Secretary to Government, NWP&O, PWD, what he termed his 'preliminary brief report on the results of the Nepalese excavations in the Tarai conducted ... during the season of 1897–98'. There is no shred of evidence that Professor Bühler received this 'preliminary report', but it would have been entirely uncharacteristic of Führer not to have sent such a copy to his patron, particularly since Bühler had collected and sent on a comparatively large sum of money to fund his Nepal expedition. What is known for certain is that on 24 March 1898 Führer sent a copy of this same report to General Khadga Shumsher Rana in Nepal. He accompanied it with a most unusual request 'with reference to a controversy lately carried on in the Indian newspapers regarding the discovery of Buddha's birthplace in the Nepal Tarai'. This concerned Dr. Waddell's very public campaign to claim credit for that discovery, which had come to a head with the publication of Dr. Waddell's charges in the *Journal of the Royal Asiatic Society*. The correspondence pages of the January 1898 issue of the same journal had carried Führer's rebuttal of Waddell's claims but also a further letter from Waddell that made additional charges, including the claim of plagiarism in Führer's monograph *Christian Tombs in the North-Western Provinces*.

It is reasonable to speculate that after seeing this issue of the *JRAS*, which he would have received as a matter of course, Bühler wrote to his collaborator in India expressing his concern and asking for an explanation, hence Führer's rather desperate appeal to General Khadga to set down what he remembered of his visit to the General's camp on 1 December 1896:

I will be extremely obliged if you will very kindly favour me with a few lines setting forth exactly what happened when I was privileged to pay you a visit on the 1st December 1896 at your camp at Padariyah, close to Rummindei [Lumbini]. You were kind enough to show me that pillar, and on seeing it, I told you on the spot that it was undoubtedly an Ashoka pillar and that an inscription would be found if a search was made below the surface of the mound. I am in need of it, as my antagonist, Dr. Waddell, has stated in the papers, 'It is somewhat amusing, after all Dr. Führer has claimed in regard to this discovery, to find not only did he *not* initiate that research, but he had nothing to do with the local discovery of the spot, not even with the unearthing of the famous pillar-edict there, which fixed the spot beyond all doubt. This digging was done by the Nepalese officials *in response to my letter* to the Government of India'.

It also seems more than probable that when Führer got back to Lucknow Museum from his Nepal excavations in mid-March he found waiting for him proof copies of his monograph *Antiquities of Buddha Sakyamuni's Birth-Place in the Nepalese Tarai.* This work was based on his earlier explorations of the Nepal Tarai in late November and December 1896 – the expedition during which the inscription on the Asokan pillar had been uncovered at Lumbini – but also included his earlier uncovering of the first Asokan pillar beside Nigliva Sagar in March 1895. Führer had actually delivered the manuscript of his *Antiquities* to the Government Press in Allahabad as early as May 1897 and the book's type had been all set for printing when the order was given to take it off the press in order to make way for an official report on the 1896 famine, for which the same type was required. Führer's manuscript had then been put to one side and seemingly forgotten by the printers. According to the Superintendent of the Allahabad Government Press, it was not until March 1898 that the printing of *Antiquities* was again taken in hand. The first printed copies were received by government departments at the end of July, which suggests that proofs may well have been available for Führer to check in March. If that was the case, it again seems entirely reasonable to suppose that he would have sent a set of these proofs to Prof. Bühler in Vienna, particularly since Führer had been at pains to thank Bühler in his Preface for his support of his work.

Antiquities of Buddha Sakyamuni's Birth-Place in the Nepalese

Tarai was duly published as Volume XXVI of the Archaeological Survey of India's New Imperial Series and (confusingly) as Northern India Volume VI. It is a most bizarre document. In keeping with its precursors in the ASI series the monograph was expected to be a work of scholarship written by a scholar for scholars, setting out in accurate detail the results of an archaeological survey. What actually appeared in print was to all intents a Buddhist tract in nine chapters, seemingly written by a Buddhist for Buddhists. The lengthy first chapter was entirely taken up with the story of the Sage of the Sakyas, detailing his birth and early life up to his enlightenment, written in the most extravagant purple prose as, for example:

> And when the Buddha, at the dawning of the day, had thus made the ten thousand worlds thunder with his attainment of omniscience, all these worlds became most gloriously adorned. And when thus he had attained to omniscience, and was the centre of such unparalleled glory and homage, and as many prodigies were happening about him as at his birth, he breathed forth that solemn utterance which had never been omitted by any of the Buddhas.

Chapter Two, entitled 'Kshemavati, or Nabhika, the Birth-place of Buddha Krakucchanda', followed much the same Buddhist course – except for one paragraph describing how the author had located the several stupas of Buddha Krakuchanda thanks to the Chinese pilgrims. The third chapter, on 'Sobhavati, the Birth-place of Buddha Konagamana' was slightly more objective. It included Führer's detailed description of the Buddha Kanakamuni relic stupa rearing its imposing head close to the Asokan pillar beside Nigliva Sagar and the imposing ruins of Kapilavastu nearby.

Three brief but perfectly sensible chapters followed on Lumbini, Asoka's pilgrimage, and the two Asokan pillar edicts. Had Führer confined himself to these three chapters his reputation as a scholar might well have survived. But they were followed by a chapter on 'Kapilavastu, the Capital of the Sakyas', in which its author quoted extensively from 'the canonical books of the Southern Buddhists'. Just eleven lines were devoted to the supposed site of Kapilavastu that the author claimed to have located and identified:

Thanks to the exact notes left by the two Chinese travellers, I discovered its extensive ruins about eighteen miles north-west of the Lumbini Pillar, and about six miles north-west of the Nigali Sagar, stretching between lat. 27°32'-38' N. [thus over a distance of nine miles] and long. 83°3'-10' E. [seven miles] in the middle of a dense *sal* forest over a length of seven miles from the villages of Amauli, Baidauli, Harnampur, and Bikuli (north-east) to Sivagarh, Tilaurakot, and Ramghat on the Banganga (south-west), and over a breadth of about three to four miles from the villages of Ramapura, Ahirauli and Srinagar on the south to the villages of Jagdispur and Nagravah on the north.

The Kapilavastu chapter was followed by a two-page essay on 'The Tharus, the modern descendants of the Sakyas', illustrated by four of the book's eight photographs. Wildly out of place though it was, this short anthropological study proposed a number of seemingly outlandish theories, two of which have since gained greater acceptance: 'The modern offspring of these Sakyas are probably the Tharus, the present inhabitants of the Tarai and the outer spurs of the Nepalese sub-Himalayas. … It is not quite improbable that they were in fact primarily an aboriginal, casteless and un-Aryan tribe of Northern India.' The sympathetic tone of the writing strongly suggests that Führer identified with the Tharus as social outcastes.

The concluding chapter of Führer's monograph capped all that had gone before. Entitled 'Historical conclusions', it was an opportunity for the author to summarise his work and findings. But the summary was cursory, the conclusions inconclusive other than the single challenging statement that the arrival of the supposedly exiled Sakyas in the hills 'forced them to develop the entirely non-Aryan and non-Indian custom of endogamy'. The work ended rather as it had begun, with a long quotation from a Buddhist text in which the ascetic Vacchagotta addresses the Sakyamuni and compares his teaching to a mighty sal tree that looses all its dead branches, twigs and bark, and yet stands 'neat and clean in its strength. It is as if, oh Gautama, one were to set up that which was overturned; or were to disclose that which was hidden; or were to point out the way to a lost traveller; or were to carry a lamp into a dark place, that they who have eyes might see forms. Even so has Gautama Buddha expounded the Doctrine in many ways'.

It is hard to find a kind word to say about this extraordinary book. Either it was written by someone far out of his academic depth who resorted to padding on a grand scale, or it is the work of someone not quite in touch with reality, so desperate to see what Faxian and Xuanzang had seen centuries ago that he willingly suspended disbelief.

If the proofs of *Antiquities* were indeed received by Bühler in Vienna and read by him they must have troubled him greatly. And if Bühler ever got the opportunity to compare those proofs with Anton Führer's 'preliminary brief report' on his most recent excavations in the Nepal Tarai he would have realised that his old student's claims to have discovered Kapilavastu – claims which he, Professor Georg Bühler, had fully endorsed and lauded in print – were bogus.

That 'preliminary brief report' was written in March 1898 as soon as Führer got back to Lucknow. It contained two indisputable successes: Führer's identification of Sagarwa lake as the site of the Sakya massacres visited by the Chinese pilgrims; and his identification of the Asokan column at the village of Gotihawa as the Buddha Krakuchanda memorial pillar seen by Xuanzang. But, crucially, what it never explained was where exactly the city of Kapilavastu was or what Führer had found there. His impressive sounding map references – 'lat. 27°32'-38' N. and long. 83°3'-10' E.' – meant that Kapilavastu city covered an area in excess of sixty square miles, not the twenty-eight that Führer himself implied.

What Führer's report also highlighted was that the copper reliquaries recovered from the seventeen Sakya stupas at Sagarwa bore the names 'of the following Sâkya heroes, viz. *Kundakumara, Junahakamara, Dhammapalakumara, Ajjunakamara, Mahimsaasakumar, Yudhitthakumar, Guttilakumara, Nandisena, Surasena, Sugaragutta, Aggidatta, Cetaputta, Giridanta, Sutasoma, Akitti, Upananda*, and *Sabbadatta*'.

These names, Führer claimed, were 'for the most part engraved in pre-Asoka characters on the outside of the caskets, in two instances written in ink inside the lid, and in three cases they are carved in the bricks forming the relic chambers'. And as well as these seventeen inscribed caskets of the slaughtered Sakyas there was also the casket covered with an ornamented copper lid found in the ruined great stupa at Sagarwa, 'on which was incised in pre-Asokan characters the following: "Relics of the Sakya Mahanama", the successor to King Suddhodana of Kapilavastu'.

Despite the presence of a capable draftsman who produced accurate drawings of the stupas' bricks with their inscribed weaponry (see p. 109), and despite a camera on hand, Führer's final report contained not a single drawing or photograph of any of these inscriptions. Führer had made his claims knowing that the Nepalese Captain had confiscated all the caskets and that it was extremely unlikely that they would ever be seen again.

'If the alleged inscriptions *had* been found,' was Vincent Smith's subsequent comment, 'he would of course have photographed them. ... They were coated with verdigris (secured by oxidation) and no inscriptions on them could possibly have been detected without very careful cleaning. ... There can, therefore, be absolutely no doubt that the alleged inscriptions were absolute forgeries.' In fact, Smith was wrong: these were not forgeries, which implies physical existence; they were plain lies.

Professor Bühler certainly received at least one communication from Führer while the latter was still in Nepal. On 21 February he wrote from Zurich to Rhys Davids in England asking for his help over the word *Sukitti* or Sukīti, occurring on an inscription found by an English planter and sent to him by Führer, adding that: 'The account, sent by Führer, of the result of the *Nepalese* excavations at Kapilavastu and the neighbourhood is *very* good. Nothing must be said about it in public. He has been ordered to send a preliminary report ten days after his return.' Führer was back in Lucknow at the beginning of March, so that his preliminary report should have been completed by mid-March. If Prof. Bühler ever saw a copy of that preliminary report the sheer audacity of Führer's claims to have found and read no less than eighteen pre-Asokan inscriptions must have set the alarm bells ringing. But, of course, there is no proof that Bühler did see it.

Nor, it must be said, is there any evidence to show that the

Professor ever knew of the revelations concerning his protégé's dealings with the venerable Burmese *pongyi* or monk Shin U Ma.

On 2 February 1898 – that is to say, when Führer was still deeply entrenched in his main dig at Sagarwa – the Government of Burma wrote to the Government of the NWP&O concerning complaints it had received from a monk named U Ma. These involved a certain Dr. A. A. Führer, Archaeological Surveyor to the Government of the NWP&O. Shin U Ma had first taken the complaints to a local government official in Burma, Brian Houghton, and had then backed them up with tangible evidence in the form of letters received from Dr. Führer. Houghton had duly passed U Ma's complaints and copies of his letters on to government headquarters in Rangoon, as a consequence of which they arrived on the desk of the Chief Secretary to the Government of the NWP&O, who passed them on to the Secretary of the Department of Revenue and Agriculture, Archaeology and Epigraphy. From there they made their way to the desk of the Commissioner of Lucknow.

As soon as he returned to his offices at the Lucknow Museum in early March Führer was confronted with the communication from Burma and asked to explain himself. According to the file, his letters to the Burmese monk went back as far as September 1896, when he had written to U Ma about some Buddhist relics he had sent him, allegedly obtained from Sravasti. The contents of this first letter indicate that the two had met while the Burmese was on a pilgrimage to the holy sites in India and had struck up a friendship not unlike that described by Rudyard Kipling in his novel *Kim* (then in the process of being written in England), which begins with a wandering Tibetan lama being greatly moved by the knowledge of Buddhism shown by the Curator of the Lahore Museum (Rudyard's father J. L. Kipling).

Dr. Führer and U Ma had then come to some arrangement for the one to send the other further relics. On 19 November 1896 Führer wrote again to U Ma to say that:

The relics of Tathagata [Sakyamuni Buddha] sent off yesterday were found in the stupa erected by the Sakyas at Kapilavatthu over the corporeal relics (saririka-dhatus) of the Lord. These relics were found by me during an excavation of 1886, and are placed in the same relic caskets of soapstone in which they were found. The four votive tablets of Buddha surrounded the relic casket. The ancient inscription found on the spot with the relics will follow, as I wish to prepare a transcript and translation of the same for you.

This letter of 19 November 1896 was written more than a year after Führer's first trip into Nepal made in March 1895 (during which he made his discovery of the Asokan inscription on the stump at Nigliva Sagar), but just before he set out on his second foray into Nepal (where he would meet up with General Khadga Shumsher Rana at Paderiya on 1 December 1896). Yet already, it seems, he had found Kapilavastu. In the year referred to in his letter – 1886 – he was still a relative newcomer to the NWP&O Archaeological Department and had yet to conduct his first excavation.

Führer's next letter to U Ma was dated 6 March 1897, three months after his much trumpeted Lumbini and Kapilavastu discoveries. In it he referred to more Buddha relics in his keeping which he would hold on to until U Ma returned to India. Seven weeks later, on 23 June, there was a first reference to a 'tooth relic of Lord Buddha', and five weeks on, on 28 August, a further reference to 'a real and authentic tooth relic of the Buddha Bhagavat [Teacher, thus Sakyamuni]' that he was about to post to U Ma.

The letters now began to come thick and fast. On 21 September Dr. Führer despatched 'a molar tooth of Lord Buddha Gaudama Sakyamuni ... found by me in a stupa erected at Kapilavatthu, where King Suddhodana lived. That it is genuine there can be no doubt'. The tooth was followed on 30 September by an Asokan inscription Führer claimed to have found at Sravasti. Then on 13 December Führer wrote to say that he was now encamped 'at Kapilavastu, in the Nepal Tarai', where he had uncovered 'three relic caskets with dhatus [body relics] of the Lord Buddha Sakyamuni', adding that he would send these relics to U Ma at the end of March. What is most odd here is that on 13 December 1897 Führer had not yet entered the Nepal Tarai, having been given strict instructions that he was not to do so until 20 December.

This bizarre hoaxing – for no element of financial fraud seems to have been involved – could not go on. The arrival in Burma of the Buddha's molar tooth seems to have been too much for the hitherto credulous Burmese monk, who soon afterwards wrote what sounds like a very angry letter protesting at the remarkable size of the tooth in question. This letter was evidently forwarded from Lucknow to Basti and then probably carried by mail runner to Führer's 'Camp Kapilavastu' at Sagarwa. It was replied to on 16 February 1898, when the Archaeological Surveyor was still encamped at Sagarwa. Writing at some length, Führer went to great pains to mollify the Burmese, declaring that he could quite understand why 'the Buddhadanta [Buddha relic] that I sent you a short while ago is looked upon with suspicion by non-Buddhists, as it is quite different from any ordinary human tooth' – as indeed it was, since it was most probably a horse's tooth – 'But you will know that Bhagavat Buddha was no ordinary being, as he was 18 cubits in height as your sacred writings state. His teeth would therefore not have been shaped like others.' In a further bid to shore up the credibility of the tooth, Führer went on to say that he would send U Ma –

> an ancient inscription that was found by me along with the tooth. It says, 'This sacred tooth relic of Lord Buddha is the gift of Upagupta'. As you know, Upagupta was the teacher of Asoka, the great Buddhist emperor of India. In Asoka's time, about 250 BC, this identical tooth was believed to be a relic of the Buddha Sakyamuni. My own opinion is that the tooth in question is a genuine relic of Buddha.

This supposed Asokan inscription was afterwards found to be written in perfectly accurate Brahmi Prakrit, its most obvious models being the many similar relic inscriptions found at Sanchi and other Buddhist sites, with which Führer was very familiar through his work on *Epigraphia Indica*.

It is highly unlikely that Führer would have wanted his old patron to know about his troubles with the Burmese monk, and there is no surviving evidence to show that he or any one else wrote to Bühler about it. Yet the fact is that the file of the Führer-U Ma correspondence was going the rounds of the concerned departments of the Government of the NWP&O in Allahabad in the spring of

1898. Because it touched on matters in Burma, which at that time came under the authority of the Government of India, it must also have been known and talked about in Government House, Calcutta. The professional opinions of senior members of the Asiatic Society of Bengal may well have been sought, the most respected among them being the editor of *Asiatic Researches*, the journal of the Asiatic Society of Bengal. This was the Swiss philologist Dr. Augustus Hoernle, a leading authority on early Central-Asian languages, who was at this time working on the decipherment of Khotanese texts written in Brahmi script (and whose own reputation was about to be badly dented by his acceptance of the forgeries of the notorious Islam Akhun of Kashgar, exposed by Aurel Stein in 1901). Philologists formed a tight circle and if Dr. Hoernle knew of the Führer-U Ma correspondence, he may well have communicated his concerns to Vienna. Whether or not Dr. Hoernle was involved, it would have been surprising if whispers of the U Ma scandal had not reached London and Vienna by the end of March or the first week of April 1898.

As for Anton Führer, nemesis was now fast approaching in the person of Vincent Smith, who corresponded with Dr. Hoernle in February and March while working with Willie Peppé on his article on the Piprahwa excavation for the *Journal of the Royal Asiatic Society*. No mention of the U Ma scandal can be found in the surviving correspondence of any of these parties, but there is just a hint of a growing desperation on the part of Dr. Führer in a letter written by him to Willie Peppé on 31 March from Lucknow Museum. Führer had been expecting him in Lucknow on the 26th, together with the Piprahwa stone coffer and its contents, but Peppé had not come and he had heard nothing from him:

> The long looked for 26th March has come and gone, and I am sorry to say I had not the pleasure of seeing you here. If you are still coming do kindly allow me to prepare coloured drawings of all the objects found in your excavations. I shall be very happy to send a man to Birdpore on any day you mention, so that he could bring a part of the valuables here, in order to prepare an illustrated report. Or, if you do not mind, you could send the things by registered

post (unpaid), and I shall return all objects with as little delay as possible.

But Peppé prevaricated, and a month later Führer had still not received the promised relics. On 21 April he wrote again to Peppé to say that he would be 'glad to receive your relics in small instalments when ever you can spare them', adding that he had 'sent Prof. Bühler at Vienna copies of the photographs and a correct impression of the [urn?] inscription. He will send you soon a printed copy of [his article in the Journal of ?] the Academy of Sciences at Vienna.' Thus suggests that when Führer wrote this letter on 21 April he had not received any recent news from Vienna.

A few days later Führer received a polite but firm letter from General Khadga Shumsher Rana in answer to his appeal for support against Dr. Waddell. The General agreed that he, Dr. Führer, 'certainly had a good share in identifying the birthplace of Buddha' – but not the major role he had publicly given himself.

At this point, no doubt thoroughly fed up with all the public bickering that had long gone on between two government servants – Drs. Waddell and Führer – the Lieutenant-Governor of the NWP&O himself stepped in to order that 'discussions of a controversial nature regarding claims to the merit of prior discovery' should be excluded from all future publications. As far as Sir Antony MacDonnell was concerned, 'Dr. Führer's share in the discovery was confined to the deciphering of the inscriptions [on the columns at Lumbini and Nigliva Sagar]', and that was it.

As Anton Führer's star began to fade so Vincent Smith's rose. In mid-March 1898, having refused to accept his resignation, the Lieutenant-Governor now offered him an immediate promotion to the post of Commissioner of Faizabad Division, to be taken up at the end of the year, and in the meantime a temporary 'acting' post as Chief Secretary to the Government of the NWP&O. This more than salved Smith's wounded pride and he accepted with alacrity. His promotion came with the additional bonus of a hot weather spent away from the open furnace of the plains in the cooling lakeside air of Naini Tal, in the foothills of the Kumaon Himalayas.

Just as Simla served as the summer capital of the Government of India so Naini Tal filled the same role as the summer capital of the Government of the NWP&O, an Elysium to which all the province's departments and headquarters staff migrated in mid-March, only returning to the plains in October. As acting Chief Secretary, Smith now found himself at the very centre of things, in direct touch with every senior government official in every department, and with the ear of the Lieutenant-Governor himself, Sir Antony MacDonnell.

Spoken of behind his back as 'our Fenian friend' because he was an Irish Catholic with nationalist sympathies, MacDonnell was a dedicated administrator but disliked and even feared by his more junior ICS colleagues on account of an ill-temper which he combined with a steely exterior. It was said of him by a friend that 'If Antony and another are cast away in an open boat and only one of them can live, it will not be Antony who is eaten'. These qualities had earned him the nickname of the 'Bengal Tiger' during his years in the Bengal secretariat and as acting Lieutenant-Governor of Bengal. A little later, Lord Curzon, as Viceroy, was to describe MacDonnell as 'a strange creature, by far the most able administrator we have in this country but ... destitute of human emotion' and regretted that 'so conscientious a worker and so able an official should not hit it off better with his own subordinates and should be, as is alleged, so suspicious and so severe towards any excepting the few whom he trusts among his own men'. Whether this was a fair assessment or not, it seems that in the case of his acting Chief Secretary the Lieutenant-Governor set aside his suspicious nature and came to rely on his judgement.

Anton Führer also took to the hills. He had long been due some local leave, which he took in early April, although in his case it meant going by train with his family to the more distant but less expensive hill-station of Mussoorie. He was still on leave in Mussoorie when he heard of the distressing news from Vienna.

The Drowning

Lake Constance, 8–9 April 1898

On the late afternoon of 8 April 1898 a stout, middle-aged gentleman with a full beard was seen sculling a hired skiff on Lake Constance, which straddles the border between Germany and Switzerland. According to eye-witnesses, he was 'rowing forward and backward for some time on one and the same spot'. Three days earlier he had walked into a hotel in the lakeside town of Lindau, booked a room but failed to sign himself in. He had spent most of 7 April rowing up and down on Lake Constance and then on the afternoon of 8 April had again resumed his rowing, having left at the reception desk of his hotel a telegram addressed to his wife in Zurich that said nothing more than 'Come tomorrow'. He was last seen on the water 'after 7 o'clock in the evening', which at that time of the year meant after dark. On the morning of 9 April the skiff was seen still on the water but overturned, unmanned and with one oar missing. Despite this discovery, two days passed before the hotel manager felt sufficiently concerned by the absence of his guest to contact the police. A search was instituted but without success and, after several days, was called off without a body being found. Indeed, the body never surfaced, which was highly unusual, raising the possibility that it had been weighted down.

Because of the lack of a corpse, his family's confusion over his whereabouts and the understandable caution of the local authorities to commit themselves, it was not until 15 April that it was established that the missing presumed drowned rower was Hofrath Doktor Johann Georg Bühler, Knight of the Prussian Order of the Crown, Comthur of the Order of Franz-Josef, Commander of the Indian Empire, Professor of Indian Philology and Archae-ology at the University of Vienna. Letters written to T. W. Rhys Davids in February show that Bühler was with his Swiss wife and their sixteen-year-old son in Zurich until he returned to Vienna on 26 February. According to Bühler, the Austrian Government had decreed an unusually early Easter vacation that year, which meant that his teaching duties at the university were to resume on 21 March and would continue over the Easter weekend itself, beginning on Good Friday 8 April. Yet it appears that, without a word to his wife or to anyone else, the Professor had abandoned his academic duties on 5 April to return to his family in Zurich – except that, unaccountably, he had stopped off at Lake Constance to go rowing.

The manner of Bühler's death at the age of sixty-one shocked philologists and historians through Europe and Asia. 'On the 8th of April last,' wrote his close friend the Sanskritist Professor Max Müller, in the *Journal of the Royal Asiatic Society* –

> while enjoying alone in a small boat a beautiful evening on the Lake of Constance, he seems to have lost an oar, and in trying to recover it, to have overbalanced himself. As we think of the cold waves closing over our dear friend, we feel stunned and speechless before so great and cruel a calamity … He who for so many years was the very life of Sanskrit scholarship, who helped us, guided us, corrected us, in our different researches, is gone.

That was the line taken by friends and colleagues alike. In India the *Indian Antiquary* printed no less than twelve extended obituaries or appreciations by his peers of the scholar acknowledged by one and all to have been the greatest among them. Several went into unusual detail on the circumstances leading up to the great man's tragic demise. 'Boating was Bühler's favourite sport, and he often liked to practice it, particularly after hard work,' wrote one of these obituarists, the historian Professor Werner Kaegi of Basle:

> On Good Friday the 8th he was induced by the beautiful spring weather to stay one day longer, 'in order to make a longer excursion,'

as he was heard saying. … He started in the afternoon in one of those long and narrow boats, the oars of which lie so lightly on the outriggers, that they are lifted even at a great distance by the wash of a steamer, if they are not held tightly as soon as the waves approach. … In the opinion of experienced people living near the lake it is highly probable that he lost one oar, which he tried to secure again, and in trying to catch it he, being a stout man, fell overboard. By this natural and simple hypothesis the terrible accident becomes perfectly plain and intelligible.

Prof. Kaegi had added this detailed explanation to his obituary because, as he explained, of newspaper reports of 'rumours circulating in Vienna as to a voluntary or violent death of Hofrath Bühler.' He went on to insist that he and the late Professor's friends 'deny most positively the very possibility of a suicide committed by Bühler for ethical or philosophical motives'.

Yet there were features of Bühler's behaviour that were hard to explain away, particularly his entirely uncharacteristic behaviour in not communicating with his wife. This his friend C. H. Tawney surmised was because 'Professor Bühler had evidently intended to surprise his family in Zurich with his visit, and had therefore given no hint of his movements, [as a result of which] they continued to correspond with him at his address in Vienna and were much distressed at receiving no answer.' It was also suggested that even the greatest of scholars might have had weaknesses that left them vulnerable to outside pressures. 'Bühler was free of all touchiness in questions of scholarship,' declared Prof. Friedrich Knauer of Kiew University, while adding that 'even men of the greatness of a Bühler are not always proof against "gnatbites"'. The newly-elected Boden Professor of Sanskrit Arthur MacDonnell took much the same line, referring to Bühler's 'high-mindedness' which 'always deterred him from doing or saying anything against those to whom he felt he owed a debt of gratitude', while also hinting at a degree of touchiness about his professional reputation: 'Had he ever been unjustifiably attacked, his aggressor would probably have had cause to repent his temerity. For Bühler, as he told me himself, kept a record of the blunders which he found in the labours of other scholars, and which he might have felt compelled to refer to in self-defence.'

Despite the defensive operation mounted by friends and colleagues the circumstantial evidence was compelling, suggesting this apparently strong and healthy man, still at sixty-one very much in possession of his faculties, had indeed taken his own life. If it was a suicide, the reasons why will never be known for certain. But some would claim that a combination of revelations concerning his former student and long-time collaborator in India lay at the heart of it; and that these revelations led the unfortunate Prof. Bühler to believe that the Piprahwa inscription, about which he had written so recently and so confidently, was nothing more than another fraud perpetrated by Führer – one with which his own name would be inextricably linked. If so, he was not to know that the chronology of events made such a forgery impossible.

It took some weeks for the news of Bühler's disappearance and presumed drowning to filter through to India. Anton Führer's response is unrecorded and can only be imagined.

To what degree the death of the world's pre-eminent Sanskritist affected the enquiry into Dr. Führer's dealings with U Ma is equally a matter for conjecture. But it is odd that what might be called the Führer scandal failed to break and that its author appeared to suffer no consequences. This may be attributed to the Government of NWP&O's determination to prevent the affair from becoming public knowledge and so cast a stain on one of its departments. Whatever was said on the subject was kept off the record and, as far as possible, out of the files, and initially, at least, the Archaeological Surveyor to the Government of NWP&O held on to his job.

However, on 8 August, four months after Bühler's death, Charles Odling, CSI, Secretary and Chief Engineer to Govt., NWP&O, PWD, received the first of 500 printed copies of Dr. Führer's long-delayed *Antiquities of Buddha Sakyamuni's Birth-Place in the Nepalese Tarai*. He was perturbed to discover that it had been printed without being submitted to his own office for approval. This did not prevent him from authorising a week later Führer's costings for a new publication: 500 copies of what was evidently intended to be an extremely lavish report on the Archaeological Surveyor's excavations of Kapilavastu – the printing to be done at the Government Presses in Allahabad, the twenty line drawings prepared at the Survey of India Offices at Dehra Dun and the fourteen coloured plates prepared by Messrs. Griggs and Sons in London, this last at a cost of £75. Odling's only proviso was that Führer's proofs for this second publication must be submitted to him before printing.

Copies of Führer's *Antiquities* now began to circulate through a number of NWP&O Government departments, with one copy landing on the desk of the Lieutenant-Governor. What Sir Antony MacDonnell's first thoughts were on reading the book are not known but his response was to ask his acting Chief Secretary, Vincent Smith, to carry out a thorough enquiry into Dr. Führer's activities that extended far beyond his Buddhist relic forgeries. Within weeks this enquiry reached its inevitable conclusion in a face-to-face confrontation between Smith and Führer in the exhibition hall of the Lucknow Museum.

'I went to Lucknow in September 1898, by order of government,' wrote Smith afterwards, 'to enquire into Dr. Führer's proceedings, and convict him of systematic falsification of his correspondence with several Governments.' One of the first questions Smith put to Führer was why a drawing on display in front of them, showing the base of the damaged stupa he had excavated at Sagarwa, bore the label 'Stupa of Mahânâman':

> I asked Dr. Führer his authority for this label, and he answered with some confusion that he found a brick with the word *Maha* on it which he interpreted as Mahânâman. He added that the brick crumbled to pieces. The story about the brick being manifestly false, I told Dr. Führer so, and drew my pencil across the label. He did not make a protest, or say a word about the alleged inscription on the casket lid [found in the same stupa]. No photograph or facsimile of that inscription exists, and it is perfectly clear that no such inscription exists. In his correspondence with the Burmese priest Uma [U Ma], Dr. Führer committed an exactly similar forgery by sending Uma a document purporting to be a copy of an inscription

> on a casket, and reading, 'Relics of Upagupta'. I charged Dr. Führer
> to his face with that forgery and he did not deny it.

Dr. Führer now took the only course of action still open to him: he resigned on the spot before he could be sacked. It was a resignation that the Government of the NWP&O was only too happy to accept.

However, there still remained the urgent questions of what was to be done with Dr. Führer's two Nepal reports – the one newly published and the other about to be printed – and who was to take over the Archaeological Surveyor's work. It was decided at the highest level that all copies of Führer's *Antiquities of Buddha Sakyamuni's Birth-Place* should be withdrawn with all speed and destroyed, and that the publication of Führer's Kapilavastu report should be abandoned. The Province's Architectural Surveyor, Edmund Smith, was made acting Archaeological Surveyor and officiating Curator of the Lucknow Museum. However, he was not thought sufficiently experienced to take on the major archaeological work that Führer had been carrying out almost single-handed for a decade. There was also the question to be resolved as to who would fill the German's place in the Nepal Tarai. This was a matter of some urgency since the Nepal Durbar had given permission for Dr. Führer to continue his Kapilavastu excavations over the coming cold weather season of 1898–99. Vincent Smith was not alone in regarding this as an opportunity not to be missed.

It was Smith who found a solution. A year earlier he had received an unsolicited archaeological report from a Bengali who styled himself Babu Purna Chandra Mukherji (written 'Mookherjee' in early reports, the word *babu* being a Bengali term of respect for an educated man but which came to be employed by the British to denote a clerk). Mukherji described himself as an archaeologist and part-time employee of the Government of Bengal. In a covering letter Mukherji had written that 'Mr. Smith might remember me as the author of the illustrated Report on Lalitpur Antiquities (Bundelkhand) which Mr. Finlay showed him at Agra at the time when the Viceroy Lord Lansdowne visited it'. The attached report was entitled *Preliminary Report on my Tour in Champaran Tarai in March 1897* and in its opening paragraph Mukherji claimed to have discovered 'the hitherto lost site of Kusinagara' in the Champaran Tarai. This was the district east of and adjacent to Gorakhpur and at this time still part of Bengal (it soon afterwards became part of the province of Bihar). Mukherji had been deputed to look for Kusinagar by the Government of Bengal but under the orders of Dr. L. A. Waddell, his instructions being 'to search for the site of the Buddha's *Parinirvana* (death) in the Jangly [jungle] tract from Rampurva, where is an inscribed Asoka pillar, to Bhikna-Thori, the Napalese [*sic*] outpost between two hills'.

Mukherji had duly scoured the area but had been unable to locate any 'Buddhistic relics' and had come away disappointed. However, on his way south from the border area he had paused at Lauriya Nandangarh and Lauriya Areraj, the sites of the two Asokan columns first brought to public notice by Brian Hodgson many years earlier. Here he did a rethink, 'constantly brooding over the extracts from Rockhill's *Tibetan Buddhism* and from Hwien Thsang [Xuanzang], which Dr. Waddell had kindly supplied me', which led him to conclude that this site and not the one at Kasia must be the real Kushinagara. In defiance of Dr. Waddell's instructions, he set about excavating the largest of the mounds near the Asokan pillar at Lauriya Nandangarh:

I employed a number of Kulies to clear the very dense and thorny jungles that covered the big mound ... and in two days' superficial excavations, I discovered that this mound of bricks, wrongly called *Gurh* (fort), represents a circular structure about 300 feet in diameter, and about 100 feet in height even now in ruins. On the north face the wall appears to be quite vertical and straight, and not sloping and round, as on the other sides. This might belong to the adjacent Vihara mentioned by H. Thsang. As I suspected before[,] this appeared to be the very stupa erected by Asoka the Great in about 260 B. C. over the remains of an anterior one, dated 543 B. C., which he broke in order to remove Buddha's burnt relics to Pataliputra and subsequently to other towns ... If the base is cleared, I doubt not, that the Vihara, the Nirvana statue, as also the inscribed pillar [as seen and described by Xuanzang], will be discovered.

A copy of Mukherji's preliminary report, already set in print but with the addition of hand-drawn drawings and notes in the Bengali's neat hand, survives among Vincent Smith's papers. On the front cover Smith has written in pencil 'mostly rubbish' and the margin of the report is littered with double exclamation marks and such comments as 'not yet justified', 'no proof', 'where is the proof?', 'not a particle of proof', 'wrong', 'pure imagination' and, finally, 'cheeky'. Yet there are also underlinings in pencil of various statements by the Bengali that had evidently excited Smith's interest. Why Mukherji should have directed this preliminary report to Smith is a mystery, but part of the answer must lie in Mukherji's already vexed relations with Dr. Waddell. The fact was that the Bengali was a man with a past – one with which Smith may not at that stage have been wholly familiar.

Very little is known about Purna Chandra Mukherji's early antecedents other than that he was 'a self-made, self-taught man', Bengali in origin but raised in Lucknow, where he found clerical work in the city as a babu (in the British sense of the word) and wrote extremely bad verse in English. But his early published work shows that Mukherji also held strong views on British rule in India that today would be described as Hindu nationalist. He felt that the English-medium education he had received had done him no favours and that Bengali Babus like himself were 'now looked on in the light of the Jews in the middle ages'. Indeed, he saw himself as a perfect example of the 'educated native', whom he described as –

one of the chief ephemeral products of British rule. He is a heterogeneous phenomenon of self-glorification and congratulation of the educational system. ... He vomits forth undigested matter. Ego and mother-country he knows not, nor cares much for them; whatever concerns non-ego and foreign country he is quite conversant [with]. ... The crow assumed the peacock's feathers amidst the laughter of all; his own class excommunicated him; the other shunned him as unworthy of the honour of their society. So our friend is in a dilemma; he is a social outlaw, while the Englishman hates him as an aping machine of his baser parts.

This portrait of a self-hating babu comes from a remarkable work entitled *The Pictorial Lucknow* written by Mukherji over the course of several years and finally published in 1883 uncompleted for lack of funds. Divided into three parts dealing with Lucknow's political history, ethnology and architecture, it was highly critical of the British Raj. The 'unjust greediness of the British Lion' had, he argued, first exploited and then destroyed the Kingdom of Oude, and had then gone on to undermine India's Hindu and Muslim cultures with Christianity and other alien ideas. Written barely a quarter of a century after what the British referred to as the Sepoy Mutiny and Mukherji called India's 'death-struggle for its right to govern itself', it made no bones about its author's admiration for the mutineers of 1857 – a stance that a few years earlier would have probably led to his transportation to the Andaman Islands:

> The [East India] Company lost its reason, not only politically and militarily, but in the civil department as well. It dared trample on the social and religious principles of the people. ... Local custom and laws were trampled under foot. Foreign codification, with her constant companions, ignorance and over-taxation, reign[ed] supreme. ... The nobles and Talukdars, civil servants and soldiers, artisans and citizens – all suffer[ed] equally ... So the fuel of anger was added to the fire of discontent. The people recoiled from their loyalty and became patriotic for their own interests. ... The chapatti, the lotus, and the impure greased cartridge gave the signal for explosion. Immediately [in May-June 1857] the Sepoys break out; the disaffected chiefs join them; and the poverty-stricken people follow them. Every one unites in the common cause, forgets reciprocal enmity, and finds a good means of retribution for numerous and conflicting grievances.

As a précis of the causes of the 1857 uprising Mukherji's summary can hardly be bettered.

However, Mukherji's *Pictorial Lucknow* was more than an attack on the ruling power. It was also a hymn to the architectural glories of the city and a call for the authorities to act to preserve the past, whether it was calling a halt to destruction of old Lucknow, which was being 'fairly improved off the face of the earth', or respecting Oude's more ancient heritage. Oude's ancient monuments, he argued, deserved better treatment than being used for 'mere metalling of roads or protective embankments to bridges'. The province's past also needed proper investigation: 'It is a well-known fact that Oudh, the ancient Koshal [Kosala], was almost the cradle of Aryan colonisation, and that the different types of the people, who, one after another, came here and rose to power and sovereign position, left vestiges of their civilisation, layer after layer, which requires a thorough search and most penetrative exploration.'

Mukherji had a talent for drawing which he developed. In 1884 he contributed a number of drawings to a report on the conservation of old buildings, and it was noted that he had an aptitude for archaeological work. The outcome was his appointment as a master draftsman in the NWP&O's PWD, the same umbrella department that employed Dr. Anton Führer. In 1887–88 Mukherji surveyed and drew up plans of antiquities in the Lalitpur subdivision of Jhansi District, afterwards published in two volumes. He then moved down to Calcutta to work for Dr. Bloch, Superintendent of the Indian Museum, as his personal assistant. After some years this arrangement ended in acrimony and dismissal, apparently over the way Mukherji exceeded his brief in collecting material for the museum in the Patna region, an area that Dr. Waddell had come to regard as his by right. He considered himself *the* authority on ancient Pataliputra and he resented what he saw as the Bengali's clumsy intrusion when the latter began to carry out excavations. As Mukherji's report on Champaran demonstrates, the Bengali evidently felt entitled to use his initiative, and his forwarding of that report to Smith may well have been a response to criticism from Waddell or worse.

Far from being warned off, Mukherji then made matters worse by again returning to Patna in the winter of 1897 to excavate under orders of the Government of Bengal – orders which appear to have originated from someone other than Dr. Waddell. His digs in and around Patna produced what Mukherji believed to be parts of six separate Asokan pillars, one found among a layer of ashes and embers, leading him to conclude a deliberate attempt had been made to split the pillars by heat, possibly the work of the anti-Buddhist Raja Sassanka in the sixth century. Smith agreed with this theory, adding that 'During the great Benares riot of 1809 the Muhammadans destroyed the pillar known as Lat Bharo by the same method'. But Dr. Waddell did not agree, describing the Babu's report as a 'wholesale perversion of truth and mischievous misdirection of work'.

Smith's initial verdict on Mukherji's report of his Patna excavations was that it was 'too crude for publication'. Yet he relented to the extent of writing an introduction to the report (now lost) and to propose that the Bengali should be authorised to superintend the Nepal Tarai excavations under his indirect supervision.

No sooner had Mukherji been appointed than Dr. Waddell came forward to demand that the appointment be rescinded and that he himself conduct the Nepal excavations. After much lobbying by Waddell and by the Government of Bengal on his behalf it was agreed that Mukherji should work 'in conjunction with and under the direction of Doctor Waddell'. It was a compromise that satisfied neither party.

When Babu Mukherji reported for duty at Lucknow on 9 January 1899 he was immediately assailed by orders from Charles Odling, Secretary and Chief Engineer to Govt., NWP&O, PWD, as to what he might and might not do. He could consult books in the Museum library but not take them out without special permission, he was to follow the rules regarding travelling allowances and, above all, he was to clearly understand that in Nepal the excavations would be carried out 'at the expense of and under the orders of the Nepal Durbar', and that all he was authorised to do was to 'indicate the places where the excavations should be made and record the results'. On the 17th of that same month Vincent Smith, who was now in post as the new Commissioner of Faizabad, came up to Lucknow to brief him in person, and on his advice Mukherji wrote a letter to Colonel H. Wylie, British Resident in Kathmandu. The letter shows the Babu to have been a man of considerable diplomatic skills – qualities that he would require in full in the days to come. He had noted the many obstacles that his predecessor had faced in trying to go about his work, particularly with regard to the way that any artefact found had immediately been removed by Dr. Führer's Nepalese escort:

> I beg therefore most respectfully and earnestly that this is not the way to conduct archaeological researches in order to achieve scientific results. Since it is my duty to superintend the excavations in the best way I shall find necessary, as also to take casts, photographs, drawings and accurate and minute notes of all our future discoveries, which require repeated examination when found, I shall feel grateful, if you kindly use your influence to get me the full opportunities for the satisfactory discharge of my duties. ... You can assure His Excellency the Prime Minister that I am a Brahman of the Orthodox school, and knowing as an Archaeologist the sacred and delicate nature of the ancient relics, no desecration or carelessness can possibly occur in my hands.

On 25 January 1899 Babu Mukherji crossed into Nepal with specific instructions from Vincent Smith: the first, to 'fix the position of the city [of Kapilavastu] ... and ascertain the positions of the gates'; the second, to make a map of the city showing its position relative to the Kanakamuni pillar at Nigliva Sagar, the second pillar stump at Gotihawa, the town of Taulihawa and the surrounding Tharu villages'.

In accordance with these orders Mukherji proceeded to Taulihawa, where he met his Nepalese escort and a labour force of fifty local Tharus. However, on the following morning he received a letter from Dr. Waddell ordering him to come at once to Nigliva village, about four miles away, where Waddell was encamped. Here he was met by Waddell who without saying a word handed him a telegram from the Government of the NWP&O instructing him to return immediately to India and report to the Commissioner at Gorakhpur, Dr. Hoey.

Mukherji had no alternative but to do as he was told. He made his way across country to Uska Bazaar railway station and caught the first train to Gorakhpur, where he presented himself at Dr. Hoey's *cutchery* or office. To his mortification he was informed that a serious complaint had been laid against him by Dr. Waddell in a telegram to the Lieutenant-Governor, and that he was to remain in Gorakhpur pending an enquiry.

No records survive of the contents of that telegram or of a follow-up letter from Dr. Waddell to the Lieutenant-Governor, but it is clear that Mukherji's behaviour at Patna and his generally seditious character had been brought to the Lieutenant-Governor's attention.

On 29 January Commissioner Hoey received a telegram from Charles Odling in Allahabad informing him that Babu Mukherji was free to return to Nepal to continue his work. On the same day letters were despatched by Odling to both Mukherji in Gorakhpur and Waddell in the Nepal Tarai. The first informed Mukherji – without so much as a word of explanation as to why he had been detained – that he 'should scrupulously avoid any action of which Major Waddell might reasonably complain and carefully abstain from doing anything likely to offend him'. The other letter told Dr Waddell that 'with the information at present before him, the Lieutenant-Governor is not satisfied that you take a correct view of Mr. Mukherji's conduct at Patna and declines to recall him'. It went on to warn Waddell that 'His Honor looks to you to adhere scrupulously to the engagement made with the Government of India, in regard to working with and on good terms with Babu Purna Chandra Mukherji'.

It is hard to interpret Dr. Waddell's behaviour as anything other than a deliberate spoiling operation to keep the Bengali archaeologist away from what Waddell evidently regarded as his territory. With Mukherji now away from the scene he put the fifty Tharus to work clearing the site beside the lake at Nigliva Sagar where Dr. Führer had first uncovered the Asokan inscription on the Buddha Kanakamuni pillar. To his surprise and satisfaction he found no evidence of a great Kanakamuni stupa in the immediate area, and to his even greater satisfaction he discovered, on digging out the Kanakamuni stump, that it was not the base of that pillar and was not set in foundations. It demonstrated not only that Dr. Führer had lied and that the Kanakamuni pillar had originally stood somewhere else.

'This pillar is not *in situ*', Waddell afterwards declared in a brief report to the Secretary of the Department of Revenue and Agriculture of the Government of India:

> Its broken end was merely stuck three feet [in fact, seven feet] into the mud bank of the Nigali-tank. ... Moreover the great stupa mound which was alleged [by Dr. Führer] in the Government report to be in its immediate neighbourhood, and the existence of which was accepted by Mr. Smith, did not in reality exist – it was a pure fabrication to reconcile this false identification with the descriptions of the Chinese pilgrims.

Dr. Waddell now needed a witness to back him up, so he downed tools and headed back to Gorakhpur: 'To attest to these important facts, which altered the whole character of my enquiry, I asked the leading archaeological authority of the North-Western Provinces, Dr. Hoey, the Commissioner of Gorakhpur, to kindly come and see these places on behalf of Government.'

By the time Dr. Waddell reached Gorakhpur Babu Mukherji was back in Nepal. He made a second rendezvous with the Nepalese Captain at Taulihawa and proceeded with him and his labour force into the sal forest north of the town. After three and a half miles they encountered the great banked enclosure known locally as Tilaura Kot. This imposing local feature struck Mukherji as an obvious place to begin his work. He may well have made enquiries and learned that the word 'kot', usually taken to mean a fort or hill, had an older meaning as a seat of government or home of a king or deity; that the word 'laura' meant a staff; and that the word 'til' could mean three. Thus one reading of Tilaura Kot was 'the royal court of the three pillars'.

Whatever his reasoning, the Babu set up his camp at the little village of Singurh outside the western wall of the kot and set the fifty Tharus to work felling trees and clearing the undergrowth. Over the next few days the workmen continued to uncover more and more of what swiftly revealed itself to be an extensive city wall, skilfully constructed of fired bricks in remarkably good condition, and surrounded by what had once been a deep moat linked to the nearby River Banganga. Mukherji himself divided his time between supervising the clearance and exploring the immediate neighbour-hood within a radius of ten miles.

His work was going well, with the Nepali officer 'co-operating with me very smoothly', when on the evening of 7 February a runner arrived with a 'chit' from Dr. Waddell ordering the Nepali Captain to stop all work and bring his entire labour force to Gotihawa. 'After nightfall' at the close of the following day, 8 February, Dr. Waddell appeared accompanied by Dr. Hoey, and they and their party made camp. No word of explanation was offered to Mukherji by Waddell until next morning when he was summoned to Waddell's tent and ordered to leave off his mapping at Tilaura Kot and start mapping Sagarwa in accordance with Vincent Smith's specific instructions to fix the position of Kapilavastu and make a map of the city. In the meantime, he was told, the Tharu workmen would be carrying out excavations elsewhere under Dr. Waddell's directions.

Not surprisingly, already strained relations deteriorated further. After the departure of the two Britons with all the diggers an agitated Babu Mukherji sat down at his tent to write a long letter of complaint. 'All our programme of works has been upset', he wrote to Mr. Odling in Lucknow:

> To upset every work without a moment's notice is a serious difficulty, and the Captain bitterly complained to me that there was no system, he and his men about 50 in number being moved here and there without a moment's notice and no courtesy. At Gotiva, five miles off, work was commenced and the Doctor ordered it to continue the next day. But shortly after he forgot all about it, telling the Captain to attend him at Ruminidei [Lumbini], last evening. But neither he nor Dr. Hoey reached the place up to this morning.
>
> I am trying my best under the circumstances and am finishing the plans already begun here before I move to Sigrava [Sagarwa] a few days hence. ... To leave half done work at every place is no work. A child even has a system of playing with his dolls.

From subsequent notes made by Waddell and Hoey it is obvious that the former had come to the Nepal Tarai with two axes to grind. His first priority was to go over the ground covered by Dr. Führer during his three forays into Nepal and demonstrate to the Commissioner of Gorakhpur that much of what Führer had claimed to have done or seen was, in Dr. Hoey's phrase, 'pure invention, an absolute lie'. This he achieved in a most satisfactory manner.

At Nigliva Sagar Hoey was shown the damning evidence of the Asokan pillar stump without foundations. 'If Dr. Führer excavated [here], he has told a falsehood as to what he saw', the Commissioner afterwards commented. 'Major Waddell exposed the whole shaft before me. The pillar is not *in situ*. I saw [at] the base a shattered end of a pillar, not a clean cut end as at Gotilva [Gotihawa], and there is no masonry pediment whatsoever'. Nor, of course, was there any sign of Buddha Kanakamuni's great stupa: 'The ruins are a pure figment of Dr. Führer's fancy. The whole passage is pure invention, an absolute lie. Nothing of the kind exists. I am appalled at the audacity of inventions here displayed'. And then there was the issue of Führer's public claim to have found Kapilavastu. 'Dr Führer has not identified Kapilavastu', was Dr. Hoey's terse judgement. 'He did not find at the place which he indicates any of the traces requisite to establish the location'.

The Commissioner of Gorakhpur was, it is said, a 'kind-hearted and genial' person and 'averse to controversy', but what Dr. Waddell had shown him on the ground forced him to conclude that plain speaking was now unavoidable. 'I was inclined to be sceptical ... when you wrote to me that you had found so little truth in the published reports of Dr. Führer's explorations', he afterwards told Dr. Waddell:

> I took advantage of my camp being in the north of Basti to go over the whole ground with you. I then came to the same conclusion at which you had already arrived, that Dr. Führer had put together absolutely false statements and added a padding of general Buddhist disquisition to make up the report to be passed through by the North-Western Provinces and Oude Government to the Government of India. It is not pleasant for me to write in strong terms of condemnation about work done under Government patronage, but it is my duty to speak out when asked, and I have therefore given notes on the points which you have selected and have not minced words.

Dr. William Hoey (seated cross-legged, wearing old-fashioned 'mushroom' sola topee) admires the Asokan pillar (out of focus, left foreground) at Lumbini, most probably taken in mid-February 1899. If so, the person seated on the ground on his right could be General Khadga Shumsher Rana. One might also expect Lawrence Waddell to be in the group, except that it is difficult to reconcile the appearance of the squatting gentleman in the military boots with published photos of Waddell. The younger person closest to the camera in the more modern cork sun helmet may be Duncan Ricketts from nearby Dulha Estate. The saddhu carrying the umbrella is the Hindu ascetic in residence in the Mahadevi temple. *(Courtesy of the Hoey family)*

Hugely gratifying as this unmasking of the man who had cheated him must have been – and doubly so to have done so in the presence of a witness as respected as the Commissioner of Gorakhpur – Dr. Waddell knew his triumph would be incomplete until he had achieved his second objective, which was to complete what his rival had signally failed to do and discover Kapilavastu himself – and to do so in the presence of Commissioner Hoey. The only problem was that he had now lost Xuanzang's guide post of the Kanakamuni pillar: 'On finding that the alleged Kapilavastu was not really that place [Sagarwa], and the local clue to its position in the original of the Kanakamuni pillar had also disappeared, I had in my search for Kapilavastu to fall back on the far distant pillar of Rummindei, discovered by General Kharga [Khadga]Shumsher , as my nearest fixed point'.

Accordingly, the two sahibs now moved from Nigliva Sagar to Lumbini, which they reached on 10 February. Here they were joined by General Khadga Shumsher and heard from his own lips how he had arranged to meet Dr. Führer at Padariya precisely because 'he knew the Lumbini Garden was there'; how the General had come fully expecting to find the inscription below the surface; and how it was he and not Führer who had then exposed the Asokan inscription on the pillar. 'Not only was this digging done by the General in the absence of Dr. Führer,' Dr. Waddell was afterwards able to report, 'but the General tells me that he himself made the rubbing of the inscription which Dr. Führer carried off as his own when he arrived later on, and it was made on Dr. Hoey's paper and with Dr. Hoey's heel-ball'.

To Babu Mukherji's great surprise that same evening the Nepalese Captain reappeared at Tilaura Kot together with all the Tharu labourers and new instructions, prompting the Bengali to write another letter of complaint to his superior in Allahabad:

> Dr. Waddell writes to me to-day from Ruminidei [Lumbini] to say that I should proceed with making detailed plans here and at Sagrava. How can I make detailed plans without opening and examining the ruins by excavations? He has sent back the Captain, who arrived here this evening with the Doctor's letter to me. He will have to remain here idling with his coolies[,] about 50 in number[,] for 10 to 15 days until the Doctor returns. For nothing he [the Captain] was taken to Ruminidei about 18 miles off.
>
> Dr. Waddell has not issued any fresh instructions beyond those of Mr. V. A. Smith, which instructions the Doctor repeats to me little by little as if I have not received the whole from you. And from the few minutes conversation I had with him the other morning I found that he wants me to do the mechanical part of the work with my intellectual eye closed. Why?

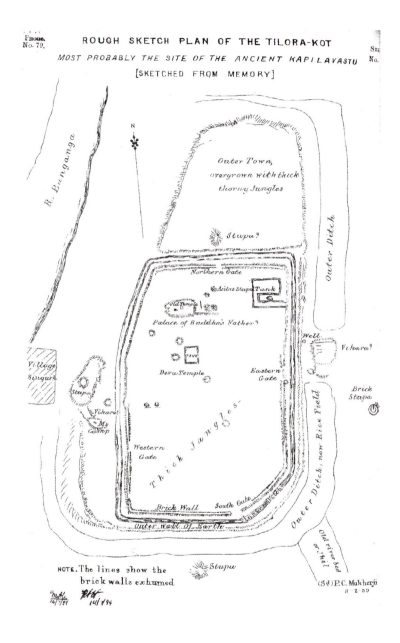

> I submit, however, to the inevitable circumstances and shall do
> my best so far as I can.

Mukherji closed his letter with a plea that the work he had achieved
in spite of Dr. Waddell should not be overlooked: 'Since I shall not
have any opportunity for showing my original work or making any
important discoveries I beg to submit a sketch-plan of the Tilora-
kot, which struck me as the most probable site of Kapilavastu, for
I could not find its vestiges at Sigrava [Sagarwa] forest as stated by
Dr. Führer.'

Signed 'P. C. Mukherji' and dated 11 February 1899, this map
of the brick-walled enclosure in the sal forest was entitled 'Rough
Sketch Plan of the Tilora-Kot, most probably the site of the ancient
Kapilavastu'.

Accompanying the sketch map was a note giving eight reasons
why, in Babu Mukherji's professional opinion, Tilaura Kot had to
be the city of Kapilavastu:

1. Xuanzang had mentioned ten deserted towns round about
   Kapilavastu and 'I have traced already some seven kots or ruins
   round about Tilora';
2. Xuanzang had described the inner wall of Kapilavastu as made
   of brick and about 14 or 15 li in circuit, and 'the inner wall of
   Tilora was of bricks, which is about 2 miles in circuit';
3. Xuanzang saw 'four stupas and viharas outside the four gates
   of the town, and a glance at accompanying sketch will show
   that they correspond here'; there was 'no other brick kot in
   the neighbourhood, nor could I find it in the forest of Sigrava
   [Sagarwa] where Dr. Führer located the Sakya town';
4. Xuanzang had described King Suddhodana's palace inside the
   city as being in ruins, over which a temple had been raised, and
   'my excavation on the north-west elevated portion of the fort
   showed that such was the fact. And the broken sculptures collected in a modern unfinished temple might represent the old
   statues mentioned by him';
5. According to Xuanzang, north of the palace were the foundations of Queen Maya's palace and a vihara, north-east of which

was Asita's stupa, 'exactly as the mounds in the sketch show';

6. Xuanzang had located the inscribed stone pillar of Krakuchanda Buddha some fifty li south of Kapilavastu, 'and Gotihava about five miles south-west of Tilora fulfils these conditions';

7. According to Xuanzang, Kanakamuni Buddha's town was thirty li north-east of Krakuchanda's town, north of which was a stupa and an inscribed pillar 'and the Nigliva pillar actually mentions Kanakamuni ... though the distance appears to be greater';

8. 'The place of massacre of the Sakyas was on the north-west of Kapilavastu and the several small stupas [excavated by Führer at Sagarwa] are on the north of Tilora'.

These were the reasons, Mukherji concluded, 'which induce me to conclude that Tilora-kot might represent the town of Suddhadana, the Buddha's father.'

The much-put-upon Bengali Babu had found what Dr. Führer and the other sahibs had passed by and missed: the ancestral home of Gautama Sakyamuni – or, to be more precise, the city of Kapilavastu as seen by the Chinese pilgrim Xuanzang in the seventh century.

Dr. Waddell was at this same time intent on the same goal. Having instructed the Nepalese Captain and his workmen to return to Babu Mukherji, he and Dr. Hoey accompanied General Khadga Shumsher north-eastwards through the Nepal Tarai to the village of Saina-Maina (today renamed Devadaha), thirty-five miles north-east of Lumbini. This was apparently at the General's invitation, for he evidently wanted them to see an excavation that he himself had conducted there, having been directed to that village by a report of an Asokan pillar, subsequently found to be false. However, he had done some digging and had uncovered a small statue of a Buddha and another of a mother suckling a child, leading him to conclude that he had found Devadaha, the capital city of the Koliyas, where Queen Mayadevi had dreamed of being impregnated by a small white elephant and where the new-born Prince Siddhartha had spent his first weeks at the home of his maternal grandfather King Suprabuddha.

From Dr. Waddell's point of view, the excursion to Saina-Maina turned out to be a wild goose chase. His overriding concern was to resolve the Kapilavastu issue and he had only accompanied General Khadga Shumsher in the hope of finding the ruins of Kapilavastu in that area. He made his excuses and left: 'I had to scour that part of the country for several hundred square miles,' he afterwards wrote, with characteristic exaggeration, 'and the difficulties of this task were all the greater as the country had never been surveyed, and the Nepalese knew little about it, and the settlers are all recent colonists mostly from British India who have cleared the forest but have no traditions whatsoever as to the ruins found there.'

Some days later Dr. Waddell turned up at the kot in the sal forest where he had left Babu Mukherji. The Babu had by this time finished his map of Sagarwa as ordered and, once back at Tilaura Kot, had made good use of the Tharu coolies released by Waddell by putting them to work excavating a number of sites within the kot's walls. This was Waddell's first opportunity to take a good look at Tilaura Kot and what he saw must have shocked him to the core: almost two miles of high brick walls complete with an outer moat laid out in the form of a rectangle, and on each of the four sides a north, south, east and west gate complete with guard house. Moreover, at the very heart of Tilaura Kot, where a section of forest had been felled to make a clearing, Mukherji's excavations were uncovering what looked suspiciously like an ancient temple which might or might not have been built over an even older palace.

Waddell must immediately have realised that the game was up; that in his desire to unmask Dr. Führer he had allowed the Bengali babu to steal much more than a march on him. Uncertain as to how to regain the initiative but determined to do something, he commandeered a party of diggers and led them out of the kot complex to a large mound a hundred yards outside its eastern walls, where he set them to work clearing the site. Perhaps he was taking his cue from Xuanzang, who had written that outside Kapilavastu's eastern gate was '*the temple of Isvara-deva. In the temple is a figure of the deva* [god or deity] *made of stone, which has the appearance of rising in a bent position. This is the temple which the royal prince when an infant entered.*'

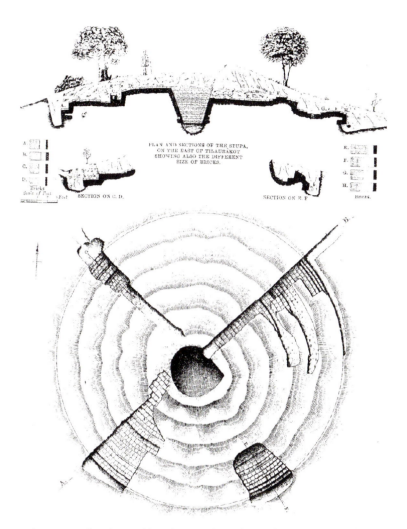

Babu Purna Chandra Mukherji's exemplary plan and cross-section of his excavation of the stupa sited outside the eastern gate of Tilaura Kot, previously dug into at the top and then abandoned by Major Waddell.

Dr. Führer had claimed to have found this same Isvara-deva temple some distance to the north-east, and it may be that Dr. Waddell was still focused on proving the German wrong. In the event, the mound revealed itself to be a brick stupa very similar in shape and construction to that at Piprahwa. On the second day he

(Above) The central mound and 'Queen Mayadevi's bathing pool' at Lumbini, photographed from the south by Babu P. C. Mukherji in March 1899. The top of the Asokan pillar can just be made out half way down the slope left of the mound topped by the brick Hindu temple.

(Below) A detail from Mukherji's map of the same area. A trial trench dug by him can be seen in both photo and map. *(From P. C. Mukherji's Report)*

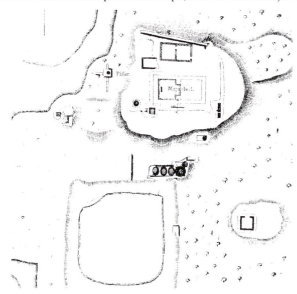

abandoned his dig and, without another word to Mukherji, headed for the Indian border.

Babu Mukherji completed the work on the stupa that Waddell had abandoned and then took his labour force to Lumbini, where he spent a week conducting a detailed survey of that complex site, complete with trial trenches, before moving on to do the same at Piprahwa.

In the meantime, Dr. Waddell had reached Calcutta, where he immediately dashed off a short report, dated 22 March 1899, which he submitted to the Secretary to the Government of India, Department of Revenue and Agriculture. 'Ultimately I found a site possessing the aggregated topographical features of Kapilavastu as described by the Chinese pilgrims,' he stated baldly and untruthfully. 'And I also found what seems to be the original position of the Kanakamuni pillar'.

Dr. Führer, it may be remembered, had linked the Gotihawa pillar to Buddha Krakuchanda, almost certainly correctly. Dr. Waddell's theory was that the Gotihawa pillar was actually the base of the Buddha Kanakamuni pillar. Finding that the bottom of the stump of the Nigliva Sagar had broken off at an angle and seeing that the top of the Gotihawa pillar had been sheared off in the same way, Waddell had concluded that all three pieces of pillar were from the one column, which had originally stood at Gotihawa. It was an ingenious theory, raised several times since, but spoiled by the fact that the diameter of the base of the Nigliva Sagar stump is greater that that of the top of the Gotihawa pillar. Recent tests have also shown that the composition of the two pillars is slightly different.

Waddell concluded his little report by drawing the Government of India's attention to the 'deplorable way in which Government is being misled over this important historical enquiry'. He begged that it should henceforward 'be treated as an imperial and not a provincial matter' – in other words, dealt with by the Government of India and not by the Government of the NWP&O. In the meantime, he urged that 'the surveyor of the North-Western Provinces Government' – meaning Babu Purna Chandra Mukherji – 'who is at present causing the Nepalese government needless trouble in excavating sites to no useful purpose, should be withdrawn without delay'. He also submitted a claim for 450 rupees to cover 'the enormous amount of unforeseen travelling which I had to perform'.

It is not known whether Waddell's expenses claim was upheld but his report was copied and passed on to the Government of the NWP&O, where it ended up on the desk of the new Chief Secretary, who passed it on to his predecessor, Vincent Smith, for his comments. Smith responded with a confidential letter the contents of which have not, alas, been preserved.

Dr. William Hoey did rather better, for in the course of his visit to Saina-Maina as a guest of General Khadga Shumsher Rana he learned that the sub-district south-east of the township was called Bhaghaura. Hoey shared the General's theory that the river which flowed down from the foothills west of the village of Saina-Maina was the ancient River Rohini, which in Buddha Sakyamuni's time had divided the Sakya country of Kapilavastu from the Koliya country of Koliygrama/Ramagrama/Devadaha. Somewhere in this region was the stupa-mound erected by the Koliyas over their one-eighth share of Sakyamuni Buddha's relics, the only one not subsequently opened by the Emperor Asoka. Although the stupa came to be known as the Ramagrama stupa, it was originally said to be at Byaghrapura, which to Dr. Hoey's ears sounded too similar to the modern Bhaghaura to be a coincidence.

Both the Chinese travellers had visited the Ramagrama stupa, both journeying east from Lumbini to get there. Unusually, it was Faxian who had provided the most valuable account of why the great emperor had failed to open up the stupa – and what had befallen it thereafter:

East from Buddha's birthplace, and at a distance of five yojanas, there is a kingdom called Rama. The king of this country, having obtained one portion of the relics of Buddha's body, returned with it and built over it a tope, named the Rama tope. By the side of it there was a pool, and in the pool a dragon, which constantly kept watch over (the tope), and presented offerings to it day and night. When king Asoka came forth into the world, he wished to destroy the eight topes, and to build (instead of them) 84,000 topes. After he

Wild elephants lay flowers at the Buddha relic stupa at Ramagrama while Naga snake divinities coil protectively round the dome. A relief from the Amaravati stupa now in the British Museum, most probably dating from the Kushan era (first third century CE).

had thrown down the seven (others), he wished next to destroy this tope. But then the dragon showed itself, took the king into its palace; and when he had seen all the things provided for offerings, it said to him, 'If you are able with your offerings to exceed these, you can destroy the tope, and take it all away. I will not contend with you.' The king, however, knew that such appliances for offerings were not to be had anywhere in the world, and thereupon returned (without carrying out his purpose).

(Afterwards), the ground all about became overgrown with vegetation, and there was nobody to sprinkle and sweep (about the tope); but a herd of elephants came regularly, which brought water with their trunks to water the ground, and various kinds of flowers and incense, which they presented at the tope.

After saying his farewells to Dr. Waddell, and most probably to General Khadga Shumsher, too, since there is no mention of the General accompanying him, Dr. Hoey made his way back from Saina-Maina towards the Indian border, but by an indirect route that took him south-east into the sub-district of Bhagahura and to the little market town of Parasi Bazaar. Four miles south of the town on a bend in the River Jharahi Hoey came upon an impressively large and quite undisturbed stupa. It was some thirty-seven miles due east of Lumbini, not that different from Faxian's five yojanas, or about thirty-three miles. This, Hoey concluded, had to be the relic stupa of the Koliyas at Byaghrapura containing the undisturbed share of Sakyamuni Buddha's remains. Modern Buddhist archaeology tends to agree with Dr. Hoey, and for religious reasons the stupa of Ramagrama remains undisturbed to this day, keeping whatever secrets it may hold.

It was not until the publication in 1901 of Babu Purna Chandra Mukherji's *A Report on a Tour of Exploration of the Antiquities of Kapilavastu Tarai of Nepal, during February and March of 1899*, that the world of archaeology first got to hear of the true identification of Kapilavastu, and who had made it. Of course, as far as the general public was concerned that honour had already been claimed by Dr. Anton Alois Führer, late Archaeological Surveyor to the Government of the NWP&O. Even so, after all the humiliations that Dr. Waddell had heaped on him, it must have been a sweet moment for Babu Mukherji when he opened the May 1899 issue of the *Theosophist* to read in print his own account of the discovery of Kapilavastu, in which he informed that periodical's readers that:

> You will be agreeably surprised to hear that though the discovery of Kapilavastu was announced to the world two years ago, Dr. Waddell and Dr. Führer each fighting for and claiming the credit of the discovery, and though the former was deputed by the Bengal Government in this year, the exact site remained unidentified, till I, deputed by the North-Western Provinces and Oude Government, was able to trace it – thanks to the great Masters who are guiding our good works.

Dr. Waddell's immediate response was to threaten to sue.

The Prince-Priest

Gorakhpur Division, 1898

The speed with which news of the Buddha relics uncovered at Piprahwa spread by word of mouth can be judged by the fact that within a week of the stone coffer's opening on 18 January 1898 a yellow-robed, shaven-headed and austere-looking Siamese *bhikku* (monk) arrived at the gates of Birdpore House demanding to speak to Peppé Sahib.

Ever since the discovery of the inscribed Asokan pillar at Lumbini in December 1896 Buddhists from Burma, Tibet and Ceylon had started coming to the area, at long last able to fulfil the pilgrim's basic requirement to visit the scenes of Sakyamuni Buddha's birth, enlightenment, first sermon and Maharaparinirvana. The subsequent discovery of what appeared to be the remains of the Buddha allotted to the Sakyas had as yet received no publicity, yet already here was a pilgrim humbly yet very firmly requesting permission to view the relics – and no ordinary pilgrim at that.

The monk was received by the Peppés as an honoured guest. He came bearing credentials, one known sponsor being a highly-respected Pali scholar of Ceylon, the Venerable Sri Subhiti, abbot of the Waskaduwe Vihara at Kulatura, and an avid collector of Buddha relics. The Ven. Subhiti had already asked for and received from the Government of Bombay a relic from a stupa excavated at Sopara. From the Commissioner of Gaya, the eminent linguist Mr. George Grierson, Superintendent of the newly-established Linguistic Survey of India, he had received a branch of the sacred *bodhi* tree at Bodgaya, and he even then was in the process of securing from Major Harold Dean of the Indian Political Service, recently

The Ven. J. C. Jinavaravansa's signed *carte de visite*, presented to Willie Peppé at Birdpore on 5 April 1898. *(Courtesy of Neil Peppé)*

returned from a military campaign in Chitral, 'at his own expenses, as a present two boxes containing some ancient sculptures of Buddhism and stone images of Buddha which were discovered by him during the same time'.

The stern-looking Siamese monk first declared himself to be the Venerable Jinavaravansa, acting as the Ven. Subhiti's agent in his quest for Buddha relics. Then, greatly to the bemusement of the Peppés', he let it be known that before renouncing the world he had been Prince Prisdang Chumsai, grandson of King Rama III of Siam and cousin of the present ruler King Chulalongkorn (Rama V). Before and after photographs, subsequently presented to the Peppés, helped to establish his bona fides.

The Ven. Jinavaravansa made an immediate impression on the Peppés, and not merely because he was a Siamese prince. In addition to a commanding presence and impeccable manners, he spoke excellent English, which was not surprising considering his upbringing and early life. Born in Siam in 1851, he had been educated in Singapore by order of his uncle the enlightened and much misrepresented King Mongkut (Rama IV) of 'The King and I' notoriety before being sent to England to study engineering at King's College, London. After becoming the first Siamese to graduate from a Western university Prince Prisdang had been accredited as Siam's ambassador to a number of countries, as well as acting as his country's treaty negotiator. In 1885 he had written the draft of Siam's first constitution but in the following year was accused by his cousin King Chulalongkorn (Rama V) of conspiring with others in writing a sixty-page petition urging him to reform or risk being colonised by a Western power. He was summoned back to Siam and appointed director-general of his country's new Post and Telegraph Department, only to resign after 'vicious' allegations were made against him by his enemies. These allegations were probably of a political nature but the official line was that, having criticised the King for his polygamy, he himself had left his wife and children for a woman he had met in Hong Kong. His response was to go into self-imposed exile in Ceylon, where in 1896 he took holy orders as a Buddhist monk at the Waskaduwe Vihara in Ceylon, soon afterwards setting out on what became an extended pilgrimage to

The Siamese Royal Prince Prisdang Chumsai. His photograph is dated from just after his fall from grace and exile to Ceylon but before his ordination as a Buddhist monk. *(Courtesy of Neil Peppé)*

all the Buddhist sacred sites – which in late January 1898 brought him to Birdpore House.

After being shown round the Piprahwa stupa and having venerated the relics found therein, the 'Prince-Priest' – as Jinavaravansa now became known to the Peppés and to the British authorities – intimated that he had come on a double mission: to secure a share of the Piprahwa relics for the Buddhists of Ceylon but also to ensure that the rest went to Siam. 'No relics of the Buddha authenticated by an inscription have ever been found and this makes the Piprahwa relics unique,' he subsequently argued in a letter to Willie Peppé. Considering 'how little importance Europeans attach to the bone and ash relics,' he was sure that the Government of India would now agree 'to do what is right and legitimate'. He then went on to explain why his cousin King Chulalongkorn was the most appropriate person to have custody of the Piprahwa relics:

1. The king of Siam is suggested as the proper person to have the custody and the right to distribute as he is the only and sole remaining Buddhist sovereign in the world;
2. When the king visited the island [of Ceylon] last year, on his way to Europe, the Ceylonese petitioned him to extend his patronage in a more direct manner and asked him to send good and learned priests from Siam to reorganise and establish the order of priesthood and unite them with the sacred order of the brotherhood of Siam, an order that has been reformed and reorganised by the late king of Siam;
3. The order of Buddhist priesthood [in Siam] is now recognised as the most strict and pure that has continued in unbroken succession from the time that Buddhism was introduced into the country, which cannot be said of any other country.

However, Peppé had already placed the Piprahwa relics at the disposal of Government, which meant that the matter was out of his hands. He therefore passed the Prince-Priest's memorandum on to the Commissioner of Gorakhpur, Dr. Hoey. On 13 April 1898 Hoey wrote formally to the Chief Secretary to the Government of the NWP&O, enclosing Jinavaravansa's memorandum. 'There is I believe,' he wrote, 'no doubt from the credentials with which he came furnished that Jinavaravansa is really the cousin of the king of Siam, but I am not prepared to recommend that the gift should be made to him'. The issue should, in his opinion, be handled at the highest level.

There were good reasons for treating the disposal of the relics with the greatest caution since a major dispute had been raging for some years at Bodhgaya between Buddhists of the newly-formed Maha Bodhi Society, led by the Ceylonese reformer Anagarika Dharmapala, and a group of Hindus over the ownership of a site the Buddhists regarded as theirs. In 1894 a near-riot had occurred at the Mahabodi temple in which Dharmapala and a number of his followers had been assaulted and injured by zealots acting for the Hindu *mahant*, or head priest, whose order had been in occupation of the temple site for some generations. The Government of India's first duty was to its own majority constituency of Hindus, yet the issue of the Buddha relics could also be turned to the Government's advantage. Hoey continued:

> It is a matter of common knowledge that the Buddhists are not satisfied because the Budh Gya temple is in the possession of the Hindus. The attitude of the Government of Bengal in this matter is necessarily one of neutrality. At the same time the connection of the British government with Buddhist countries renders it desirable that if an incidental opportunity to evince its consideration for Buddhists should arise, advantage should be taken of it to manifest its good will. Viewing the Government of India in this case as the British Government, I consider its relations with Siam, a country bordering on Burma, would justify the gift for which the application has been made. At the same time I believe that the coveted relics should be forwarded through this Government [of the NWP&O] to the Government of India and transmitted by His Excellency the Governor-General [i.e. the Viceroy] to the King of Siam.

Vincent Smith, recently appointed to the post of acting Chief Secretary and now stationed in Naini Tal, replied to Hoey on 18 May approving his actions and saying that the Lieutenant-Governor, Sir Anthony MacDonnell, had taken a keen interest in the discoveries at Piprahwa Kot, and had concluded that the finds fell into two categories:

> To the Buddhist world the actual relics are a matter of intense interest. To European scholars the accessories, e.g. the stone coffer,

the crystal vase and the small finds are the matter of interest and the two classes of objects require different treatment. The objects of interest to Europeans should be placed in a museum such as the Imperial Museum, Calcutta, and the authorities would be asked to send sets of duplicate objects to the Provincial Museum, Lucknow, and to decide whether any objects should be sent to the British Museum.

As for the relics themselves, which Smith described as 'the fragments of bone and ashes', these were, for the time being, to be 'placed in a sealed jar in the Government Treasury at Basti' pending a final decision. Smith also reported that it had been agreed that Willie Peppé should be allowed to retain 'a few duplicates' of the Piprahwa treasure for himself.

Before going on to take up his new post of Commissioner of Faizabad, Vincent Smith returned to Birdpore House where he and Willie Peppé sifted through all the gems, gold leaves and other pieces from the Piprahwa stone coffer to make an agreed division which left the Peppés with about one-sixth of the original treasure, which Willie Peppé subsequently had sealed inside four or five double-sided glass cases.

The Government of India's main share was then boxed up and, together with the crystal casket, the four soapstone caskets and the stone coffer, taken by Willie Peppé by train down to Calcutta, where on 3 August he handed them over to Dr. Bloch, Superintendent of the Indian Museum.

In the meantime both the Prince-Priest, now staying at Bodhgaya, and his religious superior in Ceylon, the Ven. Subhiti, were anxiously waiting for further news of the relics – and begging for a share of them. The Ven. Subhiti wrote to Vincent Smith to tell him that he 'would be placing me under a very great obligation if you could procure for me one of these bone relics' and, when that plea failed, he wrote directly to the Viceroy, Lord Elgin, reminding him that the Government of India's record on the preservation of Buddhist relics left much to be desired:

The great number of holy relics acquired by Cunningham from

Punjab and other places in India had been sent and placed in the British Museum in England, but they were all destroyed by a fire. On a subsequent occasion when some more were found and when they were being carried to England the ship was wrecked and they were all lost. At these the Buddhists are much grieved. Their grief is that the Piprahwa relics will also be lost if kept out. With respect to this, a pupil of the memorialist's[,] P.C. Jinawarawansa *bhiksu*, a member of the royal family of Siam[,] was sent to India by the memorialist and the Buddhist community of Ceylon to inspect the said holy relics.

It is hereby humbly requested to the British government[,] who are our rulers and who never disrespect any religion[,] that they may be allowed to have the said relics so found to be deposited in stupas to be built for the purpose and to worship, reserving to Government any share for the purpose of keeping and preserving in such museums.

On the same day on which he wrote to Hoey, 18 May, Smith also wrote to the Chief Secretary of the Government of India to inform him of Peppé's discoveries and enclosing letters from Jinavaravansa and Subhiti. He also stated that Sir Antony MacDonnell was of the opinion that 'all Buddhist countries will desire to share in relics of such sanctity' but that their disposal could be 'more conveniently decided by the Government of India'. This reluctance to recommend a course of action on the part of the Lieutenant-Governor was perhaps attributable to the fact that relations with a foreign power were not among his responsibilities – although it might well be put down to a characteristic of which the next Viceroy, Lord Curzon, was later to complain: Antony MacDonnell's reluctance to offer an opinion on any topic.

In the event, the Government of India decided in late July that the Piprahwa relics should be entrusted by the Government of the NWP&O to the King of Siam 'as the only existing Buddhist monarch for distribution on condition that His Majesty would not object to offer a portion of the relics to the Buddhists of Burma and Ceylon'. The good offices of the Prince-Priest would not be required. On 29 July Willie Peppé wrote to the Ven. Jinavaravansa in Bodhgaya to break the news, only to find that the latter had been kept fully informed: 'To me it matters not in the least who takes the relics to Siam,' replied the Prince-Priest, 'so long as the King is recognised as having claim to them as the head of the Buddhist religion, and I am only sorry that you were not selected, as I had hoped that you would be, to take the relics to Siam, but that the Siamese Govt. is to send a deputation to receive them.'

The Prince-Priest also took the opportunity to ask if he might have some examples of the relic jewels that Peppé had been allowed to keep:

> I would ask you to let me have *one* of the *Buddhist crosses* which is quite unknown in Siam, as a specimen, and one or two of the different kinds of flowers, which are the characteristic of them, as also *one trident*, for exchange with anything you may consider equivalent and like to have, either from Siam or Ceylon, and I hope you will let me have them if you could possibly spare them as souvenirs of my visit to your home.

The Prince-Priest got what he asked for and soon afterwards the Peppés were surprised to receive a parcel containing an album of Siamese postage stamps in mint condition, followed by a note from Jinavaravansa explaining that this was 'a complete collection of Siamese postage & revenue stamps which contains all the stamps are [*sic*] are in Siam even in the present day except one [sic] one "att" stamp which has since been introduced. Several of these are not issued and are therefore very rare'.

Equally determined to secure some of Peppé's share of the jewels was the Ven. Subhiti, the first of whose begging letters was written on 17 June, just as garbled press reports of Dr. Führer's activities at the 'massacre of the Sakyas' site at Sagarwa had begun to muddy the waters:

> I hear that the relics & other articles you have discovered were taken in charge of Govt, but you have been allowed to have some of those for your disposal. I hear also some false rumours given out by some people who were in India regarding these relics, i.e. that there

were only a few bone relics of Buddha and all the rest were bones of those Sakyas who were died at the battle of Widudhaba war, etc. … I am now most anxiously waiting & aiming at my mind always towards that quarter with the expectation of receiving from you some of those bone relics of every size as you have kindly intimated me your desire of doing so.

More letters followed – until their recipient finally cracked. Added to the top of one such letter, dated 8 August, is a brief note in Willie Peppé's handwriting: 'Sent him 20 relics & one gold roll 15.8.98. WCP'. These begging letters were a foretaste of what lay in store for the family, who until the remaining Piprahwa jewels were removed to England by Willie Peppé's second son Humphrey some five decades later were constantly having to deal with strangers turning up unannounced to see the collection and to beg or even demand an item for themselves.

Having willingly accepted the conditions attached to the offer by the Government of India, King Chulalongkorn of Siam deputed Phya Sukhom, a Royal Commissioner of the Ligor Circle in Southern Thailand, to head a delegation to India to receive the relics. On Tuesday 14 February 1899 Commissioner Sukhom, accompanied by his Secretary, was received by Commissioner Hoey at Gorakhpur. The party proceeded to Birdpore where Peppé showed his visitors round the site from which he had extracted the stone coffer thirteen months earlier. The party then returned to Gorakhpur, where on Thursday 16 February the relics were brought from the Government Treasury at Basti and presented 'with great ceremony' to the King's representative, who then placed them in a number of small golden pagodas specially made for that purpose. By way of exchange Peppé received from Phya Sukhom a decorated tray, initially dismissed as cheap brass-work and used for visitors' calling cards but afterward found to be high-quality silverware.

Presiding over the handover was Dr. William Hoey, representing the Governments of India and the NWP&O, who declared:

On this occasion we cannot but recall the gathering of rival kings who were prepared to fight at Kusinara for the cremated body of

A lithograph of the lost Hoey standing Buddha. This is the only known representation, taken from Hoey's and Smith's joint article in the *Journal of the Asiatic Society of Bengal*, 1895.

the great preacher of peace, among the many episodes of whose life none stand out more beautiful than his interventions between brother tribes and kingly neighbours to prevent bloodshed. Nor can we forget the events which led to the extinction of Buddhism in the Indian land where it was first propagated; one of many instances which may be cited in the history of the world in which the power of kings was used to push or crush a religious system. Reflecting on these bygone days we are entitled to congratulate ourselves that we live in an age of toleration and of wide sympathy with the faiths which others profess. As a practical illustration of this sympathy the present memorable occasion loses none of its significance.

There is one small footnote to these events. Is it possible that the missing 'third Buddha' from Dr. Hoey's collection mentioned earlier (see Chapter 4, p. 112) might have found its way to Bangkok at this time? One wonders whether the statuette could have been presented by Hoey to the Royal Envoy, Phya Sukhom, on this occasion in 1899 – or even given at an earlier date to Prince-Priest Jinavaravansa.

From Birdpore Commissioner Phya Sukhum proceeded by train to Calcutta, where he received from the Indian Museum a selection, listed as 'fragments of stone vase, gold and silver leaves, jewellery, pearl and coral', of the Piprahwa jewels now in their collection.

It is worth noting that the decision to hand over the Buddha relics to the King of Siam was taken during the viceroyalty of Lord Elgin and was already known to Peppé when Lord Curzon's appointment was announced on 11 August 1898 – Elgin himself had only been told the day before. Curzon took up office only at the beginning of 1899 shortly before the relics were handed over. The arrangements for the ceremony had presumably been made long before and it seems that Curzon had no desire to change them, being quite content that the hand-over should be done at the provincial level. The lack of reference to Piprahwa in either his or Elgin's correspondence with London suggests that they attached no great importance to it. What Curzon's private correspondence does show, however, is that he regarded himself as a friend of the King of Siam and they exchanged a number of extremely cordial personal letters both before and after Curzon took up office; in one of these the King thanked Curzon for giving his envoy 'every facility' in his mission to receive the relics.

On 9 February 1900 a third and far grander ceremony took place in Bangkok – one that in its own way mirrored that which had taken place at Kushinagara some 2,500 years earlier – at which two portions of the Piprahwa Buddha relics were presented to delegates from the Shwe Dagon pagoda in Rangoon and the Arakan pagoda in Mandalay; one portion to delegates from the Marichiwatta stupa at Anuradhapura; and two portions handed over 'conjointly with the condition of mutual agreement as to the place of deposit' to representatives of five different Buddhist sects from Ceylon: the Malwatta and Asgiriya viharas in Kandy and three viharas in Colombo. In a final ceremony the remaining Buddha relics from Piprahwa and the associated jewels were enshrined in the Golden Mount pagoda in Bangkok.

The Prince-Priest played no part in these ceremonies. Some months after his intervention at Birdpore he returned to Ceylon, where after leading a life of extreme austerity for some years he became the abbot of Dipaduttamarama Vihara in Colombo, reinvigorating that foundation and setting up a number of schools for Buddhists. The relic jewels he obtained from Willie Peppé were eventually enshrined by him in the Ratna Chetiya or Jewel Stupa at Dipaduttamarama, the building of which he had begun in 1908.

With the death of King Chulalongkorn in 1910 the Ven. P. C. Jinavaravansa returned to Siam but was prevented by the new king, his nephew Vajiravudh (King Rama VI), from attending his cousin's cremation so long as he dressed as a monk. He was afterwards forbidden to join the Siamese *sangha* as a *bhikku*. Forced to return to secular life in Siam, Prince Prisdang Chumsai continued to be treated as an outcast by the king and eventually moved to Japan, only returning to Siam after the bloodless coup of 1932 which marked Siam's transition from absolute to constitutional monarchy. He died all but forgotten in 1935.

As for the disgraced Anton Alois Führer, it seems he too may have sought refuge in the Dharma, for the February 1902 edition of the *Maha-Bodhi and United Buddhist World*, a journal edited by the notable Buddhist reformer Anagarika Dharmapala and published in Calcutta, carried a short paragraph of local news headed 'A German Buddhist Priest'. The item read in full:

> The *Ceylon Standard* remarks: 'Much interest has been excited in Buddhist and other circles at the prospect of Dr. Fuhrer [*sic*] coming to Ceylon to join the Buddhist priesthood. The Press notices recently made regarding this gentleman have given rise to grave suspicion. We understand that Dr Fuhrer will have an

opportunity given him of refuting the charges made against him before he is accepted by the leading Buddhists here as an exponent of the religion of Buddha.'

This paragraph shows that attempts by the Government of the NWP&O to keep the Führer scandal under wraps had failed, but it may also provide an explanation for Führer's bizarre behaviour. Some of his earlier frauds, such as the plagiarism of other people's work, can be put down to the actions of a man under pressure who thought he could cut corners and get away with it. Once head of his little department he began to make bold claims for the early dating of Jain sculptures excavated by him at Mathura believing he would be unchallenged, which suggests a certain academic naiveté. However, from the mid-1890s his work became increasingly focussed on Buddhist sites, and at this same time he came under pressure from his employers, the Government of the NWP&O, to demonstrate the worth of his archaeological department. His first truly outrageous claim was to have seen the great stupa of Kanakamuni Buddha at Nigliva Sagar and the ruins of Kapilavastu nearby. This was the action of a man who genuinely believed himself on the verge of a great discovery and who badly needed just such a discovery, but who had run out of time. It was a gamble and, in the event, he was desperately unlucky in failing to find Kapilavastu where he had already proclaimed it to be. But from that time onwards his actions seem also have been driven by a second factor: the discovery of Buddhism itself – a discovery intimately bound up with his readings and re-readings of Faxian and Xuanzang and his close identification with the latter in particular. Like his rivals Waddell and Smith, Führer set too much store by the directions and distances they gave and what they saw, the great difference between these three searchers being that only one took them literally.

Führer wanted to believe that the sacred landscape explored by two devout Chinese Buddhists in the fifth and seventh centuries still existed in that same idealised form in the last decade of the nineteenth century. So strongly did he believe this that he sought to make it so. The second of the reported bogus Buddha relics sent to the Burmese monk U Ma he said had come from the relic stupa of

Sakyamuni Buddha at Kapilavastu – a Kapilavastu not yet located in the geographical sense but already firmly established in Führer's mind on some metaphysical plane. This metaphysical reality may be extended to his bogus relics, for there is no evidence that he sought any financial gain from them. His sole motive appears to have been a desire to satisfy U Ma's hunger – and perhaps his own – for Buddha relics. By the time he came to write his extraordinary and fantastical *Monograph on Buddha Sakyamuni's Birth-place in the Nepalese Tarai* he was quite patently inhabiting a parallel world in which the only truth that mattered was that of Sakyamuni Buddha's homeland, as seen through the eyes of Xuanzang.

The archaeological fakery of which Anton Führer stands accused is by no means unheard of in archaeological circles. In 2000 the Japanese archaeologist Fujimori, who for two decades had been rewriting early Japanese history with progressively earlier finds, was caught on videotape salting a site about to be excavated by his team and afterwards confessed to having tampered with most of the 180 prehistoric excavations he had worked on. Biblical archaeology has also proved a rich field for those desperate to prove some aspect of Biblical truth, whether in seeking to prove the existence of Jesus by faking an inscription, as in the case of the 'James, son of Joseph, brother of Jesus' ossuary trumpeted by an American publication in 2002, or to show that Jewish refugees came to the Americas in the first century, as suggested by the ten commandments in Old Hebrew supposedly found inscribed on a rock in the desert at Los Lunas, New Mexico, in the early 1980s. Somewhat closer to home and to Dr. Führer's behaviour is the case of Frederick Bligh Bond, who in 1901 was appointed by the trustees of Glastonbury Abbey to carry out excavations at the ruins of this famous abbey in Somerset. He claimed that his excavations were guided by the psychic thoughts of a group of long-departed monks who together formed the 'Company of Avalon' and wished to see the abbey rebuilt. The trustees decided that the Company of Avalon was interfering with Mr. Bond's archaeological explorations and his engagement was terminated.

What happened to Führer after his arrival in Colombo – and to the unfortunate wife and children who presumably accompanied him – remains a mystery. They simply disappeared from public notice. As the news item from the *Ceylon Standard* shows, the press were on to Dr. Führer. The scandal made good copy and reporters would have pursued him wherever he went – unless he and his family travelled under a different name. It would be nice to think that, whatever surname Anton Alois may or may not have assumed, he and his family found peace and a sanctuary in which to rebuild their lives.

As for the man who believed that Führer had robbed him of the glory due to him, Dr. Waddell continued to demand redress. It is clear from the guarded responses in the files of the Government of the NWP&O that Dr. Waddell made a series of complaints to the Government of India, charging the Government of the NWP&O with 'official defamation' by publishing Dr. Führer's Buddha's birthplace monograph, which he claimed had injured his 'character and reputation'. The result of the Government of the NWP&O widely circulating 'this falsified report ... has already been to ruin my reputation amongst the leading Orientalists in Europe and America. Relying on this book as the authoritative pronouncement of Government, they have been led not only to exclude me from all share of the discovery, but to regard me as the impostor in the matter'. As if this were not enough, Waddell also complained that he had been publicly defamed 'both in my official and private capacity' by an employee of the Government of the NWP&O, a 'dishonest agency which Government has been and is still employing', despite having been 'utterly discredited as an Archaeologist by all competent authorities to whom he is known, by the Indian Museum, the Asiatic Society of Bengal, and the Bengal Government'.

This unnamed 'dishonest agency' was, of course, poor Babu P. C. Mukherji, and the public defamation of which he was accused was his crowing remark made in *The Theosophist* about 'Dr. Waddell and Dr. Führer each fighting for and claiming the discovery' of Kapilavastu. In view of 'this person's defamatory attack', Waddell demanded the requisite redress, which was that he should be allowed 'in conjunction with Dr. Hoey, to complete the exploration of the Kapilavastu region', of which he possessed 'unique knowledge'.

If no redress was forthcoming he would 'take whatever steps he may deem necessary to vindicate his honour in this matter'.

However, Sir Antony MacDonnell evidently had more important things to think about and he passed Dr. Waddell's complaints on to Vincent Smith, no doubt judging him to be the person best qualified to deal with them, even though the latter was now in his new post as Commissioner of Faizabad and was no longer his acting Chief Secretary. Smith dealt with Waddell tactfully and unambiguously. The first issue was easily dealt with. 'I see nothing in Dr. Führer's unfortunate book which in any way concerns Major Waddell's honor, character, or reputation,' he concluded. 'The little note, page 29 of the monograph, which Major Waddell calls "an attack" on him is merely a correction of a bearing, and the correction is not without justification'. By withdrawing the book from circulation, destroying the remaining stock and striking it from the Archaeological Survey of India series the Govt. of the NWP&O was doing all that was required of it.

The issue of Waddell's complaint against Mukherji should have been a more straightforward matter to deal with because it was the word of an officer of the IMS against that of a temporary employee of the Govt. of the NWP&O and a troublesome one at that, with a history of complaints against him. Smith summoned Mukherji down to Faizabad, heard his side of the story and read his full report of his explorations in the Nepal Tarai. It soon became clear to him that the Bengali had excelled himself, not only in relation to his work at Tilaura Kot but also at Lumbini where, quite apart from his two weeks of mapping and excavating, he had also used his status as a Brahmin to make a thorough search of the Hindu temple that straddled the main stupa. In the antechamber he had found, among a number of severely damaged sculptures, a large bas-relief which appeared to have been deliberately broken in two and its features defaced. Within the main shrine itself was a second and much larger bas-relief showing a group of similarly defaced figures, the largest of which had also lost its head when the sculpture had been broken in two. This Mukherji could not immediately identify – until a more thorough search under the floor of the antechamber revealed the missing head. Once the two sections

The famous Mayadevi bas-relief from Lumbini, drawn by P. C. Mukherji's draftsman Sohan Lal. *(From P. C. Mukherji's Report)*

had been reunited it immediately became clear that the largest of the figures was Mayadevi, with her right hand reaching up above her to grasp the branch of a sal tree as she gave birth. Beside her stood her sister Prajapati reaching out towards her, with the figures of Brahma and Indra looking on. At her feet, severely defaced, was the outline of the infant Siddhartha, already standing.

Mukherji had thought the panel to be of a style similar to the workmanship he had seen while excavating at Pataliputra and he had no hesitation in calling it Mauryan and most probably damaged by Muslim iconoclasts, a view shared by Smith, neither recognising that first Führer and then Hoey had seen the Mayadevi figure intact (see p. 135). So by a quirk of fate the discovery of a now world-famous statue, first identified as Queen Maya giving birth by Anton Führer, and again identified as such quite independently a few months later by William Hoey, is today credited to the man who brought back the first image of it, Purna Chanda Mukherji.

Having read Babu Mukherji's extensive and fully illustrated report Smith wrote to Dr. Waddell to ask if he had anything to add to the latter's very brief report written after his return from Nepal. He got no reply, which led him to put on record that 'Major Waddell has unfortunately preferred not to communicate to the Government of the North-Western Provinces and Oude the conclusions at which he has arrived concerning the topography of the Tarai, and I am consequently not able to deal with his criticisms quite so easily as I could if he had expressed himself frankly'. He then read the PWD's file containing all the correspondence relating to the recent explorations, including all the charges made against Mukherji by Waddell.

On 25 May 1899 Smith wrote to the Lieutenant-Governor, first giving his judgement on Babu Mukherji:

> I have the honor to say that I think Mr. Mukerji did excellent work this year in the Nepalese tarai. He displayed great activity and industry, working with keen enthusiasm, and I have every reason to believe that his surveys and drawings are as accurate as was possible in the circumstances. I consider him an acute and careful observer, though his theories may not always command assent. … I expect that his final report will add materially to our knowledge of the Buddhist antiquities of the Tarai.

On the issue of Dr. Waddell, Smith was careful to restrict himself to diplomatic language:

> I regret that Major Waddell has declined to work in co-operation

with Mr. Mukherji, and I am ignorant of his conclusions. ... I regret that I am unable to support the proposal that the exploration of the Kapilavastu region should be completed by Messrs. Waddell and Hoey. Nor can Major Waddell claim to possess unique knowledge of the country to which he paid a flying visit. ... Mr Mukherji was in the country for two months and traversed the same ground as Major Waddell: so far as I know, Major Waddell did not take any plans, drawings or photographs. The draftsman and photographic apparatus remained with Mr. Mukherji, whose knowledge of the various localities must, I should think, be more extensive than that of the rival explorer.

I have never seen Major Waddell, and know him only from his writings. I do not wish to say anything which could give offence, and therefore abstain from assigning reasons for my opinion that it is not desirable to entrust to him the duty of further exploration. ... I fail to see the necessity for the steps which Major Waddell desires to take in vindication of his honor.

Dr. Waddell undertook no further archaeological explorations on Indian soil. In September 1900 he received orders to join the expeditionary force being assembled to put down the Boxer Rebellion in China. On his return he was despatched to the North-West Frontier to take part in a campaign against the Mahsuds. A year later he was involved in yet another frontier campaign, this time in Swat. His hour of glory came in 1903 when he managed to persuade the Government of Bengal that he was the right man to accompany Col. Francis Younghusband on his mission to Tibet as the expedition's archaeologist. His role in that shoddy imperial adventure as cultural commissar has been told elsewhere, but it is fair to say that his behaviour as the expedition's looter-in-chief was exactly what was to be expected of the man who tried and failed to destroy the reputation of a better man who stood in his way.

Babu Purna Chandra Mukherji's *Report on a tour of exploration of the antiquities in the Terai, Nepal, the region of Kapilavastu, during February and March 1899* was duly published in 1900 in Volume VI of the Archaeological Survey of Northern India series. It came with a laudatory prefaratory note by Vincent Smith, now retired from Government service and thus freed from the con-straints which had hitherto prevented him from discussing Anton Führer's deceptions in the Nepal Tarai. Its publication restored Mukherji's reputation as an archaeologist and led to the publica-tion of his long-delayed report on his excavations of Patna.

Lord Curzon was installed as Viceroy in Calcutta on 3 January 1899. None before or since came better prepared. One of his main concerns was to thoroughly overhaul Indian archaeology, which he criticised as having 'no supervision, no control'. Addressing the Asiatic Society of Bengal in February 1900 he promised a new order in which conservation would go had in hand with excavation, epigraphy and the proper provision of museums. 'It is,' he declared, 'equally our duty to dig and discover, to classify, reproduce and describe, to copy and decipher, and to cherish and conserve'. As part of this process a new Surveyor General or Inspector General of Archaeology was required, as in the days of General Cunningham, but someone thoroughly versed in the latest and most scientific techniques. Vincent Smith's name appears to have been put forward for the post but was rejected by Lord Curzon, who wrote privately to the Secretary of State for India that he was 'not the man we want for the new Director-General of Archaeology. He is an amateur, a dilettante and not a man of science'. Instead, twenty-six-year-old John Marshall was appointed, a thoroughgoing professional from the British Museum who had learned his trade under Sir Arthur Evans on Crete but with no experience of India.

The arrival of John Marshall in India in 1902 marked the begin-nings of the modern era of Indian archaeology. Greater security along India's North-West Frontier meant that the Buddhist civilisation of Gandhara now became the main focus of Marshall's work. One of its casualties was Babu Mukherji, whom Marshall employed not as an archaeologist but as a *pandit* or learned man. 'Without the advantage of a scientific training,' wrote Marshall, 'Babu P. C. Mukherji showed himself ungrudgingly devoted to his work and possessed of a variety of useful knowledge which was not infrequently turned to good account'. The Babu's last known contact with Vincent Smith was made in January 1902 when he wrote to him in England. Only the postscript survives among

Smith's papers, but from this it is clear that Mukherji was still eager to complete the work he had begun in the Nepal Tarai in 1899:

As Pandit of the Bengal Survey, I am touring in Behar. I have been last month to the ruins of Bawangurh, near Tirveni, where you once suggested to me that Ramagrama or San-mo might be found. … Since the question of the identification of Kapilavastu is now almost set at rest, thanks to you for the opportunity you gave me, would it not be better if you recommended to the Govt. of India in connection with your Prefatory Note & the programme of tour I sketched in my Report [on Kapilavastu], for an exhaustive exploration of the region from where you locate Sravasti & Kusinara to Vaisali, embracing a sufficient tract to settle all doubtful points about the Chinese Pilgrims' line of route. I wish to do that work under your supervision. … This is a great and important work. P. C. Mukherji.

How Smith responded to this appeal is not known. The Bengali Babu is believed to have died of fever in 1903, soon after the publication of his book *The Indian Chronology: Buddhistic Period*, in which he argued that Vincent Smith in his *Asoka; The Buddhist Emperor of India* (1901) had got his early chronologies all wrong; that the Sandrocottus of the Greeks was not Chandragupta but Asoka: that there had been two Asokas, one Mauryan and one from the Nanda dynasty; and that it was not Asoka but his grandson Samprati who had put up the inscribed rock edicts – unsupported claims that did nothing to diminish his reputation as a maverick. Although overshadowed by his fellow Bengali, the pioneer Indian archaeologist Rajendra Lala Mitra, sometime President of the Asiatic Society of Bengal, Babu Purna Chandra Mukherji deserves to be better remembered by his countrymen, not least for putting the home town of the Buddha Sakyamuni back on the map.

Smith's introduction to Mukherji's Kapilavastu report was not quite his last appearance in print in India. Dr. Führer's years of work on the excavations on the Jain stupas at Mathura had never been published, although a large number of photographic plates, maps and drawings of excellent quality had been prepared. It was decided that something must be done and the task was given to Smith to salvage what he could and get it into print. Smith's *The Jain Stupas and Other Antiquities of Mathur*a was published in 1901 as Volume XX of the Archaeological Survey of India's New Imperial Series. In his Introduction Smith set out the known history of the excavations at Mathura beginning with General Cunningham in 1871 and ending with Dr. Führer's series of excavations between 1888 and 1896. He quoted briefly from Führer's reports as the Lucknow Museum's curator, almost without comment other than to note that one seemingly important inscription highlighted in Führer's final report of 1896 had not been found and that, until it was, 'no inference from it can be safely drawn'. Rather than dwelling on Führer's reports he directed the reader to the impressions and photographs sent by Führer to the late Professor Bühler, which the latter had 'admirably edited' and published in Volumes I and II of *Epigraphia Indica*, adding that 'the necessarily restricted plan of the work precludes me from attempting any elaborate discussion of the numerous topics of interest suggested by the plates'.

Vincent Smith retired from India in 1900, having been preceded by William Hoey, who went home on leave at the end of 1899 and formally retired soon after. Both men had put in enough service in India to be able to claim the generous pension of £1,000 per annum that was one of the major perks of being a member of the Heaven-Born. From 1903 to 1905 Dr. Hoey was Reader in Hindustani and Indian History at Trinity College, Dublin. In 1906 he moved to Oxford, where he was attached to Jesus College as the University Lecturer in Hindustani preparing ICS probationers for their service in India. During this time he published *Urdu Praxis: a Progressive Course of Urdu Composition* (1907) and *A Memorandum on the Training of Selected Candidates for the Civil Service of India as Probationers in England* (1913). Until shortly before his death in 1918 he remained an active fellow of the Royal Asiatic Society – the records showing, for example, that in October 1913 he took part in a round table discussion on the dating of King Kanishka that included Vincent Smith and Dr. L. A. Waddell. Shortly before his final retirement in 1916 he published a booklet entitled *Going East*, no doubt based on the advice he gave to his students and full of practical tips drawn from his own Indian experience. These ranged from the right clothing to buy – 'You want one topi for show and one for use'– to appropriate behaviour – 'Take but little alcohol in any form at any time, and never any until after sunset … Always keep Quinine in 5 grain tabloids; but don't dose yourself continually. There is a drug habit known as "Quinine Habit", which is most dangerous' … 'Wherever you may be stationed, in whatever capacity, learn the vernacular'.

The booklet ends with what could be seen as a summation of Dr. William Hoey's philosophy for getting on in India:

> You are to spend the best years of your life in exile. Study the people around you, their interests, customs, sorrows, superstitions and simple joys. Ballad, folklore and fairy tale are the literature of the humble villagers whom you meet in camp and jungle. The forest track, the cover of the sambur, the haunt of the tiger, the buried ruins, the inscribed stone, all are in their keeping. To enter into their life will gain their confidence, and relieve the tedium of your exile.

For Vincent Smith retirement from the ICS meant leaving one career in order to take up a second. He initially settled in Cheltenham from which he commuted to Dublin, where he had been appointed Reader in Indian History and Hindustani at the University of Dublin, but his tenure there was brief. His first major work, *Asoka, the Buddhist Emperor of India*, was published in 1901 and followed three years later by his *Early History of India*, in which he controversially followed Anton Führer's lead in declaring Buddha Sakyamuni and his fellow Sakyas to be non-Aryan and 'sturdy hillmen'. This history subsequently became the first part of what was to be his *magnum opus*, the *Oxford History of India*, first published in 1919. In 1910, after several years of academic isolation, he moved to Oxford to join St John's College and became a curator of the Indian Institute. A second major disappointment was his failure to get elected to the Readership in Indian History after having served as deputy reader. However, he and Dr. Hoey were mainstays of the Indian Institute for the better part of a decade, during which time Smith contributed scores of papers to learned journals on Indian numismatics and history.

Smith continued to maintain that both Sravasti and Kushinagar were still waiting to be found in the Nepal Tarai. However, in 1907 John Marshall's right-hand man Dr. J. P. Vogel recovered from Kasia no less than 463 seals 'belonging to the Convent of the Great Decease' one showing a 'flaming pyre'. A year later, one of John Marshall's new generation of Indian archaeologists, Pandit Daya Ram Sahni, excavating at Cunningham's Jetavana-Sravasti at Saina-Maina found a copper plate in a monastic cell recording the grant of six villages to 'the community of Buddhist friars, of which Buddhabhattaraka is the chief and foremost, residing in the great convent of holy Jetavana'. Further excavations at Kasia Kushinagar in 1911–12 produced more seals, three showing a coffin between sal trees, as well as a fifth century copper-plate with an inscription indicating it was 'deposited in the (Pari)nirvana-caitya [Maharaparinirvana stupa], and thus testifies that the stupa in which it was found was called by that name and that this spot was believed to be the place of Buddha's death in the fifth century'.

What held up much better was a hypothesis Smith had first put forward in his introduction of P. C. Mukherji's *Report on a tour of exploration of the antiquities in the Terai, Nepal, the region of Kapilavastu, during February and March 1899*. Unable to reconcile the two Chinese pilgrims' very different accounts of Kapilavastu and its surrounds, he had re-examined their directions and distances and found Faxian to be much less accurate than Xuanzang. Faxian's unreliability allowed Smith to propose that Faxian and Xuanzang had gone to two quite different Kapilavastus:

The later traveller [Xuanzang] started from the stupa of Kasyapa north of Sravasti and made his way direct to the ruined city on the Banganga [Tilaurakot]. Doubtless he travelled along the road which still exists skirting the foot of the hills through Tulsipur and Panchpirwa in the Gonda District. His predecessor [Faxian] would have followed the same road for most of the way, but in the final stages he must have diverged to the south and marched direct to Palta Devi, or Krakuchandra's town [Faxian's 'Na-pei-kea'], to which he

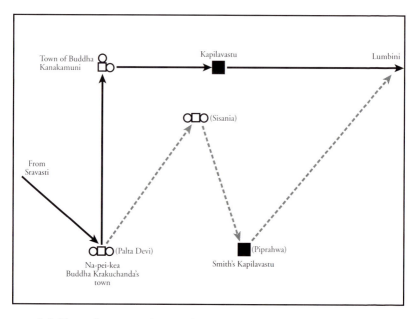

Solid lines show Faxian's route from Sravasti to Kapilavastu and on to Lumbini. Dotted lines show Vincent Smith's proposed route by way of Piprahwa

reckons the distance to be twelve yojanas. Fa-hien then moved on five miles to the north-east (he calls it north), and reached Sisania, from which he marched five miles to the south-east (he calls it east), and so arrived at Piprava [Piprahwa], or Kapilavastu, from which the Lumbini garden was distant nine or ten miles. … He found Konagamana's town more or less directly on the road from Krakuchandra's town to Kapilavastu. He was not interested in the Tilaura-Kot town, and, therefore, passed it by.

In brief, it was Smith's case that Xuanzang's direct route had led him to Kapilavastu II – now Tilaurakot – but that Faxian's more southerly route had taken him first to the town of 'Na-pei-kea' – now Palta Devi in Basti District – and then to the original Kapilavastu I – now the Piprahwa complex.

Palta Devi, according to Smith, was to be found 'in a bend of the Jamuar River, about three miles on the British side of the border' and about six miles west of Birdpore. Francis Buchanan on his pioneering survey eighty years earlier had noted Palta Devi as a Shiva temple built over 'a considerable ancient edifice'. The temple was also well known to Willie Peppé, who had himself seen there 'a broken pillar, worshipped as a Mahadeo … said to extend deep into the ground' which he believed to be Asokan. Owing to religious sensitivities he had been unable to examine the pillar more carefully.

The other modern site referred to by Smith was the village of Sisania (today Sishaniya Pandey) inside Nepal and about five miles north-west of the Piprahwa stupa. Smith had passed close to Sisania on his way to visit Dr. Führer's excavation at Sagarwa but not close enough to see the ruins there, which had first been brought to his attention by Babu Mukherji, who had declared them to be the remains of an ancient town. According to Smith's theory, this was the site of Buddha Kanakamuni's town, first visited by Faxian and then by Xuanzang. As for the Asokan pillar which Xuanzang had seen there, that had subsequently been moved to its present site beside the Nigliva Sagar, perhaps by a Buddhist Pala king in the eleventh or twelfth century: 'Considering that Firoz Shah conveyed the Asoka pillars at Delhi, one from Mirath (Meerut), and the other from Topra near Ambala [Umballa], no difficulty need be felt about the transport of the Konagamana pillar eight or thirteen miles. Coolies are cheap, and with enough coolies anything can be moved.'

What Vincent Smith could not explain was why, if Faxian visited the Piprahwa stupa complex as Kapilavastu, he made no reference to the stupa there as the reliquary of the Sakyas' share of Buddha Sakyamuni's relics. 'I cannot offer any plausible explanation,' he admitted, 'which is the more strange, because Fa-hien in his account of Kushinagara alludes to the legend of the division of the relics.' What Smith might have proposed was that by the time the Chinese pilgrim came to that region the countryside had reverted to jungle: '*In it there was neither king nor people. All was mound and desolation. Of inhabitants there were only some monks and a score or two of families of the common people.*' The few remaining Buddhists would not have been able to read the Brahmi script on the Asokan pillars, and may no longer have known what they represented. The monks relied on oral transmission, verbal accounts handed down from one generation to the next. After gaps in occupation these would inevitably have become corrupted over time.

Smith's 'two Kapilavastus' theory found few supporters at the time, even his old friend and some-time rival William Hoey describing it as 'thin'.

Smith belonged to a generation of administrators who took a paternalistic view of British rule in India. His studies of Indian history led him to conclude that India was unsuited to democratic self-government and his last foray into the public arena was an unwise attack made at the age of seventy-one on the Montagu-Chelmsford proposals for Indian political reform of 1919, which he criticised as pandering to the 'spirit of make-believe' he believed was prevalent in Indian politics. He died in Oxford, in February 1920, his last work, an article on 'The Invasion of the Punjab by Ardashir Papakan (Babagan), the first Sasanian King of Persia, A. D. 226–41', being published posthumously in the *Journal of the Royal Asiatic Society* in April 1920.

As for those who had ruled over the tarai in Smith's time, Sir Antony MacDonnell served briefly as the President of the Indian Famine Commission in 1901 before resigning on the grounds of ill-health and returning to London. It was expected that he would return to India as the Governor of Bombay but he surprised everyone by taking up an offer to become the administrative head of the Irish Government as Permanent Under-Secretary of State for Ireland, where his known nationalist sympathies eventually made his position untenable, leading to his resignation in 1908 at the age of 64. He was then given a peerage as the first Baron MacDonnell. On the creation of the Irish Free State in 1921 he was proposed as a senator but declined to take it up. He died without male heir in 1925.

MacDonnell's opposite number across the border, General Khadga Shumsher Rana, continued to bide his time as Governor of the Western Tarai until the death of his elder brother in March 1901. The third brother, Rana Shumsher, had already died so in the absence of General Khadga Shumsher in exile the position of ruling Prime Minister passed to the liberal-minded fourth brother

Deva Shumsher, whose unsuitability for the post was shown by his attempt to abolish female slavery in the kingdom. Before his surviving elder brother could summon his allies and march on Kathmandu the other members of the satrabhai met and forced Deva Shumsher to abdicate in favour of the fifth and most able of the brothers, Chandra Shumsher, who became Maharaja and Prime Minister of Nepal in June 1901. In 1903 ex-Prime Minister Deva Shumsher and General Khadga Shumsher made a joint attempt to seize power while Chandra Shumsher was away in Delhi attending the Edward VII Coronation Durbar, but the Prime Minister had been kept fully informed of their plotting and the outcome was that both the two exiled brothers were banished from Nepal for life. The former was given a mansion in the hill-station in Mussoorie and a pension, while his more dangerous elder brother was forced to live at a greater distance from Nepal. He settled in a lakeside villa in Sagar, in the heart of the Central Provinces (now Madya Pradesh) and miles from anywhere.

That the General continued to retain an interest in Buddhist archaeology is shown by a series of articles he contributed to the *Pioneer* in 1904, in which he speculated on what still lay waiting to be discovered in the Nepal Tarai. Three remarks of his are of particular interest to modern archaeologists. The first concerned the derivation of the name of Tilaura Kot: 'The term *Laura* is equivalent to *Laguda*, a Staff. The Asoka pillars would seem to have been called *Laguda* by the common folk. Tilaura Kot was so called because it contained three pillars.' What the General was too polite to explain to his English-speaking readership was that another meaning of the word *laura* was 'phallus', which in a culture that worshipped the male generative organ as a Shaivite symbol would be a perfectly appropriate term to describe a large pillar rising out of the ground. If this was correct there should have been a third Asokan pillar in the area – which led directly on to the General's second observation. This related to the Shaivite temple known as the Towleshwar Mahadev built in the late nineteenth century at the crossroads in the centre of the town of Taulihawa, three miles south of Tilaura Kot:

The temple of Towleshwar Mahadev attracts the attentions of every careful researcher after Buddhistic 'antiquities' and relics by its particular position, i.e. on the raised ground which must always be a stupa; also by the few stone images of the Buddhistic period lying about the place in a state of ruin. I saw a few old 'recluses' there and by pumping the least reluctant member of the community came to know that formerly the mound was topped by a linga, which he affirmed was without end, and built over it the present temple of Towleshwar Mahadev, or the Shiva of Towlihawa. The Linga itself seemed to have been hewn out of a piece of Asoka's pillar although the priest of the temple denied it. I was further told that the *Anauta Lingh* [i. e. the lingam stone] was *Rakta Murti* [red statue] i.e. of a red colour which was characteristic of the red stone of Asoka's pillars. It is a pity that the search for pillars was not made two decades ago, when it lay bare and had not been covered by such a big temple. The 'mystery' of the pillar will, in consequence, remain unsolved for ages to come.

The General believed that this overlooked Asokan pillar in Tauli-hawa had been placed there by Emperor Asoka to mark the site of the relic-stupa of Buddha Krakuchanda. However, a more plausible theory is that Tilaurakot's Towleshwar Mahadev temple was built around the base of the Buddha Kanakamuni Asoka pillar by Hindu immigrants at some point in the nineteenth century after the upper part of the pillar had been pulled down or broken off. Part of this upper section was then removed to its present site at Nigliva Sagar, where it was deliberately broken in two, perhaps so that the upper section could be used as a roller for crushing sugar cane.

To this day the lingam in the Towleshwar Mahadev temple remains so covered in vermilion powder and offerings that it is impossible to determine what exactly it is. Archaeologists seeking to examine the stone have always been rebuffed by the temple authorities, although it has been suggested that some of these same archaeologists, being good Hindus, have not pressed the matter too hard.

The General also speculated on the real location of Sravasti, believing, like Führer, Smith and Mukherji before him, that it remained undiscovered in Nepal's Western Tarai. He believed it to be located thirty-six miles north of Nepalganj, ninety miles north-west of Tilaurakot in the Surkhet valley:

> The valley is almost desolate now – majestic sal trees and bamboo topes growing in solitary grandeur around it – and is interspersed with a few straggling hamlets of which the names of Ramrikad, Deovali, Danda deserve a mention. A friend of mine, who at my request inspected the places, tells me that 'Ramrikad', or the beautiful arrow of Bhimsen, means nothing but an octagonal pillar tapering towards the top. Can this be one of the pillars mentioned by Hienthsiang [Xuanzang]? … The place is said to contain some interesting ruins. Unfortunately, the information reached me at the fag end of my touring season, when the much dreaded malarial fever makes its appearance. I have, therefore, included the examination of this place in my program for next year, when I hope to be able to test the correctness, or otherwise, of my surmise bordering on conviction that Surket is the real Sravasti.

Unfortunately, politics and exile intervened, and General Khadga never got to test his theory. From that day to the present no serious effort has been made to explore the Surkhet area.

According to family legend, General Khadga made one last attempt to return to Nepal in the 1910s. He arranged to meet his younger brother Prime Minister Chandra Shumsher at the India-Nepal border, where the two of them conferred for five minutes out of earshot, after which the brothers turned their backs on each other and returned to their respective homes. The General sub-sequently spent a decade repairing his family's fortunes through clever investments in Calcutta. Once he was satisfied that his children were well provided for he bade them farewell and moved to the holy city of Varanasi (Benares), where he abandoned his comfortable lifestyle to become a *sanyasi*. He died there in 1921.

Only one other member of the ever-expanding Rana family ever showed any interest in archaeology: Chandra Shumsher Rana's third son Kesher Shumsher, who liked to call himself 'Kaiser'. A great dilettante, best remembered for his library and the 'Garden

(Above) The Mayadevi temple and Asoka pillar at Lumbini as it was in 1930, photographed by Humphrey Peppé.

(Below) The Mayadevi temple photographed by Humphrey Peppé a decade after Kesher Shumsher Rana's disastrous excavations and restoration. *(Courtesy of Neil Peppé)*

of Dreams' he had built to his own design in his palace grounds in the heart of Kathmandu (now beautifully restored and open to the public), he most unwisely decided to do some archaeology at the Lumbini site, which had remained untouched since P. C. Mukherji's visit in 1899. Between 1933 and 1939 Kesher Shumsher Rana carried out a number of brutal excavations rather in the style of Dr. Führer but with much less excuse, given that archaeological method had made great strides on the sub-continent over the intervening three decades.

As photos taken in the early 1930s show, the site was desperately in need of conservation, but Kesher Shumsher's conservation took the form of demolition. In the name of archaeology he demolished many of the smaller stupas that surrounded the original Mauryan stupa and destroyed most of the ornately decorated brick platform that had been built about it in Gupta times. Then in the name of restoration he replaced the crude little brick Hindu temple with an even cruder version set on a modern brick platform with railings. At the same time the original 'Mayadevi bathing pool' was dug away, reshaped into a rectangle and provided with stone steps in the manner of a Hindu bathing ghat.

Under the oppressive rule of the Ranas no word of criticism or foreign interference was allowed. The restoration of the Shah monarchy in 1951 first opened Nepal to the modern world but did little to improve things. It took the visit of the UN Secretary General U Thant to Lumbini in 1967 to get the Government of Nepal – which, to all intents, meant the Hindu monarch King Mahendra – to take an active interest in the country's Buddhist heritage. The Buddhist U Thant let it be known that he was deeply distressed by the condition of the site of the Buddha's birthplace and this shamed the king into setting up a committee to restore Lumbini and turn it into a centre of international pilgrimage. A Japanese architect was brought in to design the Lumbini Master Plan, creating three areas linked with walkways and a canal, with the Mayadevi Sacred Garden complex at one end, a monastic zone in the middle and a secular zone at the other end. Even so, it was not until 1992 that a major recovery programme was begun to restore the Mayadevi temple, involving archaeologists from the Japan Buddhist Federation, the Government of Nepal's Department of Archaeology and the Lumbini Development Trust. What little was left of the original Mauryan central stupa was almost totally stripped away to reveal a base made up of some fifteen chambers, surrounded by a square circumambulation path – a floor not so dissimilar from that of the damaged stupa uncovered by Dr. Anton Führer at Sagarwa. At its centre was found an irregularly shaped slab of rough conglomerate rock, with a natural 'footprint' at its centre. Its significance remains undetermined but its careful positioning at the centre of the stupa raised over it suggests that it was intended to be a marker stone representing the exact spot on which the child Buddha was born.

Sad to say, once the area had been stripped back to basics it was covered by a new temple, designed by the Nepal Institute of Engineering, in every way as inappropriate and as hideous as its predecessor. Critics are assured that this is temporary but to date no alternative plans have been put forward to do what is required, which is to restore the area to something closer to its original Asokan form and to give it back its sanctity.

The Aftermath

1900–2008

On 6 June 2004 the then general secretary of the Buddhist Society in London and a volunteer were together making a photographic inventory of the Society's possessions at their premises at 58 Ecclestone Square. In what is known as the Rupa cabinet in the Society's lecture room they found a small cardboard box with a label on the lid on which was written in ink in Willie Peppé's distinctive handwriting '"Relics of Buddha" from the Piprawah Stupa Birdpore Estate Gorukhpur N.W.P. India 1898'. Inside, nestling in each of twelve compartments, were twelve jewels from the Piprahwa stupa: two pearl-like objects, two necklace beads, four flower-petal-shaped gems of different colours, and the remaining four stones cut in various shapes and sizes.

Although the box was known about, no one at the Buddhist Society was quite sure how long it had been in the Rupa cabinet or where it had come from. Yet it had certainly been with the Society for some years and probably dated from the first period of the Society's history, which went back to 1907 and the formation of the Buddhist Society of Great Britain and Ireland.

The handwriting, the date on the box, the archaic spelling of 'Gorukhpur' and the use of 'NWP', which was abandoned in 1903 when the province was renamed the United Provinces, all suggested very strongly that Willie Peppé had presented the twelve jewels as a gift before returning to India and Birdpore in the autumn of 1900. The most likely explanation is that the box came to the Buddhist Society indirectly through Prof. Thomas Rhys Davids or his widow Caroline Rhys Davids (who spoke to the

Society on the subject of Buddhist archaeology in 1930), but that they had originally been presented by Willie Peppé to the Royal Asiatic Society on 10 April 1900.

On that date Peppé was a guest of the RAS at their premises at 22 Albemarle Street when their Honorary Secretary, Rhys Davids, gave an illustrated lecture on the Piprahwa excavation and its significance. The Society's records show that Peppé afterwards answered questions from the floor and received a vote of thanks, proposed by Rhys Davids and seconded by Dr. William Hoey, for 'the great services he had rendered to the history and archaeology of India'. However, there is no record of a box of Buddhist reliquary jewels being presented at that occasion or at any other time, although it should be said that the Society's records are far from complete after two changes of address subsequent to its occupation of 22 Albemarle Street.

A striking feature of Rhys Davids' lecture was the stress he laid on the authenticity of the Piprahwa excavation: 'The careful excavation of Mr Peppé makes it certain that this stupa had never been opened until he opened it. The inscription on the casket states that "This deposit of the remains of the Exalted One is that of the Sakyas, the brethren of the Illustrious One." It behoves those who maintain that it is not, to advance some explanation of the facts showing how they are consistent with any other theory. We are bound in these matters to accept, as a working hypothesis, the most reasonable of various possibilities. The hypothesis of forgery in this case is simply unthinkable.'

After these unusual opening remarks Rhys Davids went on to consider what the Piprahwa Kot might represent: 'If this stupa and these remains are not what they purport to be, then what are they?' The inscription, he believed, was 'worded in just the manner most consistent with the details given in the [*Mahanibbana*] *Suttana*' – except that later texts such as the *Asokavadana* had described how Emperor Asoka had opened the original Buddha relic stupas in order to redistribute their contents. So how, he asked, were the inscribed casket at Piprahwa and Asoka's removal of the Buddha relics to be reconciled? He believed he had the solution:

Though the sceptics – only sceptics, no doubt, because they think it is too good to be true – have not been able to advance any other explanation, they might have brought forward an explanation which has so far escaped notice. It is alleged, namely, in quite a number of Indian books that Asoka broke open all the eight stupas except one, and took all the relics away. This is a remarkable statement. That the great Buddhist emperor should have done this is just as unlikely as that his counterpart, Constantine the Great, should have rifled, even with the best of intentions, the tombs most sacred in the eyes of Christians.

Indeed, this was how Asoka's Buddhist contemporaries had at first viewed his actions, so that when he went to break open the first of the stupas at Rajgir he met fierce resistance and was forced to bring in his army to enforce compliance. But then Rhys Davids went on to draw the attention of his audience to a passage from the *Asoka-vadana* which he believed had been corrupted over time: 'Having given back the relics, putting them distributively in the place when they had been taken, he restored the stupa. He did the same at the second, and so on till he had taken the seventh bushel; and restoring the stupas he went on to Ramagama'. Clearly something was wrong here, for the emperor would not have removed the relics from the stupas merely to put them back. Surely, the passage was meant to convey that Asoka, having removed the relics, then gave back some portion of the same relics, otherwise why would he have had the stupas restored. Thus the Piprahwa stupa had been opened by Asoka, its Buddha relics removed, then restored with some portion of the original relics returned.

No record was kept of what else was said at the RAS meeting, but Rhys Davids' opening remarks sound very like a riposte or an answer to doubts raised. If doubts were already circulating, this might offer an explanation as to why – assuming Willie Peppé *did* donate his box of jewels to the Society – they were subsequently removed from their premises, perhaps in 1907 when Rhys Davids (to all intents a Buddhist himself), stepped down as Honorary Secretary of the RAS. That Rhys Davids continued to support the authenticity of the Piprahwa excavation can be seen from remarks made in his book *Buddhist India*, published in 1903, in which he offered a new twist to Smith's 'two Kapilavastus' theory: 'The old Kapilavastu was probably at Tilaurakot. But Peppé's important discoveries at the Sakya Tope (at Piprahwa) may be the site of a new Kapilavastu built after the old city was destroyed by Vidudhabha.'

What can be said with certainty is that Willie Peppé left London with the thanks of Indology's great and good ringing in his ears and joined his family on holiday in Scotland. So far as is known he carried out no further excavations on the Birdpore Estate. However, the long shadows cast by the activities of Dr. Anton Führer continued to darken Piprahwa.

Rhys Davids was succeeded as Honorary Secretary at the RAS by the much less Buddhistically inclined John Faithful Fleet, ex-ICS, who belonged to an earlier generation than Smith and Hoey and was separated from them by the fact that he spent his Indian career in the Bombay Presidency. Fleet came out to Bombay in 1867, having studied Sanskrit at University College, London, under Professor Theodore Goldstücker – another of that remarkable band of German scholars who dominated Indology at that period. His duties as an administrator did not prevent Fleet from continuing his Indian studies, which brought him into the circle of Professor Bühler, who had preceded him to Bombay by four years, and other philologists at Bombay University. In 1883, thanks to General Cunningham, Fleet was appointed to the specially created post of Epigraphist to the Government of India, a position he held until the Epigraphical Department was closed down five years later. Besides co-editing the *Indian Antiquary*, Fleet's most important contribution to Indian studies was his work on Gupta inscriptions and early Indian chronology, scholarship that proved immensely valuable to Smith and other historians.

Fleet retired from the ICS in 1897 after thirty years service, and a decade later took over from Rhys Davids at the RAS, where he exploited his privileged position to the full, particularly when it came to publishing in the *Journal of the Royal Asiatic Society*, which carried in excess of ninety articles by him between 1907, when he took over from Rhys Davids, and his death in 1917. A cursory analysis of these contributions reveals that for a period of approximately five years commencing in 1905 his scholarship was focused on early inscriptions written in Brahmi. His starting point was the Piprahwa inscription, on which he published no less than three readings in as many years. In 1905, by starting his translation at a different point in the ring of Brahmi lettering from his predecessors, he came up with:

> Of the brethren of the Well-famed One, together with children and wives this receptacle of relics of Buddha, the Blessed One of the Sakyas.

This reading provoked a strong response from a number of Continental scholars, beginning with the French philologist Silvain Lévi, who argued in *Journal des Savants* that the Piprahwa relics were actually those of the Sakyas slaughtered by King Vidudhaba and that the correct reading of the inscription should be: 'C'est ici les reliques des Çākyas, frères bienheureux du saint Bouddha, avecs leurs soeurs, leurs fils et leurs femmes [Here are the relics of the Sakyas, blessed brothers of the saint Buddha, with their sisters, their sons and their wives]'. Fleet was forced to revise his reading, now declaring, in line with Lévi, that the relics could not be those of Buddha Sakyamuni: 'The record in fact commemorates ... an enshrining of relics, not of Buddha himself as his hitherto been believed, but of his kinsmen, with their wives and children and unmarried sisters. And now we see the meaning of the curious articles, numbering more than seven hundred, which were found in the stupa along with the inscribed vase.'

To arrive at this conclusion Fleet had to reinterpret two key words: *sakiyanam* and *sukiti*. The first, he declared, did not relate to the Sakya clan at all but could only be a noun or adjective expressing a relationship: 'Discarding the suggestion which I made on the previous occasion, I find the natural meaning of the word *sakiya*, as used here in one of the ordinary meanings which belong to it as the Pali form of the Sanskrit, *svakiya*, own, meaning belonging to oneself'. As for *sukiti*, Fleet took this to mean 'possessed of good fame' and so 'a special appellation of Buddha, used here in a more or less sentimental or poetical fashion, to denote him as "the Well-famed One". While he had been unable to find such a word used as an epithet for the Buddha in Buddhist literature, he had found in the *Mahavastu* in a list of such names ending in *kirti*, so it might well have been a local appellation.

But this now raised the ire of two more French scholars: the eminent and by now elderly French Orientalist Auguste Barth, who had published critical remarks on British archaeology in India and had a reputation as a sceptic, and his more junior colleague Emile Senart. The latter now intervened to defend the interpretation towards which he believed the late Prof. Bühler been working at the time of his death, one in which the word *sukiti* was to be read as a personal name in the genitive. Thus the inscription should read:

> This receptacle of relics of the blessed Buddha of the Śakyas (is the pious gift) of the brothers of Sukirti, with their sons and with their wives.

M. Auguste Barth took the same view but had a lot more to say:

> Dr. Fleet accepts, in effect, Professor Rhys Davids' now so improbable interpretation of *Sukiti* as a designation of the Buddha; from Professor Lévi he takes over the latter's general conclusion that we have to deal with the relics of the victims of the massacre. But then *Sakiyanam* at the end can no longer be an ethnical name, as 'the Sakyas of the Buddha' would have no sense in any language. So he makes it an adjective, representing it as from the Sanskrit *Savakiya*, '*suus proprius*' with the mean of 'relations, kinsman'. … On this frail basis Dr. Fleet would build an entire long chronological edifice.

Barth proposed the following reading:

> This receptacle of relics of the blessed Buddha of the Śakyas (is the pious gift) of the brothers of Sukīrti, jointly with their sisters, with their sons and their wives.

He also went on to pour cold water over the entire business of relics, declaring that the Piprahwa inscription –

in no way tends, even indirectly, either to strengthen or to weaken the accounts of the distribution of the ashes, or their removal by Asoka, or of the destruction of Kapilavastu and the Sakyas; nor does it supply us with materials for constructing a chronological system; it simply makes us acquainted together with the name of an unknown personage, no doubt some local *raja*, with the existence (after so many others, teeth, frontal bone, alms bowl, hair, even the very shadow) of new relics of the great reformer, relics probably more ancient, and which [some] may, if so inclined, suppose more authentic, than any others.

Faced with this heavyweight assault, Fleet admitted defeat on the meaning of the word *sukiti*, declaring 'I now abandon my opinion that there is any reference to Buddha in the word in question' – while adding, as if *sotto voce*, 'But who is Sukiti?' So it came about that the opinion of M. Auguste Barth, who had the strongest claim to the mantle of the late Hofrath Georg Bühler, prevailed, and the majority of Western scholars came to accept his view that, even though the inscription was most probably 'not later than Asoka', it did not relate to the original Sakya deposition of Buddha Sakyamuni's relics.

Barth's reading continues to find general acceptance to this day. Writing in 1991 the German archaeologist and scholar Herbert Härtel noted that the opening *iyam salilanidhane budhasa bhagavate* was quite different from the usual Buddhist reliquary inscriptions from the Gandharan region and from Central India, all confidently dated to the second century BCE. He ascribed the inscription to 'a more familiar, a Sakya tribal connection'. However, he also believed that Piprahwa's steatite reliquary vases could not have been produced before the second century and the magnificent crystal casket not earlier than the first century BCE. More recently the distinguished American epigraphist Richard Salomon has stated that 'the weight of scholarly opinion nowadays is in favour of dating such early records as the Piprahwa, Sohgaura, and Mahasthan inscriptions as contemporary with or later than Asoka', while adding that he himself has little faith in dating on palaeographical grounds alone, 'especially when, as in the case of Mauryan period inscriptions, we have a very little corpus to work with. Such palaeographic dates are rough estimates at best, guesses at worst.'

None of these scholars dealt directly with the question of fakery, but the spectre of Anton Führer was never far away. Any hopes that the damage to Indian archaeology had been contained following his resignation were dashed when in January 1912 an article with the innocuous sounding title of 'On Some Brahmi Inscriptions in the Lucknow Museum' appeared in the *Journal of the Royal Asiatic Society*. Its author was the relatively youthful German scholar Dr. Heinrich Lüders, who had studied at Georg Bühler's old *alma mater* of Göttingen University before coming to Oxford to work in the Library of the Indian Institute from 1895 to 1899. Some time after his appointment as Professor of Indic Philology at Berlin University in 1909 Lüders made an extensive tour of Buddhist and Jain sites in India, in the course of which he visited Lucknow Museum. Three years earlier Vincent Smith had written to the *Journal of the Royal Asiatic Society* expressing concern at the state of affairs at the Lucknow Museum, where the new curator, Babu G. D. Ganguli, had complained to him that Dr. Führer's collection of Jain sculptures from Mathura remained uncatalogued and that 'a large number of the inscribed sculptures are lying scattered in the Museum without any sort of label on them'. Lüders duly inspected the sculptures, and on his return to Germany went into print to demonstrate with chapter and verse how someone had invented a number of inscriptions supposedly excavated at Ramnagar in Rohilkhand 1891–92, in some instances basing them on genuine inscriptions logged in *Epigraphia Indica*. More critically, Lüders also drew attention to some Brahmi characters inscribed on the back of a Jain statue from Mathura in the Lucknow Museum, done so crudely as to cause him to declare that 'I am not sure whether the pages of the *Epigraphia Indica* are really the proper pages for such a joke. … I cannot help declaring this inscription to be a forgery. The decision of the question who is responsible for it I leave to the readers of this paper'. Since Dr. Anton Führer had excavated the Jain statue in question at Mathura in 1891–92 and in his report had even drawn attention to the remarkably early date it carried, there remained little doubt as to who the culprit was.

In the late 1920s Willie and Ella Peppé retired from India, having sold their summer retreat in Mussoorie to a Sikh maharaja and after handing the management of the Birdpore Estate over to their second and third sons, Humphrey and Lionel. Willie's last public association with the Piprahwa excavation appears to have been in 1932, when he was due to address the Buddhist Society in London on the subject but was unable to do so after becoming seriously ill. His health continued to deteriorate and he died in Welshpool in 1936. Meanwhile in India, his two sons Humphrey and Lionel had married their cousins, the sisters Elfie and Vivienne Parry. Lionel subsequently joined the Royal Navy, leaving the running of the estate entirely in the hands of his elder brother. From a short note on the Piprahwa stupa written by Humphrey Peppé in retirement it is clear that the family's collection of relic jewels continued to draw pilgrims to Birdpore House, and to cause them problems: 'Many Buddhists from Burma and Ceylon, pilgrims from Lumbini, have been shown them, and also VIPs who have come to the Basti District or visited the Lumbini Garden. Some have tried to take them from me.'

In 1952, five years after Independence, the Government of India abolished the zamindari system and nationalised all such estates, paying minimal compensation to their owners in the form of bonds redeemable in annual increments over a period of forty years. According to Humphrey Peppé, 'this really tore the whole fabric of rural life in the Provinces. In many cases of bad zamindars this was beneficial to the villagers, but in others disastrous.' It marked the end of the Peppé connection with the estate which the family had established and built up over more than a century of struggle. The only way they could redeem their bonds was to sell them at half their face value. They also sold what little property was left to them, including Birdpore House, which became a Government Inspection Bungalow providing accommodation for touring government officers. Humphrey Peppé was allowed to rent three rooms on the ground floor while he stayed behind in India in an attempt to secure the compensation money due to them. During this same period the Piprahwa area came under the ownership of the Archaeological Survey of India by compulsory purchase.

Just before Christmas 1956 Peppé was asked to vacate his rooms for VIPs who were due to arrive on 25 December. He went to stay with friends but on returning home on Boxing Day found Birdpore House still very much occupied. 'I found the house swarming with VIPs, officials, police and all the children from the nearby bazaars and villages,' he afterwards recalled. 'I think there were thirty-eight cars parked on our one time tennis lawn, apart from numerous tents etc. However, it was worth it.' The VIPs turned out to be the young Dalai Lama and the Panchen Lama, who were on a pilgrimage tour of India as part of the celebrations for the 2,500th anniversary of Buddha Sakyamuni, as calculated by the Tibetan calendar:

> I asked the District Magistrate how I was expected to greet him, the God-King. He suggested the ordinary Indian salutation, both hands raised almost to the level of the face, with palms together and fingers extended. He introduced me to the Dalai Lama, who in the most friendly way took one of my hands in both of his, and put me at my ease immediately; the Panchen Lama followed his example. The former was quite a young man of about twenty-one, I think, of Mongolian type, about the same height as myself, dressed in a sombre dark reddish brown robe of thick woollen material, draped off one shoulder. He was clean shaven and his head very closely cropped all over.

The two Tibetan leaders had come to Birdpore to venerate the Piprahwa stupa before moving on to Lumbini, but they also asked to see the jewels in the Peppés' possession: 'They spoke through an interpreter but evidently understood a great deal of English. They were both charming, and showed a great interest in the objects I had to show them.'

Three year later Mrs Elfie Peppé was spending a last Christmas with her husband in his rented rooms at Birdpore House when the Dalai Lama paid a second visit. This was a year after the Dalai Lama had fled Tibet in the wake of the failed Tibetan uprising against the Chinese occupation. 'He seemed extremely interested in everything Western,' recalled Elfie Peppé of their meeting –

The ancient bas-relief of Queen Mayadevi giving birth to Buddha Sakyamuni, photographed at Lumbini by Neil Peppé in 1958. The round white objects are flower offerings left by pilgrims. *(Courtesy of Neil Peppé)*

asking innumerable questions about the history of the estates, the countries in Europe we had visited, and our intended voyage back to England. I offered him an enlarged photograph that my son Neil had taken of the ancient stone carving depicting Buddha's birth, which was in the temple he had just seen that afternoon [at Lumbini], and he insisted that we both sign our names on the back, with the date, and – making a little joke – even the time … There was about him a spirituality, yet with a warm friendliness, which impressed me strongly.

Soon after the Dalai Lama's visit the Peppés left Birdpore and India for good.

In February 1962, after a gap of more than six decades, the Archaeological Survey of India returned to the Nepal Tarai to carry out a survey at and around Lumbini, at the request of His Majesty's Government of Nepal. The person deputed was the then Superintendent and later Director of the ASI, Mrs. Debala Mitra. In February 1962 she and her party set up a base camp at Lumbini and after making a thorough survey of the area, during which they examined no less than thirty-six sites, they settled on two of them: Lori-Kudan and Tilaurakot. The site at Lori-Kudan, just south of Taulihawa town, had last been surveyed by P. C. Mukherji and, on the basis of its four large mounds, identified by him as 'the famous Nyagrodha Monastery, where Suddhodana received his son as the Buddha' and where the Sakyamuni's aunt and step-mother Prajapati had presented him with a gold-threaded robe. Debala Mitra's findings disappointed those expecting evidence of early Buddhist occupation, for her main conclusion was that the imposing and finely decorated buildings uncovered were 'the remains of three Brahminal temples … none … earlier than the eighth century A. D.' She found no inscriptions or dateable objects and her report was subsequently criticised as quite literally super-ficial by Nepali archaeologists, in that most of her excavation work had been restricted to clearance of the mounds and had not gone deeper than ground level. Since then no further excavation work has been carried out at this important site to prove or disprove its earlier Buddhist credentials. As far as the Lumbini Development Trust is concerned Lori-Kudan remains the site of the Nyagrodha Monastery.

Moving on to Tilaurakot in March of the same year – a timing that would have been unthinkable even two decades earlier but was now possible thanks to DDT and paludrine – Mitra dug a hundred-foot trench that cut though a section of the enclosure's northern rampart and into a part of the Kot's interior. The trench uncovered no structures other than a number of terracotta ring wells. The shards of pottery recovered from the trench included significant amounts at the lowest level of the distinctive black early pottery found in North India known to archaeologists as Northern Black Polished Ware or NBPW. Mitra's meticulous analysis of these and other artefacts led her to conclude that while 'the settlement of the town may go back to about the 6th century BC, if not earlier', the occupation of the area excavated had not begun until the third century BCE, with few signs of occupation continuing after the start of the Christian era. Although a number of coins were found, only two could be dated – to the first and second centuries BCE. Almost 200 human or animal terracotta figurines – of which more than fifty were of elephants – were ascribed to the same period. Also found in large quantities were beads, mostly of terracotta and bone but including glass, agate, rock-crystal, carnelian, chalcedony, garnet, amethyst, jasper and topaz. Superficially these invite comparison with those found at Piprahwa in 1898 but none come close to matching the delicate lapidary work that is such a distinctive feature of the Piprahwa treasure.

Mrs. Mitra's findings came as a great shock to Nepal's still fledgling Department of Archaeology, which immediately began planning an excavation programme using its own domestic archaeologists. These began at Tilaurakot in 1967 under the leadership of the Department's most senior officer, Jara Nanda Mishra, and continued under Babu Krishna Rijal, with additional excavation being undertaken by a Japanese team from Rissho University. Their work, spread over a decade, was summarised by B. K. Rijal as the discovery of 'a net-work of the part of Suddhodana's palace complex. ... The bastions and watchtowers ... are comparable to ancient cities in India dating to the eighth–sixth century BC' – conclusions criticised by Western archaeologists as utterly untenable. Nor did these conclusions do any favours to the early work carried out by J. N. Mishra, in the course of which he uncovered two well-constructed stupas in the jungle less than half a mile north of Tilaurakot which became known as the *jodi* or 'twins'. The largest he found to have been constructed in four phases, beginning in the fourth century BCE and ending in the second century BCE.

What Mishra also demonstrated was that Mrs. Mitra had been extremely unlucky in the placing of her trench, for his own work showed extensive occupation of the site during the Mauryan, Sunga and Kushan periods, and, in particular, a great deal of strengthening of the walls and their four gates during the Kushan era. Although evidence of earlier occupation was limited, Mishra established nine levels of occupation at Tilaurakot, beginning in about 700 BCE – a date that his successor sought to push back by several centuries with no real supporting evidence. Rajal's one undisputed coup was his unearthing in 1973 of a hoard of thirty-one silver punch-marked coins in a trench just outside the western ramparts. Although an exact chronology of North Indian punch-marked coins based on the various symbols stamped on them has still to be agreed upon, Rajal was probably on firm ground in asserting that the coins ranged from pre- to post-Mauryan, and equally correct in stating that they demonstrated that in the third and second centuries BCE the inhabitants of the town within Tilaurakot's walls had enjoyed 'a comfortable urban life with sound economic base marked by organised trade and commerce'.

It was at this point that nationalist archaeology first reared its head, beginning with Mrs Debala Mitra's book *Buddhist Monuments*, published in 1971, in which she wrote that the city of Kapilavastu remained unidentified: 'Although we explored a large part of the area which formed part of the ancient country of Kapilavastu and excavated extensively Kodan and limitedly Tilaurakot, we did not find anything in favour of the identification of Tilaurakot with Kapilavastu'. She went on to argue in favour of Kapilavastu being on the Indian side of the border: 'The inscription on the reliquary found within the main stupa at Piprahwa coupled with Piprahwa's correspondence with Fa-hien's [Faxian's] bearing and distance of Kapilavastu in relation to Lumbini raises a strong presumption for Piprahwa and its surrounding villages like Ganwaria being the site of Kapilavastu'. The conflicting literary evidence from Xuanzang and Faxian Mitra resolved by the simple expedient of repositing the Nyagroda complex *north* of Kapilavastu, in defiance of both Xuazang's and Faxian's directions which had placed it on the south side. 'Nyagrodharama represents Piprahwa,' she wrote, so it followed that 'the remains of Kapilavastu are to be sought in the mounds immediately around Piprahwa and not in the distant site of Tilaurakot.'

From a strictly archaeological viewpoint there were solid grounds for excavating at Piprahwa and near the neighbouring village of Ganwaria just to the south, where 'ancient habitation mounds' were covered in pottery shards that included NBP ware. As for Piprahwa itself, Mitra went on to declare: 'Intensive excavation in the monasteries at Piprahwa is likely to yield some monastic seals or sealings which usually furnish the name of the establishment. If they are found, they will prove conclusively [the] identity of Piprahwa and the adjoining sites with Kapilavastu or otherwise.'

Even before these astonishingly prescient words had appeared in print Mitra's colleague, K. M. Srivastava, Superintending Archaeologist of the ASI's Mideastern Circle, had begun work at Piprahwa, driven, he would afterwards aver, by a 'firm belief in the identification of Kapilavastu.' His 'primary objective,' he declared, 'was to locate the lost town of ancient Kapilavastu and thereby settle the long standing controversy.' This absolute conviction of Srivastava's that he was destined to locate Kapilavastu was uncomfortably similar to the beliefs that drove Führer some seventy decades earlier. Coming so hard on the heels of Mitra's remarks, it inevitably led to cries of 'foul' from India's neighbour to the north. It also demands that his results be examined with the utmost scientific rigour.

The first thing that Srivastava's extremely professional excavation of the Piprahwa stupa exposed was a *pradakshinapath* in the form of a ring of burnt bricks, which had been subsequently been built over. The uncovering of this ring allowed Srivastava to determine the exact centre of the stupa, and a well was then dug down to reach the point where in 1898 Willie Peppé had located the giant stone coffer. 'That Peppé was satisfied with the massive stone box, which contained the inscribed casket, was apparent from the cutting,' wrote Srivastava. 'Certain concrete evidences

The bricks covering the two chambers before their opening, showing how the chambers had been set into the earth below the brick stupa, the lowest layers of which can be seen above. From K. M. Srivastava's *Excavations from Piprahwa and Ganwaria*, 1996. *(Courtesy of K. M. Srivastava)*

were present before Peppé, which led him to believe that there were no relics below. Both the circular pipe, which led him to the box, and the burnt-brick courses of the stupa came to an end. Peppé, therefore, could not imagine earlier relics below.'

Srivastava chose to go on digging, and almost immediately came across two sets of six large bricks laid flat and separated by a 65-centimetre-wide section of yellow clay, each brick measuring 42 × 80 × 37 centimetres. Further excavation revealed that these bricks covered two small chambers:

> When the three courses of brick of the northern chamber were removed, a soapstone casket came to light. By the side of the casket and separated by a brickbat, one red ware dish with incurved sides

The broken red ware and the undamaged soapstone reliquary casket *in situ* after the opening of the northern brick chamber. From K. M. Srivastava's *Excavations from Piprahwa and Ganwaria*, 1996. *(Courtesy of K. M. Srivastava)*

and wide mouth was observed. The dish was covered by another dish of the same size ... broken into three pieces. ... The maximum diameter of the casket was 7 cm, whereas of the dish 26 cm. The height of the casket was 12 cm. It contained charred bones.

In the southern chamber two red dishes of the same type as before and again laid one on top of the other were uncovered, both smashed into pieces. Two courses of brick lower was a second soapstone casket considerably bigger than the first, its lid broken. Here, too, charred bones were found inside. The red dishes in both brick chambers appeared to be empty, although Srivastava thought that they 'probably contained ash'.

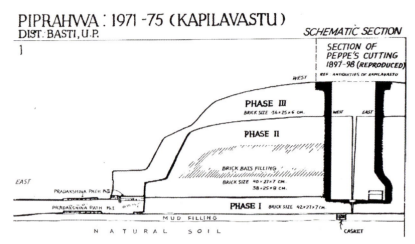

Srivastava's cross-section of the Piprahwa stupa, showing the three phases of its construction and Peppé's earlier trench. From K. M. Srivastava's *Excavations from Piprahwa and Ganwaria*, 1996. *(Courtesy of K. M. Srivastava)*

It was Srivastava's view that the two soapstone relic caskets were 'contemporaneous to the early period of Northern Black Polished Ware, which could be dated to fifth–fourth century B. C., i.e. earlier in date than the inscribed relic casket discovered by Peppé at a higher level. The dishes found in the chamber confirmed the above-mentioned date.' This generous dating enabled him to declare categorically that 'The finding of the earlier caskets established that the stupa in which they were found was built by the Sakyas over the mortal remains at Kapilavastu, sometime in fifth century B. C.. This indication was already available in the inscription on the casket found by Peppé, which mentioned both Buddha and his community Sakya.'

More convincingly, Srivastava was able to show that the Piprahwa stupa had been built in three distinct phases, marked by diminishing brick sizes, the first twelve layers of the largest bricks having being laid on piled-up earth, with the two brick chambers at the centre. He was equally convincing in arguing that the third and final phase of building, when the base of the stupa was converted from a circular shape into a square one, niches added for Buddha images, and the height of the central dome increased, had taken place during the Kushan era.

A year later Srivastava and his team turned their attentions to the complex of buildings surrounding the stupa, first unearthed by W. C. Peppé and subsequently by P. C. Mukherji. Srivastava was at this stage still convinced that this was Kapilavastu and, as he afterwards admitted, began work on the large quadrangular monastery on the stupa's north-eastern flank 'with the primary objective of unearthing inscriptional evidence to confirm the belief', a perfectly reasonable statement, given that inscriptions in the form of monastic seals have helped to identify a number of major Buddhist sites. Re-excavating the several structures beside the stupa Srivastava established four structural phases in their building, each more elaborate and larger in scale than the last. It became clear from the amount of charred wood uncovered and from a mound of burnt rice found in one of the cells that the complex had been abandoned after a devastating fire, which Srivastava assigned to 'the beginning of the fourth century or the last quarter of the third century A. D.'. But what was undoubtedly the high point of the excavation was the discovery in March 1973 of two seals and no less than seventy-seven sealings on baked terracotta tablets fired bright red, mostly found scattered in cells in the main monastery adjoining the stupa at its north-east corner.

The writings or pictographs on the two seals could not be identified but when the sealings had been cleaned they were found to bear a variety of legends. Of these, thirteen sealings carried the same legend in Kushan Prakrit script, which according to Srivastava read: *'Maha kapilavastu bhikshu sanghasa'*, or, 'Of the community of Buddhist monks of great Kapilavastu'. Even more remarkably, no less than twenty-two sealings carried all or parts of another slightly more elaborate legend. According to Srivastava, this read: *'Om devaputra vihare Kapilavastusa bhiku sanghasa'*. The first word is the sacred primordial syllable *om* found in Hindu and Buddhist mantras. The word *devaputra* translates as 'son of the gods/divine son', an honorific known to have been used as a title for the Kushan kings Kanishka (c. 126–150 CE) and his successor Huvishka (c. 150–193 CE), so that the entire legend reads

'*Om* of the community of monks of Kapilavastu in the monastery of Kanishka/Huvishka'.

Srivastava had no doubts as to what the sealings represented, declaring that he had made 'an epoch-making discovery by settling the location of ancient Kapilavastu, which had been eluding the archaeologists for more than a hundred years'. However, the manner in which his findings were initially suppressed by the ASI led Srivastava himself to complain that, far from receiving 'world wide acclaim', his discovery was 'deprived of the recognition and remained behind the curtain. Instead of any applause for the meritorious work, the news continued to be a victim of suppression for a period of three years'. Whatever the reasons for this suppression (which seems to have involved internal professional jealousies), they raised doubts in the minds of the international community of epigraphists, doubts which could easily have been resolved by allowing the sealings to be subjected to full academic scrutiny. Instead, a combination of official interference and misplaced national pride have quite unnecessarily cast yet another shadow on Piprahwa, unnecessary because even though grumbles about lack of transparency continue to this day, the sheer number of sealings involved make it impossible that Srivastava's readings are wide of the mark, certainly as far as the all-important letters *ka-pi-la-va* go. They demonstrate beyond doubt is that the monastic complex at Piprahwa at the time of the Kushans was intimately linked with the name of Kapilavastu. 'The Kushan kings were closely attached to the sacred site,' Srivastava believed. 'It was only under their patronage that the stupa and the eastern monastery were embellished in their third stage of construction ... during the time of Kushan emperor Kanishka, and all viharas surrounding the Great Stupa seem to have been amalgamated into one composite *Bhikhshu Sangha*, which assumed the title of *Maha Kapilavastu Bhikhshu Sangha*'.

But, of course, the Piprahwa stupa and its surrounding monastic complex did not in themselves constitute the city of Kapilavastu, which Srivastava now sought among the high mounds at nearby Ganwaria. A trial trench cut in 1972 produced such a rich crop of shards and artefacts that Shrivastava and his colleagues committed themselves to a full-scale excavation of a site that extended over 1,000 yards from north to south and about 900 from east to west.

The two largest mounds had been ransacked, either for their bricks or for buried treasure. Despite this loss, the excavations revealed them to be viharas very similar in structure and size to the eastern monastery at Piprahwa. Elsewhere there were shrines and what Srivastava categorised as residential structures, but not enough to demonstrate that in its final phase this had had been anything other than very extensive religious complex. Srivastava then set out to establish what lay under the bricks, sinking deep trenches at a number of points to expose the earlier city which he believed had been inhabited by the Sakyas. The results led him to conclude that Ganwaria had been through four distinct periods of habitation:

> Period I, dateable between 800 and 600 B. C., was characterised by fine grey ware; black polished ware; red ware vases and dishes with reddish rim and greyish bottom; Period II was distinguished by the appearance of Northern Black Polished Ware, a red ware painted in black horizontal bands and other associated wares. … A date of between 600 and 300 B. C. was assigned to the period; Period III belonged to Sunga times with its beginning in the second century B. C. and end by the beginning of the Christian era … characterised by numerous variety of characteristic terracotta figurines; Period IV was characteristically Kushana, dated from the beginning of the Christian era to the close of the third century. Buddha heads and other terracottas in large quantity, Kushana coins, beads of terracotta and semi-precious stones and terracotta sealings were the principal antiquities.

The news of Srivastava's discovery of Kapilavastu inside Indian territory was finally broken by the *Times of India* on 24 January 1976 under the headline 'Buddha's Lost City of Kapilavastu Found'. Much was made of the relics found in the two brick chambers which, after being put on special display at the ASI's headquarters in New Delhi, went on a three-month tour of Sri Lanka. According to Srivastava, his identification of Piprahwa-Ganwaria as Kapilavastu caused 'a great uproar among a particular set of scholars', by which he meant chiefly archaeologists and politicians in Nepal, where the news was received with outrage and talk of an Indian plot to deprive Nepal of its hitherto undisputed claim to be the homeland of the Buddha. But there were also international scholars on hand to point out major flaws in Srivastava's case. The most glaring of these was that during the Kushan period when the Kapilavastu seals were made the Ganwaria site was patently a large monastic site and not a city. There was also the awkward fact that the Ganwaria site had no city wall and, indeed, no eastern gate as described by Faxian. Furthermore, it was on the wrong side of the sites linked by both Chinese travellers to Buddhas Krakuchanda and Kanakamuni. For Siravastava's case to be accepted, much clearer evidence of Gotihawa as a city and not a religious site has to be forthcoming, as well as the discovery of an Asokan pillar or two to the south and west.

These concerns have not prevented the ASI from finishing off its admirable restoration of the sites of Piprahwa and Ganwaria with signs declaring them to be Buddha Sakyamuni's Kapilavastu. Nor have they prevented the state of Uttar Pradesh from rebranding that area as Kapilavastu and the Indian Tourist Development Corporation from promoting it as such, with scores of Indian tour operators now including Piprahwa as such in their 'Footsteps of the Buddha' pilgrim tours.

The response of the Government of Nepal is most clearly seen in the exaggerated claims made for Tilaurakot as Kapilavastu made in B. K. Rijal's *Archaeological Remains of Kapilavastu, Lumbini, Devadaha* published in 1979.

The result of two countries claiming Kapilavastu as their own has been to cast what Herbert Härtel has called 'a highly deplorable political shadow', with Nepal and India indulging in a 'tug-of-war' in which 'publications of the subject have partly left the scholarly level, and prejudices suppress the argumentation'. That is the situation today, although Härtel's fellow countryman Max Deeg has more recently (2003) conducted further archaeological and epigraphical research which has led him to declare his conviction that 'the Kapilavastu which the Chinese pilgrims Faxian and

Xuanzang saw is the modern site of Tilaurakot on the Nepalese side of the border.' What helped Deeg arrive at his conclusions are two recent programmes of research. The first was a geophysical survey of the Tilaurakot site carried out in 1997 by a team from Bradford University led by Professors Robin Coningham and Armin Schmit. Using ground-penetrating radar that produced sub-surface images, they were able to reveal the existence of a major street running east and west through the site, with side streets running off it at right angles, clear evidence of a town or city. Returning three years later, the team excavated a trench in the centre of the site and collected pottery shards at the lowest level of habitation which they dated to between 1000 and 600 BCE. They also collected samples for carbon-14 dating, the results of which after calibration gave a 95 per cent probability for a dating of 760–370 BCE, as well as a strong lower boundary peak of 541 BCE with a 92 per cent probability – readings which could hardly be more perfect for those looking for hard archaeological evidence that this site was occupied throughout the sixth and fifth centuries BCE but then ceased to be occupied, at least for a period, early in the fourth century BCE. Yet the fact remains that Tilaurakot still awaits the large-scale excavation its importance demands. Only then will we know its true significance in the story of Buddha Sakyamuni.

The second advance was the thorough survey of the countryside between the Banganga River and Lumbini carried out in 2001–02 by an Italian team led by Professor Giovanni Verardi of the University of Naples. Using GPS and remote sensing techniques, Verardi's team identified no less than 136 archaeological sites in that area, of which no less than 110 were previous unknown. The team also carried out excavations at and around the Asokan pillar at Gotihawa, showing conclusively that the pillar and associated brick stupa had indeed been raised in the Asokan era, as might be expected, and restored in the Kushan era. They found no trace of any mud stupa preceding the one built of fire-baked bricks and no trace of any relic deposit, confirming that this was a memorial rather than a funerary site. Settlement in that area had begun in the eighth century BCE.

What lingering doubts remain about the authenticity of

Tilaurakot as Kapilavastu are very largely due to a failure of will on the part of the Lumbini Development Trust, which has achieved little in the twenty-three years of its existence beyond alienating the local Madeshis and saddening millions of Buddhists the world over. Nepal's Department of Archaeology also bears some responsibility even though it can plead lack of funds and political interference from above. As for His Majesty's Government of Nepal, retired ministers can point to far more important issues they had to deal with, not least a civil war and empty coffers, but the fact remains that they repeatedly came and saw and made promises and did nothing, this despite the fact that in 1997 UNESCO tried to shame the Government of Nepal into doing something by declaring Tilaurakot a World Heritage Site.

Tilaurakot as it is today would be immediately recognisable to P. C. Mukherji, for very little has changed since 1899. Cattle and buffalo roam at will across the site, people from the nearby village use it as a latrine and picnickers from Taulihawa see it as a convenient place to leave their rubbish. In the monsoon season pools of water flood the central 'palace' area and the western gate. The votive offerings of clay elephants and other creatures left by local Tharus at the little brick temple at the heart of the enclosure are the only signs that anyone cares. In the absence of any attempt at conservation the walls first exposed by Mukherji are crumbling away, while the bricks of the Eastern Gate provide souvenirs for overzealous pilgrims. But the painful fact is that very few pilgrims do go to Tilaurakot. No services exist to get them there and there are no services once they get there, so that only the most determined traveller makes the effort.

Now that the last in a line of royal so-called patrons has been shown the door of his palace things must change, for now a real opportunity has presented itself for Kapilavastu-Lumbini to be put firmly on the map – not just for visiting Buddhists and tourists, but for the local Madeshis and the Nepal Tarai, too. With bold, imaginative, politics- and corruption-free planning, funds could be raised from the Buddhist world not simply to restore and conserve Kapilavastu but to make the Kapilavastu-Lumbini area the Ankor Wat of Nepal, a site worthy of its glorious past.

The last words must go to Piprahwa and the relics uncovered there.

In 2001, the ghost of poor Anton Führer reappeared in the form of a complex conspiracy theory, conceived largely by an Englishman named Terence Phelps. Phelps went on the World-wide Web to make a number of claims based on extensive and impressive research, one of them being that the real Kapilavastu was to be found just inside Basti district midway between Basti and Gorakhpur at a site first explored by Archibald Carlleyle. Of greater relevance here is Phelps' assertion that not only the Piprahwa inscription but also the two Asokan pillar edicts at Lumbini and Nigliva Sagar are fakes and part of some elaborate hoax or conspiracy involving not just Dr. Führer but several of the individuals featured at length in these pages. These theories are available for inspection on the internet as *Lumbini on Trial: the Untold Story*. The detailed chapter and verse set down in the preceding pages should in themselves be enough to convince any fair-minded reader that any claims of forgery or conspiracy involving the 1898 excavation at Piprahwa are baseless.

In June 2004 came the rediscovery of the Buddhist Society's Piprahwa jewels, which indirectly led the present writer to the home of Neil Peppé, son of Humphrey and grandson of Willie. He had in his possession what remained of the Piprahwa jewels granted to the family by the Government of the NWP&O in 1898, as well as various papers and photographs, of which extensive use has been made throughout this account. One curious item was a sealed glass test tube half full of carbonised or petrified rice grains, labelled and bearing the inscription 'Rice found at the Piprahwa stupa, discovered by W. C. Peppé, Birdpur Estate in 1889. The rice appears to have petrified'. Neil Peppé believed these grains had been collected by his grandfather from the bricks of the stupa, which he remembered as being full of rice husks. A sample was made available by their owner for radio carbon testing at RCD Locking and the Radiocarbon Laboratory of the University of Groningen and produced an impressive result of a 65.6 per cent probability level for 55–135 CE, and a 95.4 per cent probability level for 20–220 CE, in other words, slap-bang in the middle of the Kushan era, and the kingship of King Kanishka.

Also among Neil Peppé's treasures was a loose collection of larger and cruder stones and beads which he did not recall had ever been boxed up by his grandfather into display cabinets like the rest. Among them was a small object scarcely one centimetre high, white enamelled and rounded at one end and black and jagged at the other. This on closer inspection appeared to be part of a molar tooth. It was taken with some excitement to the Natural History Museum in London where it was examined by Robert Kruszynski of the Human Origins Group, who declared it to be non-human and probably the cheek tooth of a piglet. It was subsequently sent to the Advanced Microscopy Centre at the University of Leicester, where it was examined by a forensic pathologist who gave his opinion that it was 'non-human and could possibly be canine'. The tooth was then sent to carbon-14 testing but insufficient material was available and it was therefore decided that the test should be abandoned.

It is this writer's opinion that this tooth fragment is something of a red herring, and that it and the other loose items with which it was mixed came not from the Piprahwa stone coffer at all but from a badly smashed soapstone vase full of clay uncovered by Willie Peppé at an earlier stage of his excavation – at a depth of ten feet and just before he reached the top of the central 'pipe'. Peppé had described the contents of this smashed vase as 'some beads, crystals, gold ornaments, cut stars etc', but no further reference was ever made to either pot or contents. The inference has to be that Peppé did not connect them with the much finer jewels and beads from the coffer and simply put them to one side. Again, it is this writer's view that the animal tooth fragment and the attendant items should be ascribed to the third and final (Kushan) phase of the rebuilding of the Piprahwa stupa. Not only do the jewels and beads match the larger and clunkier items found elsewhere in India in reliquary vases from the Kushan period but that was also a time when Buddhist relic worship had developed into a cult not unlike Christian relic worship in Medieval Europe when 'fakes' of saints' bones abounded.

At about this same time Terence Phelps gained an ally in Andrew Huxley of the Law School at the School of Oriental and African

Studies (SOAS), London. Huxley presented a paper at SOAS in January 2006 entitled 'A fraudulent scholar in Burma: Rev. Dr. Anton Führer (1853–1930)' in which he highlighted the Führer-U Ma correspondence. Misleading reports of a 'Buddha tooth' and Neil Peppé's collection had now begun to appear in national newspapers and on the internet. For want of scholarly examination the claims of the conspiracy theorists were in danger of being accepted at face value. With the support of the Royal Asiatic Society, this writer organised an informal one-day conference specifically to consider all aspects of the Piprahwa excavations. Thanks to the kindness of Viscount David Lascelles, this was held at the new conference centre at Harewood House, Yorkshire, on 8 July 2006.

Among those present were three scholars of international repute: the historian Richard Gombrich, Boden Professor of Sanskrit at Oxford, and the epigraphists Richard Salomon, Professor of Asian Languages at the University of Washington, and Oskar von Hinüber of the University of Freiburg. Among those invited to present papers were Terence Phelps, Andrew Huxley and Neil Peppé, the latter presenting a sequence of previously overlooked letters written by Vincent Smith and Anton Führer to Willie Peppé during the time Peppé was working on the excavation. Since Phelps's paper 'The Piprahwa Deceptions' and Huxley's 'Georg Bühler's death and its implications for Piprahwa' have not been published it would be improper to comment on them here. However, it has to be said that, with the exception of these two speakers, those who saw and heard the whole evidence presented and the opinions of the highly qualified historians, archaeologists and epigraphists present, came away with no doubts as to the validity of the Piprahwa excavation of 1898. Here it is worth highlighting some closing remarks made by Prof. Salomon on the wording of the Piprahwa inscription:

> Normally, a clever forger will borrow terminology and style from genuine inscriptions, but the relatively few reliquary inscriptions that were known at the time of the discovery of the Piprahwa inscription have no significant textual resemblance to it. The Piprahwa inscription is unusual, for example, in using *nidhane* as the

term for 'reliquary' or 'container,' which is nowhere else so used. If a scholarly forger was making up a fake inscription, he would have been likely to have borrowed a term such as *samudaga* or *mañjūṣa* from the recently discovered Bhattiprolu inscriptions. ... Forgeries tend to be either blatant imitations of genuine inscriptions, or totally aberrant texts, and if the Piprahwa inscription were a forgery – which I am certain is not the case – it would belong to the latter category. But this kind of forgery can be convincing only if done by a very clever and learned forger, and I do not see any evidence that A. A. Führer, the suspect in this case, was capable of this. Despite its anomalous character in comparison to other relic inscriptions, the Piprahwa inscription rings true in all regards. Its language, for example, is a good specimen of Ardhamāgadhī [regional or archaic Maghadi], as manifested, for example, by the dialectally characteristic epenthesis in the last word, *sakiyānaṃ* = Sanskrit *śākyānāṃ*. It would have taken a very brilliant linguist indeed to come up with such an excellent imitation of this little-documented language, over one hundred years ago; this is in theory not impossible, but it seems very, very unlikely. In short, it is hard to imagine that Führer, or anyone else for that matter, could have created such a convincing forgery.

Whatever Anton Führer did in Lucknow or in the Nepal Tarai, and whether or not his behaviour affected Prof. Georg Bühler in any way, the excavation carried out by William Claxton Peppé was not interfered with in any way – not by Führer, nor by Smith nor any other person. The finds and the inscription were genuine, as are those uncovered by K. M. Srivastava at that same site. Which begs the final question: what was the Piprahwa stupa and its contents all about?

The best hypothesis we are ever likely to arrive on the basis of what we know at present at is that the Kapilavastu in which the Prince Siddhartha grew to manhood was a settlement enclosed within a walled palisade beside the modern River Banganga, pretty much where the ruins of Tilaurakot are today. The leaders of the Sakya and Koliya tribes lived in substantial longhouses or roundhouses of thatch and unplaned timber that fully exploited the natural resources available. The brick walls we see at Tilaurakot today are chiefly expressions of the piety of the Mauryan, Sunga and Kushan rulers who rebuilt Kapilavastu conscious of the weight of Buddhist oral history hanging over them. Few among those international historians and archaeologists who know the subject doubt that Tilaurakot is the city of Kapilavastu seen by Xuanzang, and what doubts remain can best be resolved when the scores of ancient sites currently lying neglected east of the River Banganga between Sagarwa lake and the Indian border have been properly excavated – to say nothing of the full-scale excavation of Tilaurakot by Nepali and international archaeologists working together, followed by full-scale conservation and sensitive reconstruction. Few among those same international scholars outside India doubt that the Ganwaria-Piprahwa complex is essentially a large Buddhist monastic site that came into its fullest development during the Kushan era, only to be largely abandoned following a fire or some catastrophic event towards the end of the third century CE.

If Faxian did indeed come to that same southern site a century later and mistook it for Kapilavastu, he found there '*neither king nor people. All was mound and desolation. Of inhabitants there were only some monks and a score or two of families of the common people*'. Earlier on his journey the local inhabitants or local guides had been able to direct him to the Maharaparinirvana sites of the Buddhas Krakuchanda and Kanakamuni, but here, at what he supposed was Kapilavastu, they had nothing to tell him of the site of the deposition of the Sakyas' share of Buddha Sakyamuni's ashes. Two centuries later the better-informed Xuanzang went through much the same process but did far better than Faxian in describing the pillars raised by Asoka honouring Buddhas Krakuchanda and Kanakamuni. Yet this is rather like Sherlock Holmes and the dog that failed to bark in the night. Both Faxian and Xuanzang failed to mention the site of the deposition of the Sakya's share of the Sakyamuni relics, despite the fact that their pilgrimages to Kapilavastu, Lumbini, Ramagrama and Kushinagar were primarily to honour Buddha Sakyamuni. Why? Not because it did not exist, but because *no one knew where it was*. The link with the past had been broken.

We have no reason to doubt the validity of the account of the division of the Buddha Sakyamuni relics from the funerary pyre given in the Maharaparinirvana *suttanta*, any more than there is to doubt the stories of Emperor Asoka's disinterment and redistribution of those same relics. There almost certainly was a deposition of a share of the Sakyamuni's remains in Sakya country and, if Sakyamuni's reported instructions were followed, that site was not at Kapilavastu city but at a prominent position beside a well-travelled highway or cross-roads. Patently, all knowledge of that site was lost at some time in Buddhist history, most likely with the social breakdown that came at the end of the Kushan era.

So now to an archaeological interpretation of Piprahwa Kot, where a number of conflicting issues have to be resolved in order to arrive at a coherent solution. There is no reason to doubt the compelling evidence of K. M. Srivastava's sealings found in the great monastery east of the stupa, showing that in the Kushan era this was a monastic site with royal patronage linked with Kapilavastu, just as there is no reason to doubt Srivastava's findings that the four religious buildings surrounding the stupa evolved with it in three main stages, culminating in the Kushan buildings we see today as restored by the ASI. This shows that not only the Kushans but their predecessors, too, held the Piprahwa stupa in high regard. Srivastava's excavation of the stupa also showed that the two brick chambers containing the lowest level of reliquaries had been laid into mud filling above the natural and undisturbed soil, suggested an original stupa of piled-up mud. That, too, is thoroughly convincing.

What are not so convincing are three particular claims made by Srivastava. The first is that the two soapstone reliquary vases from the two brick chambers predate the very similar soapstone reliquary vases found in Peppé's stone coffer. Srivastava offers no evidence to show that they do. All four vases are to all intents identical, almost certainly made at the same place at the same time. His second claim is that these same two soapstone vases found by him are 'contemporaneous to the early period of Northern Black Polished Ware, which could be dated to fifth–fourth century B. C.'. This has also to be rejected. It would be hard to find outside India any scholar of the early Buddhist period prepared to say that any of the small soapstone vases found in Buddhist stupas from Afghanistan down to Madras predate the second century BCE. What this means is that even Emperor Asoka, who died within two or three years of 235 BCE, is out of the frame, never mind anyone earlier.

Srivastava's third claim is that the two sets of red ware dishes found with the two soapstone reliquary vases are contemporaneous. This is not necessarily so. There is no reason why this red ware type should not predate the soapstone vases by at least a century. Srivastava offers no thoughts as to why these seemingly empty red dishes should have been there at all, but almost as an aside remarks that they may have contained ash. What this suggests is that the red dishes have a far better claim to have been the *original* reliquaries placed in the mud stupa than do the two soapstone vases.

This leads us on to a feasible scenario in which bone and ash relics are laid in a mud stupa, possibly as early as the end of the fifth century BCE. The original reliquary that contained these relics may not even have been the red dishes but something far simpler. A century later there is nothing to show that these are the Sakyas' share of the relics of Buddha Sakyamuni other than oral tradition. However, a decision is taken to act on that tradition and to preserve the mud stupa properly. The relics are placed in two red dishes with two similar dishes placed over them as covers. They are returned to their original hole in the mud stupa, which is now protected by chambers made up of large slabs of brick forty inches long and twenty-seven inches wide. A simple brick stupa, round but not necessarily dome-shaped, is laid over them, constructed of the same type of large bricks as those used for the two chambers. This first brick stupa can be described as early Mauryan period and falls comfortably within the reign of Asoka the Great.

Indeed, Emperor Asoka cannot be excluded absolutely from the secene. The archaeological evidence shows that he erected at least three pillars within walking distance of Piprahwa: one to Buddha Saykamuni at Lumbini; one to Buddha Kanakamuni now lying at Nigliva Sagar; and the third, most probably to Buddha Krakuchanda, at Gotihawa. Since the Lumbini pillar commemorates the site of Buddha Saykamuni's birth and Xuanzang records an Asokan pillar commemorating his death at Kushinagar and another pillar at Pataliputra commemorating the site of one of the eight deposition sites of Saykamuni's ashes, it is highly likely that Asoka also raised pillars at the other deposition sites, including that of the Sakyas.

The fact that neither Willie Peppé nor Babu Mukherji nor K. M. Srivastava found such an Asokan pillar at Piprahwa does not mean that such a pillar did not stand there 2,000 years ago. All three archaeologists saw no need to excavate the low ground immediately west of the stupa, mostly taken up with what was once a tank or ritual bathing pond. A column may well have toppled into the tank centuries ago, and even if such a column had been removed traces of its foundation would remain – a hypothesis which a geophysical survey could resolve without any need for digging.

But Emperor Asoka and the soapstone vases recovered by Peppé and Srivastava have nothing in common, for the general consensus among archaeologists outside India is that they cannot date from earlier than the second century BCE – which forces us to ask: who, then, built the great stone coffer with all its remarkable contents?

By the end of the third and the beginning of the second centuries BCE the Mauryan dynasty was already in decline before being brought to an abrupt end by Pusyamitra Sunga c. 185 BCE. Of Asoka's successors, not a great deal is known and very little supported by archaeological evidence. But there is one possible contender, albeit a shadowy one.

Asoka's eldest son was by his first wife, who was a Jain. He was named Kunala and because he rejected the Buddhism adopted by his father he was blinded, supposedly by Asoka's youngest wife, a Buddhist, and excluded from the line of succession. Asoka named as his successor a younger, Buddhist son, Dasarathu, but when Kunala's son, Samprati, came to court to plead for his father Asoka was so impressed by his manly character that he named him as Dasarathu's successor. When Asoka died c. 235 BCE he was duly succeeded by Dasarathu, who reigned for eight years before his death c. 227 BCE. His Jain nephew Samprati then took over the throne of Magadha – at which point the Jain, Brahminical and Buddhist accounts diverge widely. According to the Jain chronicle

Pataliputrakalpa, Samprati lived for fifty years and became to the Jains what his grandfather had been to the Buddhists: a model promoter of Jainism who built many new Jain temples and restored many old ones. He was followed by a cousin or nephew named Salisuka, who by Brahminical tradition, recorded in no less than three *Puranas* or ancient texts, was an evil man because he applied Asoka's Dharma and was duly punished by the gods by ruling for only a short time. But the Buddhist texts tell a quite different story. They claim that the Jain Samprati ruled for less than a decade before being succeeded by the noble Buddhist ruler Salisuka, who ruled for twice as long – from about 218 to 200 BCE – before being succeeded by the last three Mauryan kings, none of whom ruled for longer than eight years.

One interpretation of the differences in these accounts is the division of Asoka's empire, with Samprati and his predominantly Jain successors ruling in Gandhara and Western India, and Salisuka and his Buddhist descendants in Magadha and Central India. There is very little to go on here, except for the intriguing detail that Salisuka and his apparent rival Samprati were also known by a number of secondary, honorific names, greatly adding to the confusion of who was who and how long each ruled and where. Yet Salisuka was undoubtedly an ardent promoter of Buddhism and so emerges out of the fog of that period as the strongest contender for the role of the ruler who may, or may not, have involved himself in the stupa at Piprahwa.

There is no doubt at all that it was Asoka the Great who erected the Asokan rock and pillar edicts, because he puts his name to his work. But, despite what the *Asokavadhana* has to say on the matter, the emperor who ordered the eight Buddha Sakyamuni relic stupas to be opened and their contents redistributed may not have been Asoka, but one of his successors, the most likely candidate being his great-grandson (or grandson) Salisuka, possibly derived in part his name *suka* – 'shining one'.

The collective evidence from the Piprahwa stupa allows the possibility that no earlier than 200 BCE – and even that is pushing it to the chronological limit – a powerful raja whose suzerainty extended from the middle Ganges to the foothills of the Himalayas decided to carry on the sacred work of spreading the Dharma started by the revered Asoka by redistributing the relics of Buddha Sakyamuni. The raja orders the simple brick stupa erected by Asoka over the Sakyas' share of the relics south of Kapilavastu to be opened. The red ware dishes are taken from their brick chambers, all the bone fragments removed and the dishes returned to their chambers. However, on the ruler's instructions, a few bone parts are also returned, but now enshrined in two state-of-the-art caskets of soapstone, specially made for this purpose and turned on lathes, perhaps the first of their kind seen in these parts. The brick chambers are resealed.

But the ruler is growing old and knows he is coming to the end of his time. He wonders if he might have gained more merit had he himself had been present at the reburial of the Buddha Sakyamuni relics or even if sufficient respect was shown. So he leaves his splendid capital at Pataliputra, crosses the great river and sets out on the royal highway marked with the pillars his illustrious predecessor raised. He takes with him the finest gifts his kingdom can supply: a magnificent reliquary of crystal like no other; garlands of flowers, but of the kind that will never wither – not only of gold leaf, which are easily made, but of cut precious stones, the finest examples of lapidary work that the country has ever produced, the product of hours of the most delicate handicraft of which his jewellers are capable. Nothing to match these little carved flowers and leaves will be found in any other Buddhist reliquary on the sub-continent. He also takes with him a coffer hewn from one great block of stone from the same quarries on the Ganges upstream of Kashi from which his great-grandfather (or was it grandfather?) had his edict pillars cut. This, too, is unique. Nothing to match it will be found in any other stupa.

And when, finally, the ruler arrives in some state at the Sakya stupa he has also thought to bring with him two more of the new soapstone reliquary vases, containing just a few more bone fragments of the Sage of the Sakyas, so that he can make his own personal deposition. These, along with the crystal casket, the flowers of gold and precious stones, an assortment of other small treasures of various kinds, he himself places with the utmost reverence into the stone coffer at the centre of the round, flat, brick-built stupa that Asoka built. But then at the last minute the ruler realises that he has left no record of what is being deposited here. He calls for an inscription to be added to one of the reliquary caskets.

So now we come to the small matter of the Piprahwa inscription, undoubtedly genuine but perplexing in that it can be read as a relic either of Buddha Sakyamuni, or the Sakyas, or as a relic of Buddha Sakyamuni gifted by the relatives of someone called Sukiti. What we can also say about the inscription is that it was crudely done and lacked sophistication, suggesting either an early form of Magadhan Prakrit or a very provincial form of the same. Let us go with the second hypothesis.

The ruler calls for a scribe but none are immediately to hand so he has to fall back on a local man, an inexperienced oaf who does his best to scratch a few words around the top of the lid of one of the caskets. Inevitably, in his terror, he botches it. He misses the genitive in 'of the Sakyas' and has to add it above the line, and he is uncertain how the ruler's name should be spelled and is afraid to ask. So instead of writing 'This receptacle of relics of the Blessed Buddha is the precious gift of Salisuka and his brothers – *salisukanambhati* – with his sisters, sons and wives', he writes *sukitibhatinam*, which in 2,300 years' time will have learned men arguing over who exactly Sukiti was and why this was the gift not of Sukiti himself but of Sukiti's brothers, sisters, sons and wives.

But the words are written and the sweating scribe assures his lord that he has got it right. Never having had to trouble himself with reading or writing, the ruler has to take the man at his word. So the lid is placed on the stone coffer at the centre of the brick stupa, the ruler retires to his chariot or his palanquin and the clay plasterers and the bricklayers step forward to begin the work that millennia later will be identified by K. M. Srivastava as Phase II of the Piprahwa stupa. Three centuries later fresh orders come from another ruler, this time a king of the Kushans, ordering enlargements, with niches where statutes of Bodhisattvas can be placed, and the addition of a processional path so that pilgrims can more easily circumambulate the edifice. The surrounding monasteries are also enlarged and for two centuries the stupa and its attendant monasteries resound to the chants of monks and pilgrims before the fatal assault that ends in fire and smoke, followed by the encroachment of the jungle, the return of the sal forest and the pipal trees that will in time give this collection of mounds its particular name of Piprahwa.

Acknowledgements

My first thanks must go to Neil Peppé, family custodian of his grandfather William Claxton Peppé's treasures and papers, for whom life has not been easy these last few years, not least because of some of the issues discussed in this book. However, without his unstinting support this book could not have been written and my hope is that now the story has been told fully the cloud that has hung over the Peppé connection with Piprahwa will be lifted. I am also extremely grateful for the generous support that Viscount David Lascelles gave in hosting and feeding our little one-day conference on Piprahwa in June 1996 at his new conference centre at Harwood House, to say nothing of the support provided by the Harewood Trust's Director Terry Suthers and staff. Another valued supporter of the conference was John Eskenazi, of John Eskenazi Ltd, who made it possible for three organic artefacts from Piprahwa to be scientifically tested as far as that was possible. Also supporting the conference with its imprimatur was the Royal Asiatic Society, with the associated Society for South Asian Studies making it possible for Rakesh Tewari of the UP Archaeological Department to attend. Among those who spoke formally or informally at The Harewood Conference my special thanks to Prof. Richard Gombrich, Prof. Oskar von Hinüber, Prof. Robin Coningham, Dr. Madhuvanti Ghose, Dr. Julia Shaw, Dr. Lance Cousins, Dr. Rakesh Tewari, Dr. Andrew Huxley and Terry Phelps, and to Prof. Richard Salomon for allowing me to quote an extract from his unpublished paper. Another organisation which took an active interest in this project was the Buddhist Society of London; my special thanks its officers, staff and members, especially Dr. Desmond Biddulph, Louise Merchant and Tsugumi Ota, and, indirectly, Ven. S. Dhammika.

As to my research in the UK, my thanks to: Dr. Rosie Llewelyn-Jones of BACSA; Kathy Lazenblatt, Librarian at the Royal Asiatic Society; Dr. Gillian Evison, Curator, South Asian Collection, and Emma Mathieson, Curator, Modern Asian Collection, Indian Institute Library, at the Bodleian, Oxford; Françoise Simmons, Librarian, and Catherine Sutherland, Deputy Librarian, Faculty of Asian and Middle Eastern Studies, Cambridge; John Falconer, Curator of Photography, and Andrew Cook, Curator of Maps, British Library; Dr. Jennifer Howes, Curator, Helen George, Headley Sutton and his unfailing helpful front desk team, Tim Thomas, Paul Carter, John Chignoli and Dorian Leveque, Asia, Pacific and Africa Collection, British Library; Norman Cameron, Secretary, and staff at the Royal Society of Asian Affairs. Finally, my special thanks to Sheila Hoey Middleton and Lawrence Middleton for so kindly reading through my manuscript at an early stage, for making many helpful suggestions and corrections, for allowing me free use of their research, and for directing my own into some neglected corners.

In India my special thanks to Dr. K. M. Srivastava for allowing me to quote from his work and to reproduce some of his photographs and drawings of his Piprahwa excavations, and to Prof. Himashu Ray of Jawaharlal Nehru University for so generously making her research at the Indian National Archives available to me. My thanks also to: Ram Advani in Lucknow; Dr. Rakesh Tewari of the UP Archaeological Circle and to the Director and staff at the Lucknow Museum; and The Director, Archaeological Survey of India. My thanks to Aman Nath in Delhi for his hospitality, and to Anish Goel and other supporters of Shri S. N. Goenka's Vipassana movement for looking after me in Mumbai.

In Nepal my first thanks must go to the Rai family and, in particular, Binod Rai, who on this occasion to his more familiar services as expedition leader and organiser took many of the colour photographs for this book. Among the many in Kathmandu who helped me in my researches my thanks go to: Lisa Choegyal; Dr. Basanta Bidari; Kiran Man Chitrakar; Prabakar S. Rana; Deepak S. Rana; Dr. Ajaya S. Rana; Bidur Dangol; Harihar Raj Joshi; and Pankaj Pradhananga. For their support, advice and hospitality my thanks to H. E. the British Ambassador Andrew Hall and Kathie

Hall; Morna Nance, Director, British Council; Janet Rockwell of 'Heaven's Door'; Jim Edwards; Ambika Shrestha; Sangeeta Thapa; Pratina Rana Pandé; Ted and Ellen Riccardi; and Charles and Pam Gay. In the Nepal Tarai, my thanks to Dr. Keshab Man Shakya, the incoming Vice-Chairman of the Lumbini Development Trust and members of his staff, especially Sunil Dahal and Gyanin Rai; also to Hem Sagar Baral, Dinesh Giri and staff at the Lumbini Buddha Garden; and to the Tharu people of Sonbarsi village for their hospitality.

Finally, my thanks to the team at Haus Publishing.

Notes on Sources

Abbreviations: Indian Office Library, British Library – IOL, BL; Archaeological Survey of India – ASI; Royal Asiatic Society – RAS; North-Western Provinces and Oude – NWP&O; *Journal of the Royal Asiatic Society – JRAS*; *Asiatic Researches – AR*; *Indian Antiquary – IA*; *Epigraphia Indica –EI*; Peppé Papers – PP; *Dictionary of National Biography – DNB*; *Dictionary of Indian Biography – DIB*; Asiatic Society of Bengal – ASB; *Journal of the Asiatic Society of Bengal – JASB*.

Preface. A Winter in Nepal

Anyone who still believes that Edward Said's *Orientalism*, 1978, and his follow-up should be taken seriously should read Ibn Warraq, *Defending the West: A Critique of Edward Said's Orientalism*, 2008, the most incisive of a number of critical studies on the subject.

The quotation from the Government of Bihar is taken from *South Asia Intelligence Review*, 2007.

Prologue. The Return of the Wanderer, c. 405 BCE

The account of the Mahaparinirvana of Sakyamuni Buddha is based on the *Mahaparinibban Suttanta*. I have also drawn on *The World of Buddha*, translated by Peter Leggatt as it appeared in consecutive issues of *The Middle Way* from February 2001 to May 2002 and three articles by J. F. Fleet: 'The Tradition about the Corporeal Relics of Buddha', *JRAS*, April and July 1907; 'The Day on which Buddha Died', *JRAS*, January 1909.

The traditional origins of the Sakyas and Koliyas are given in the *Divyavadam* (trans. Cowell and Neil, 1886). According to the *Dighanikaya* (trans. Rhys Davids and Carpenter, 1890) the Sakyas settled in the lower slopes of the Himalayas. The linking of the Sakyas to the *sal* tree was first made by William Hoey in a letter, *JRAS*, April 1906, p.453: 'the application of the word *śāka* in Northern India is to the *sāl*-tree ... the *sāl*-tree is also called *sāku* throughout the districts and provinces bordering on Nepal. ... The Nepal Taria forests ... . are essentially *sāl*-forests, and Śākya obviously means "the people of the *sāl*-forests". The issue of whether it was pork or mushroom that the Sakyamuni ate is one that is fiercely debated among scholars of Buddhism (eg. W. Hoey, *JRAS*, December 1906, p.881, note); I have chosen to follow the literal version.

The dating of the Buddha is discussed in Heinz Bechert, ed. *The Dating of the Buddha*, 1992 and more recently Lance Cousins, 'The Dating of the Historical Buddha: A Review Article', *Indology*, 2007, *www.indology.info/papers/cousins*. I have chosen to follow the still unchallenged reading of Prof. Richard Gombrich in his paper 'Discovering the Buddha's Date', first read at the International Association of the History of Religions Conference in Rome in 1990 but subsequently revised and most recently read at the Harewood Piprahwa Conference, June 2006. An account of the First Buddhist Council, most probably held in the last decade of the fourth century BCE, is given in the *Cullavagga* of the *Vinaya Pitaka* and in the *Mahavamsa*. For early Buddhist history I have consulted Ed. H. Bechert and R. Gombrich, *The World of Buddhism*; the now outdated T. W. Rhys Davids, *Buddhism: being a Sketch of the Life and Teachings of Gautama, the Buddha*, 1886, 'Asoka and the Buddha Relics', *JRAS*, July 1901, and *Buddhist India*, 1903; Vincent Smith, *Asoka: the Buddhist Emperor of India*, 1903; J. F. Fleet, 'The Rummindei Inscription and the Conversion of Asoka to Buddhism', *JRAS*, April 1908; and John S. Strong, *The Legend of King Asoka: a Study and Translation of Asokavadana*, 2002.

1. The Opening: Piprahwa kot, 18 January 1898

My reconstruction of W. C. Peppé's opening of the Piprahwa stupa is based on the private letters and papers in the Peppé family papers (PP), as described in my (unpublished at the time of this publication) article 'What Happened at Piprahwa'. These include a bound pamphlet with photographs entitled *The Piprawah Stupa on the Birdpore Estate Containing the Relics of Buddha*, written by W. C. Peppé in the first person, possibly a first draft before he wrote his article 'The Piprahwa Stupa, containing relics of Buddha', *JRAS*, July 1898. The remarks about Willie Peppé's character and the closing remark about digging deeper made by Mrs. Peppé is taken directly from Vivienne Peppé's unpublished MS 'The Story of the Peppés', 1983, all PP.

Details of the life of Vincent Smith are found in 'Vincent Smith' by Prof. C.S. Srinivasachari, *Eminent Orientalists: Indian, European, Indian*, Ed. Anon., 1922. His outspoken character is mentioned in his first entry in the *DNB*, written by S. V. Fitzgerald, subsequently revised in later editions. The quotations from Vincent Smith's letters to Willie Peppé are drawn from correspondence in PP. I have also drawn on W. C. Peppé, 'The Piprahwa Stupa, containing relics of Buddha, by William Claxton Peppé, Esq, communicated with a note by Vincent A. Smith, ICS, MRAS', *JRAS*, July 1908.

Details of the Battiprolu excavation are in Alexander Rea, *South Indian Buddhist Antiquities, ASI, New Imperial Series*, Vol. XV, 1894.

Some details of the academic life Georg Bühler are taken from 'Dr. Buhler' by Prof. M. S. R. Iyengar, *Eminent Orientalists: Indian, European, Indian*, Ed. Anon., 1922 and from obituaries written by Max Müller in *JRAS*, July 1898, and Max Müller and eleven others in *IA*, Dec. 1898.

The first quoted account of the *tarai* is from Francis Buchanan/Hamilton's *An Account of the Kingdom of Nepal and of the Territories Annexed to this Dominion by the House of Gorkha*, 1815 (Buchanan changed his surname to Hamilton in later years, causing a great deal of confusion). The first European to write about the Tharus at some length was none other than Anton Führer in Chapter 8 of his notorious *Antiquities of Buddha Sakyamuni's Birth-place in the Nepalese Tarai*, 1898. The disputed origins of the Tharus are discussed in Arjun Guneratune, *Many Tongues, One People: the Making of Tharu Identity*, 2002, and in Subodh Kumar Singh, *The Great Sons of the Tharus: Sakyamini Buddha and Ashoka the Great*, 2006.

Details of the settlement of the Gorakhpur Tarai, the travails of the European 'capitalists' and the subsequent histories of the Gibbon and Peppé families are taken from three sources in PP: W. Gibbon, *The Gorkhpoor Tarai in Days Gone by*, privately printed in Birmingham, 1890; W. C. Peppé, *Letter addressed to the Settlement Officer of the Basti District in the North Western Provinces of India, recounting a history of the Birdpore Estate from the date it was granted to the Proprietors, to the present time; extending over a period of Fifty Years*, privately printed in Mussoorie, 1899; and Vivienne Peppé, unpublished MS 'The Story of the Peppés', 1983. The account of the enforced resettlement of the Tharus is given in Gibbon's *Gorakhpoor Tarai in Days Gone by*, PP.

Details of the life of General Khadga Shumsher Jung Bahadur Rana came from conversations with two of his great-grandsons: Dr Ajaya S. J. B. Rana and Deepak S. J. B. Rana; also Percival Landon, *Nepal*, Vol. I, 1927; Silvain Lévi, *A Notebook of Sojourn*, translated by S. Mitra and edited (alas, with many omissions and errors) by Harihar Raj Joshi, 2006.

2. The Reading: Birdpore House, 19 January 1898

The reconstruction of the Peppé family's examination of the Piprahwa reliquaries and their contents is based on the Peppé letters and papers in PP as described above in Ch. 1, and W. C. Peppé, 'The Piprahwa Stupa, containing relics of Buddha, by William Claxton Peppé, Esq, communicated with a note by Vincent A. Smith, ICS, MRAS', *JRAS*, July 1898. Also to be found in PP are: a rough copy of a deposition about those present at the opening of the stone coffer from the Piprahwa stupa; a recycled letter from Pandit Misra, Magistrate of Basti, to Peppé; a hand copy of the Piprahwa inscription with a note from Peppé, to which a translation and further note from Smith has been added; a series of letters from Smith and Anton Führer's to Peppé. See also my unpublished article 'What Happened at Piprahwa', Ch. 1 above.

An account of the activities of the early British Orientalists and the discovery of the roots of Buddhism in India, including the part played by Francis Buchanan/Hamilton, is given in Charles Allen, *The Buddha and the Sahibs*, 2003. Buchanan's remarkable reports of his field-work are to be found in the British Library MSS Eur.

K156–75, his exploration of the Indian Tarai in Vol. II of *Topographical Account of the Northern Part of the District of Gorakhpur and its Antiquities*, in three vols. edited by Montgomery Martin, *History, Antiquities, Topography and Statistics of Eastern* India, 1838.

The Sen dynasty seal is reproduced in W. F. Gibbon, *The Gorakhpoor Tarai in Days Gone By*, 1890, in PP.

For accounts of the Mauryan dynasty I have drawn on the *Ashokavadana* and the *Divyavadana* but also Vincent Smith, *Asoka: The Buddhist Emperor of India*, 1901; R. C. Majumdar, *Ancient India*, 1977, Romilla Thapar, *A History of India*, Vol. I, 1966, John Keay, *India: A History*, 2001, B. N. Mukherjee, *Ancient India*, 2003. Asoka's links with Nepal are considered in Daniel Wright, *History of Nepal*, 1877, and Lama Taranath, *History of Buddhism in India*, 1971. The seventeenth Asokan inscription lists the pilgrimage sites visited by Asoka. The quotation about Chandragupta's conquests is from Kshmendra's *Brihat-Katha-Manjari*. Smith's account of Asoka's pilgrimage is taken from *Ashokavadana*, of which he wrote, erroneously, that 'the chronology of the romance [the *Ashokavadana*], which places Asoka only a century after the death of Buddha, is manifestly erroneous'.

A. C. L. Carlleyle's account of his supposed discovery of Kapilavastu is given in his 'Report of Tours in Gorakhpur, Saran, and Ghazipur', ASI Reports (Old Series) Vol. 22, 1885. Alexander Cunningham's confirmation of his claim to have discovered Kapilavastu is from his Introduction to A. C. L. Carlleyle, *Report of Tours in the Central Doab and Gorakhpur in 1874–75 and 1875–76*, which also contains Carlleyle's account of his discoveries of Kushinagar and the Rampurva pillar. A modern translation of Xuanzang's *Report of the Western Regions of the Great Tang* is given in Max Deeg, *The Places Where Siddhārtha Trod: Lumbini and Kapilavastu*, 2003.

Anton Führer's reports are in: *The Sharqi Architecture of Jaunpur, with Notes of Zafarabad, Sahet-Mahet and Other Places in the North-Western Provinces and Oude*, ed. by James Burgess, 1889, ASI New Series Vol. I, NWP&O Vol I.; *The Monumental Antiquities and Inscriptions in the North-Western Provinces and Oude, described and arranged by A. Führer, PhD*, 1891, ASI (New

Series) Vol. II, PWP&O Vol. II; *Progress Report of the Epigraphical Section for the Working Season of 1895–6*, 1897, ASI NWP&O 1895–97; *Extracts from Lucknow Museum Reports of 1888–89, 1889–90 and 1890–91*; see also Vincent Smith, *The Jain Stupa and Other Antiquities of Mathura*, 1901, ASI New Imperial Series Vol. XX, NWP&O Vol. V.

3. The Expected Visit: Birdpore House, 27 January 1898

For details of Smith's visit to Birdpore and his reports of Piprahwa stupa contents see Chs. 1 & 2 above, PP. As well as the list of items presented by Vincent Smith in 'The Piprahwa Stupa', *JRAS*, October 1898, three different lists of the Birdpore relic items are to be found in the PP, as well as Smith's second tentative translation of the Piprahwa inscription, undated.

For details of the ICS career of William Hoey I am much obliged to Sheila Hoey Middleton, also Hoey's remarks in 'Exploration of the Birthplace of Buddha in the Nepal Tarai', *Government, NWP&O PWD Proceedings for August 1899. Building and Roads – Miscellaneous*.

The quoted comments on Dr. Bühler's contribution to Jain studies are taken from Prof. K. S. R Iyengar's essay in *Eminent Orientalists, Indian, European, American*, 1922. The quoted judgement on Smith's work is contained in Prof. C. S. Srinivasachari's essay in the same work. For Smith's early scholarship on Gupta coins see: 'A Classified and Detailed Catalogue of the Gold Coins of the Imperial Gupta Dynasty of Northern India, with an Introductory Essay', *JASB*, 1884; 'The Coinage of the Early or Imperial Gupta Dynasty of Northern India', *JRAS*, January 1889; 'Observations on the Gupta Coinage', *JRAS*, January 1893; 'Further Observations on the History and Coinage of the Gupta Period', *JASB*, 1894.

For my sources on early Indian history see Ch. 2 above. Quotations from Faxian are from James Legge's translation, *A Record of Buddhistic Kingdoms: Being an Account by the Chinese Monk Fa-Hiuen of his Travels in India and Ceylon (A.D. 399–414) in Search of the Buddhist Books of Discipline*, 1886. Quotations from Xuanzang are from Samuel Beal's translation, *Si-Yu-Ki: Buddhist Records of the Western World by Hiuen Tsiang*, 1884.

Führer's closing quotation is from his *Progress Report of the Epigraphical Section for the Working Season of 1895–6,* 1897, ASI NWP&O, 1895–97.

4. The Unannounced Visit: 'Camp Kapilavastu', 28 January 1898

V. Smith's account of his foray into Nepal and his meeting with Dr Führer are to be found in: *Government, NWP&O. PWD Proceedings for August 1899. Building and Roads – Miscellaneous. Exploration of the Birthplace of Buddha in the Nepal Tarai. File No. 49 Mis.;* and in *Annual Progress Report of the Archaeological Survey Circle (Epigraphical Section) NWP&O, for the year ending 30 June 1899,* 1899; Smith's Introduction to Babu Purna Chandra Mukherji, *A report on a tour of exploration of the antiquities in the Terai, Nepal, the region of Kapilavastu, during February and March 1899, with a Prefatory Note by Mr Vincent A. Smith,* No. XXVI, *Part of the Imperial Series, and Vol. VI of Archaeological Survey of Northern India,* BL SW196/26/2; and Vincent Smith's critical 'Note on the Exploration of Kapilavastu', dated 3 January 1898, *Government, NWP&O PWD Proceedings for August 1899. Building and Roads – Miscellaneous.*

A. Führer's account of his exploration and excavations in the Nepal Tarai are to be found in: his letters to W. C. Peppé, PP (see also Ch. 1 above); 'Archaeological Survey N-WP and Oude Circle: Progress Reports of the Epigraphical Section in the Working Season of 1893–94, 1894–95, and 1895–96, in *Progress Reports of the Epigraphical and Architectural Branches of the NWP&O,* 1892–1903; and 'Exploration of the Birthplace of Buddha in the Nepal Tarai', printed in *Archaeological Survey, NWP&O Circle Progress Report for the Epigraphical Section for the Working Season of 1897–98.*

W. Hoey's explorations are in V Smith and W. Hoey, 'Notes on the Sohgaura Copper-Plate', *Proceedings of the ASB,* 1894; Smith and Hoey, 'Ancient Buddhist Statuettes and a Candella Copper-plate from the Banda District', *JASB,* 1895. Hoey also describes his dealings with Gen. Khadga S. J. B. Rana in *Government, NWP&O, PWD,* etc already cited above in this chapter. Smith and Hoey's third collaboration on Gupta coinage is listed above Ch. 3. As regards Dr Hoey's Gupta statuettes, a mystery surrounds the whereabouts of the missing third Buddha statuette: see Sheila E. Hoey Middleton, 'The Third Buddha', *Journal of South Asian Studies*, Vol. 18, 2002.

Dr. L. A. Waddell's early published work included *Discovery of the exact site of Pataliputra and description of the superficial remains*, 1892; *The Birds of Sikkim*, 1893; *The Lamasim of Sikkim*, 1894; *The Buddhism of Tibet or Lamaism, with its Mystic Cults, Symbolism and Mythology and its Relation to Indian Buddhism*, 1895; and *Report on the Excavations at Pātaliputra (Patna)*, 1903. Waddell's version of the events of 1895–96 is given in his letter 'The Discovery of the Birthplace of the Buddha', *JRAS*, January 1897. His memorandum was read at the August meeting of the ASB and published as 'The Birthplace of the Buddha and its Asoka Monuments' in *JASB*, 1896, together with a note on 'A Tibetan Guide-Book to the Lost Sites of the Buddha's Birth and Death', *JASB*, 1896. The charge of plagiarism made against Dr. Führer is referred to in Waddell's letter above, based on Stanley Lane-Poole's complaint in a letter published in the *Athenaeum* on 28 September 1895. Waddell's letters to Hoey and his map of Rajdhani is among Smith's papers in the Indian Institute Library at the Bodleian, Mss. Eng. Misc. C794.

The first accounts of the discovery of the Lumbini pillar are given in G. Bühler, letter 'The Discovery of Buddha's Birthplace', *JRAS*, April 1897; V. Smith, letter 'The Birthplace of Gautama Buddha', *JRAS*, July 1897; L. A. Waddell, letter 'The Discovery of the Birthplace of the Buddha', *JRAS*, July 1897.

Prof. Georg Bühler's reading of the Nigliva sagar pillar inscription first appeared in *The Academy* in April 1895, his first reading of the Lumbini inscription in 'The Discovery of Buddha's Birthplace', *JRAS*, 1897; his summation in 'The Asoka Edicts of Paderia and Nigliva', *EI*, Vol. V, 1898.

Dr. A. Führer's notorious *Antiquities of Buddha Sakyamuni's Birth-Place in the Nepalese Tarai*, written in 1897 but not published until 1898, was suppressed on publication and all copies withdrawn and destroyed. Fortunately, Dr. Harihar Joshi tracked down a copy in Pakistan which he laboriously copied and published in Kathmandu in 1996, for which he deserves much credit (although readers should be aware that the copying is imperfect). Details of

Dr. Führer's 'discoveries' are given in '*Archaeological Survey*' etc already cited above in this chapter.

The sources of the translations of Faxian and Xuanzang are cited in Ch. 3.

An account of Dr. Führer's faking of inscriptions is given in H. Lüders, 'On Some Brahmi Inscriptions in the Lucknow Museum', *JRAS*, 1912.

5. The Return: Birdpore House, 29 January 1898

For an account of Smith's movements in the Nepal Tarai see: his critical 'Note on the Exploration of Kapilavastu', dated 3 January 1898, in *Government, NWP&O. PWD Proceedings for August 1899. Building and Roads – Miscellaneous. Exploration of the Birthplace of Buddha in the Nepal Tarai. File No. 49 Mis.*; and his introduction to Babu Purna Chandra Mukherji, *A report on a tour of exploration of the antiquities in the Terai, Nepal, the region of Kapilavastu, during February and March 1899, with a Prefatory Note by Mr Vincent A. Smith*, No. XXVI, *Part of the Imperial Series, and Vol. VI of Archaeological Survey of Northern India*.

Details of Smith's collaboration with Peppé are given in: W. C. Peppé, 'The Piprahwa Stupa, containing relics of Buddha, by William Claxton Peppé, Esq, communicated with a note by Vincent A. Smith, ICS, MRAS', *JRAS*, July 1908; V. Smith, letter 'The Piprahwa Stupa', *JRAS*, Oct. 1898.

Prof. Bühler's letter to Peppé is quoted in his 'Preliminary Report' cited in Ch. 2 above, also in J. H. H. Peppé, *The Piprawah Stupa on the Birdpore Estate Containing the Relics of Buddha*, a twelve-page pamphlet, undated, now in the Peppé Papers, Cambridge Centre for South Asian Studies. This pamphlet is clearly linked to W. C. Peppé, 'The Piprahwa Stupa, containing relics of Buddha, by William Claxton Peppé, Esq. communicated with a note by Vincent A. Smith, MRAS', *JRAS*, 1898.

Hoey's account of his visit to Lumbini is given in *Government, NWP&O, PWD* etc quoted above. Smith's account of his foray into Western Nepal is given in 'Kausambi and Sravasti', *JRAS*, July 1898.

The quarrel between Drs. Waddell and Fuhrer is set out in their letters in *JRAS*, July 1897 and Jan 1898.

Führer's forays into the Nepal Tarai are described in 'Archaeo-logical Survey N-WP and Oude Circle: Progress Reports of the Epigraphical Section in the Working Season of 1893–94, 1894–95, and 1895–96, in *Progress Reports of the Epigraphical and Architec-tural Branches of the NWP&O, 1892–1903*. His 'preliminary brief report' dated 23 March 1896, 'Nepalese Excavation in the western Tarai', was printed in *Government, NWP&O PWD Proceedings for August 1899. Building and Roads – Miscellaneous*; a significantly altered progress report, 'Exploration of the Birthplace of Buddha in the Nepal Tarai', was printed in *Archaeological Survey, NWP&O Circle Progress Report for the Epigraphical Section for the Working Season of 1897–98*. For critical accounts of the same by Waddell, Hoey and Smith see the first para in Ch. 4 above.

The quotes from Silvain Lévi's diary are taken from Silvain Lévi, *A Notebook of Sojourn*, translated by S. Mitra and edited by Harihar Raj Joshi, 2006.

For Führer's and Smith's letters to Peppé see PP in Ch. 1 above.

Führer's desperate letter to Gen. Khadga Rana and the latter's reply is printed in *Government, NWP&O, PWD, Proceedings for August 1899. Building and Roads – Miscellaneous* and in *Annual Progress Report of the Archaeological Survey Circle (Epigraphical Section) NWP&O, for the year ending 30 June 1899*, 1899.

The remarkable Führer–U Ma correspondence was rediscovered by T. A. Phelps in the National Archives of India, *Govt. of India Proceedings Part B, Dept. of Revenue and Agriculture, Archaeology & Epigraphy, Aug. 1898*, File No. 24 of 1898, Proceedings Nos. 7–10, and referred to by Andrew Huxley in his paper *Georg Bühler's Death and its implications for Piprahwa*, read at the RAS Hare-wood Conference on 8 July 2006. While acknowledging my debt to Phelps and Huxley in this respect I cannot agree with most of the claims made in that paper.

Lord Curzon's references to Sir Antony MacDonnell are taken from his correspondence with Lord George Hamilton, Mss. Eur. 111/158–59, IOL, BL, with special thanks to Laurence Middleton for tracking them down. Other sources are Philip Woodruffe (Philip Mason), *The Guardians*, 1954; David Gilmour's *The Ruling Caste*, 2005; *DNB*; *DIB*.

6. The Drowning: Lake Constance, 8 April 1898

Details of Prof. Bühler's career, last days and drowning are given in the obituary notices by Prof. Max Müller carried in *JRAS*, July 1898, and by A. A. MacDonnell and eleven others in *Indian Antiquary*, 1898. Bühler's letters to Rhys Davids are in the Rhys Davids Archive, Library of the Faculty of Asian and Middle Eastern Studies, Cambridge, RD T/8 Gen. Corresp. For that information I am indebted to Andrew Huxley's unpublished paper *Georg Bühler's Death and its implications for Piprahwa*, read at the RAS Harewood Conference on 8 July 2006.

Details of the processes leading up to the publication of Führer's *Antiquities of Buddha Sakyamuni's Birth-Place in the Nepalese Tarai* are set out in *Government, NWP&O. PWD Proceedings for August 1899. Building and Roads – Miscellaneous. Exploration of the Birthplace of Buddha in the Nepal Tarai. File No. 49 Mis.* This same key publication includes Smith's account of his confrontation with Führer, an account of Waddell's appointment to supervise Mukherji, his treatment of Mukherji, Mukherji's response and Waddell's essentially bogus preliminary report on his identification of Kapilavastu

Details of P. C. Mukherji's early career and dismissal in 1894 are found in: Upinder Singh, *The Discovery of Ancient India: Early Arcaheologists and the Beginnings of Archaeology*, 2004; the *Indian Museum Annual Report, April 1894 to March 1895*, 1895; and Frederick M. Asher, 'The Former Broadley Collection, Bihar Sharif', *Artibus Asiae*, Vol. 32, Nos 2–3, 1970. Smith's comments on P. C. Mukherji's Patna excavations are contained in Vincent A. Smith, 'Asoka Notes No. X', *Indian Antiquary* Vol. XXXVII, 1909. Smith's copy of Mukherji's *Preliminary Report on my Tour in Champaran Tarai in March 1897* is to be found among Smith's papers in the Indian Institute Library at the Bodleian, Mss. Eng. Misc. C794. So, too, is Dr. L. A. Waddell's brief untitled report of his foray into Nepal in February 1899, dated 22 March and addressed to Secy. Govt of India, Dept. of Revenue and Agriculture.

Babu Mukherji's remarkable *The Pictorial Lucknow*, 1883 (in which he spells himself 'Mookherji'), was reissued in 2003. For a full account of his exploration of the Nepal Tarai and his excavations see Babu Purna Chandra Mukherji, *A report on a tour of exploration of the antiquities in the Terai, Nepal, the region of Kapilavastu, during February and March 1899, with a Prefatory Note by Mr Vincent A. Smith*, No. XXVI, Imperial Series, and Vol. VI, Archaeological Survey of Northern India, BL SW196/26/2.

Dr. W. Hoey's report on what he saw at Nigliva and Lumbini is included in *Government, NWP&O. PWD Proceedings for August 1899. Building and Roads – Miscellaneous. Exploration of the Birthplace of Buddha in the Nepal Tarai. File No. 49 Misc*. Hoey's identification of Ramagrama is referred to by Smith and Mukherji in *A report on a tour of exploration of the antiquities in the Terai*, above and in Sukra Sagar Shrestha, 'Ramagrama Excavation', *Ancient Nepal*, 2006. The remarks on Hoey's character are taken from an obituary carried in *The Oxford Magazine*, 3 May 1918.

7. The Prince-Priest: Gorakhpur Division, 1898

The two prime sources for this chapter are the letters in PP and the official correspondence now in the National Archives of India relating to the disposal of the Piprahwa relics: *1899 Foreign Department, External A Pros. April 1899, nos. 92–11*. These last were found in the National Archives of India by Dr. Himanshu Ray, for whose scholarship and generosity in making them available to me I am greatly indebted.

For details on the life of the 'Prince-Priest' Prisdang Chumsai Jinavaravansa I have drawn on a note by Sumet Jumsai in a leaflet on the Ratna Chetiya Dipaduttamarama in Colombo, for which I am indebted to Ven. S. Dhammika. See also V. Charkam, 'The Life and Times of Prince Prisdang', which can be accessed on *www.geocities.com/raimnforest/vines/8769*.

For a possible solution to the mystery surrounding the whereabouts of Hoey's missing third Buddha statuette, see Sheila E. Hoey Middleton, 'The Third Buddha', *Journal of South Asian Studies*, Vol. 18, 2002.

Smith's initial support for Führer's claims for his discovery of Kapilavastu is quoted a letter from Waddell, to the Secy. GoI, Dept. of Rev. and Ag.. No. 41-A, dated Calcutta 22 March, 1899, Smith Papers, Indian Institute Library, Bodleian. Dr. Waddell's account of his actions in the Nepal Tarai in January-February 1899 are contained in the same letter.

Details of Waddell's charges and Smith's enquiry and judgement are to be found in *Government, NWP&O Public Works Department Proceedings for August 1899. Building and Roads – Miscellaneous. Exploration of the Birthplace of Buddha in the Nepal Tarai. File No. 49 Mis.* See also Babu Purna Chandra Mukherji, *A report on a tour of exploration of the antiquities in the Terai, Nepal, the region of Kapilavastu, during February and March 1899, with a Prefatory Note by Mr Vincent A. Smith*, No. XXVI, Imperial Series, and Vol. VI, Archaeological Survey of Northern India, BL SW196/26/2.

Waddell's inglorious later career has been charted in Charles Allen, *Duel in the Snows: The True Story of the Younghusband Mission to Lhasa*, 2004.

Mukherji's last letter to Smith is among Smith's papers in the Indian Institute Library at the Bodleian, Mss. Eng. Misc. C794.

For a Nepali view of modern Lumbini see novelist Munjushree Thapa's essay 'The Buddha in the Earth-Touching Posture' in *Tilled Earth*, 2007.

8. The Aftermath, 1900–2008

Rhys Davids's lecture was entitled 'Asoka and the Buddha Relics', subsequently published in *JRAS*, July 1901.

J. F. Fleet's three readings of the Piprahwa inscription were in: 'Notes on Three Buddhist Inscriptions', *JRAS*, October 1905; 'The Inscription on the Piprahwa Vase', *JRAS*, January 1906; 'The Inscription of the Piprahwa Vase', *JRAS*, January 1907. Fleet's rivals were Silvain Lévi, *Journal des Savants*, 1905; M. Senart, *Journal Asiatique*, 1906, and M. Barth, *Journal des Savants*, 1906. Sadly mention of Fleet, 'The Inscription on the Sohgaura Plate', *JRAS*, 1907, had to be omitted for reasons of length.

H. Hartel's essay, 'Archaeological Research on Ancient Buddhist Sites', is published in H. Bechert Ed. *The Dating of the Historical Buddha*, 1991.

H. Lüders's exposure appeared as 'On Some Brahmi Inscriptions in the Lucknow Museum', *JRAS*, 1912.

Smith's letter on the state of affairs at the Lucknow Musuem appeared in *JRAS*, October 1905.

Humphrey and Elfie Peppe's accounts of their two meetings with the Dalai Lama and their post-Independence vicissitudes are given in two short accounts included among PP.

Debala Mitra's accounts of her survey and excavations in the Nepal Tarai and Basti District are given in: *Excavations at Tilaurakot and Kodan and Explorations in the Nepalese Terai*, 1972; and *Buddhist Monuments*, 1971.

For J. N. Mishra's work at Tilaurakot see 'Tilaurakot Excavations', *Ancient Nepal*, 1977. For B. K. Rijal's work at Tilaurakot and elsewhere see: *Archaeological Remains of Kapilavastu, Lumbini and Devadaha*, 1979; and *100 Years of Archaeological Work in Lumbini, Kapilavastu and Devadaha*, 1996. Summaries of their explorations, with extracts from earlier excavations and surveys are also found in Basanta Bidari, *Lumbini: A Haven of Sacred Refuge*, 2002, and *Kapilavastu: The World of Siddhartha*, 2004.

For K. S. Srivastava's work at Piprahwa and Ganwaria see: *The Discovery of Kapilavastu*, 1986; and *Excavations at Piprahwa and Ganwaria*, 1996.

For Max Deeg's recent research see 'The Places where Siddhārtha Trod: Lumbinī and Kapilavastu', *Lumbini International Research Institute Occasional Papers*, 3, 2003.

Robin Coningham's and Armin Schmidt's work at Kapilivastu is still unpublished other than as press-reports which can be accessed on the internet. I am grateful to Robin Coningham for the results of the carbon-dating.

For Prof. G. Verardi's work see 'Excavations at Gotihawa and a Territorial Survey of Kapilavastu District of Nepal', *Lumbini International Research Institute Occasional Papers*, 2, 2002.

For a summary of Ramagrama see Sukra Sagar Shrestha, 'Ramagrama Excavation', *Ancient Nepal*, 2006.

Another invaluable tool for a history of the archaeology of Nepal was Gitu Girt, *Art and Architecture: Remains in the Western Tarai Region of* Nepal, 2003 (which would have been all the better with the provision of a map).

I am grateful to Richard Salomon for allowing me to draw on

his unpublished informal paper, 'Observations on the Piprahwa inscription and its Epigraphic content', which he read at the Harewood Conference, June 2006.

Among those who challenged K. M. Srivastava's readings of the Piprahwa seatings were Hartal (cited above) and Deeg (cited above).

Index